Dear Teri,

I very much hope
you enjoy the book.
See you at
Croucled House,
Castlefield Bowl,
Summer 2021!

All the best,

Teri

POP
LIFE

The Story of a Minor
Musical Expedition

Tom Kirkham

novum 🪁 pro

www.novum-publishing.co.uk

© 2018 novum publishing

ISBN 978-3-99064-301-3
Editing: Hugo Chandler, BA
Cover: Eleri Stedman
Cover design, layout & typesetting: novum publishing
Author's photo: Tom Kirkham

The images provided by the author have been printed in the highest possible quality.

www.novum-publishing.co.uk

Contents

Acknowledgements

There have been many pivotal figures responsible for keeping this minor musical expedition alive. I am however acutely aware that the acknowledgements page is invariably the least interesting section within all but the dullest of books. Hence, I shall be brief.

I'd like to afford the highest praise imaginable to Caitlin, my perpetually optimistic editor, and Emma, my creative consultant, whose role predominantly comprised trying to stop me slagging off Adele, for fear it might lose me readers.

Next, I'd like to thank every one of my erstwhile expedition companions. This list is as comprehensive as memory allows, so apologies if I've neglected anyone. Sincere and heartfelt thanks go to Laura, Joe, Alex, Lewis, Frances, Sash, Christine, Chris, Yulia, Zowie, Frances II, Mel, Abi, Dana, Brett, Philip, Jonathan, Agatha, Joe II, Giles, Miki, Hannah, Catrin, Lexi, and of course, the old devils Rick and Brendan.

Special mentions must go to my good friends Rhys and Eleri. I've lost count of the number of shows we attended together along the way, and I couldn't have made it through this journey without them.

Finally, a note on the title. I originally wanted to call this book 'Dance, Music, Sex, Romance', in the ultimate tribute to The Purple One, whose unassailable genius and majesty will remain with me for now and always. However, upon realising that my account lacked at least three of these quintessential qualities, I was forced into a hasty rethink. "Pop Life" is the standout track from the 1985 Prince album Around the World in a Day, and it feels perhaps a little more appropriate. After all, *"Life it ain't real funky. Unless it's got that pop…"*

Prologue

It's April 21ˢᵗ, the year is 2016, it's eleven twenty p.m. and I'm slumped at the glass table in the front room of my Camden flat listening to "Purple Rain" and blubbing my heart out. I've been drinking heavily, but that hasn't stopped me recording a commemorative podcast in Prince's honour with my best friend Emma (aka Dr. Bearhead). My housemate Philip has just been in to check on me, but now I'm alone once more, trying to edit the podcast recording down to size, while simultaneously bellowing out the words to "Take Me with U" at the top of my voice.

Prince wasn't supposed to die. Like the annual new Woody Allen film or Arsenal F.C.'s spring collapse in form, his records are one of life's great certainties. How can there not be a new Prince album this year? The news of his passing has put me all at sea and I have no idea what to do next. So, I just carry on listening, crying, singing and basking in music so powerful that I can hardly believe it's real. *How can music possibly be this good?*

I feel compelled to write about music right now because, like many of my contemporaries, my life began with music. The earliest memories I have are of my dad playing me "Starman", "Get It On" and "Yellow Submarine". Aged seven I borrowed and never returned a cassette from Richard, an older kid who lived across the street from me, containing on it albums by Jesus Jones and James. Introductions to Oasis and Pulp followed a few years later. By age fourteen I was diversifying in the directions of Marilyn Manson, Lamb, Björk and Kate Bush, before changing course once more and discovering Steely Dan and The Smiths, two bands who have next to nothing in common other than a sense of humour. R.E.M.'s often overlooked classic "Reveal" co-incided with my eighteenth birthday. In the summer of my nine-teenth year I discovered pop music; twelve months later I was immersed in Johnny Cash and his country vibes. In early 2004 I suffered temporary insanity and developed a six-month long obsession with Amy Lee of Evanescence, during which time, I held myself hostage to the "Fallen" album, until eventually, like any Stockholm Syndrome sufferer, I found that I'd become rath-er fond of it.

But nothing compared to Prince, and now I feel as though I need to tell a story about music, simply because I can't think of any other way to deal with his not being there. I need to keep him alive for the sake of my sanity. Not that I have a great deal of sanity left to cling to. My mental health is a disaster zone – I'm half expecting the UN to rock up in my head in a belated attempt to stabilise the region.

Last year was a catastrophe, the last nine months have been hell and now Prince is gone. All I have for company and comfort is my longstanding cat Mr. Kitten, and he's asleep.

Over the course of 2014 to 2015 I've endured acrimonious break-ups, moved flats multiple times and moved cities twice. I've been forced to leave my job, my band has ground to a halt and I'm plagued by insufferable anxiety and depression, a con-sequence of several months spent sitting on my own in the front room, with nothing but my increasingly morose thoughts for company. Despite my years of servitude, Mr. Kitten has done nothing to help, the useless bastard – he's slept happily through my discontent, through endless hours spent pacing up and down in the flat, whipping myself up into an exasperated frenzy, try-ing to figure out how on earth things managed to go so wrong.

My life has unravelled. I'm broken, bereft of motivation, an abject failure. Do you hear that Mr. Kitten? A failure!

Back when I was twenty, I prophesised that this day would come, though admittedly I had expected it to arrive within the week rather than thirteen years later. Boy was I a fun twenty-year-old to be around! Still, at least back then I was younger, thinner, more alive and more inclined to believe in Kate Bush's eternally optimistic sentiment that, *"I just know that something good is gonna happen. I don't know when. But just saying it could even make it happen."*

I need to go to bed soon, but before I do I must apply antiseptic cream to my newly minted David Bowie tattoo, my first inking, and an earnest attempt to comprehend the enormity of such a monumental loss to music. And now Prince. It's too much to bear, and all I can do to contain my grief is to carry on writing and listening.

Weeks 1–3:
Dead and Born and Grown

Where does the time go? This perennial question of those unfortunate enough to be nearing the end of this mortal coil also afflicts us thirty-somethings, as we battle to comprehend what the hell we're doing with our lives. It seems even more pertinent in London, where entire generations are locked in arrested development, unable to transcend the mundane yet compulsive tendency to meet, eat, drink, party, hang (as in over), hair of the dog and repeat. Choose a random week from your diary of three years ago and the chances are it was defined by this pattern of activity. We are of course now cursed by the blight of the Facebook Memory, an automated tool with the unhappy knack of delivering everyday reminders that you've been doing the same fucking thing for the best part of a decade, except that back then you were younger, and your hair probably looked ridiculous.

When periodically we arrive at rare moments of introspection it can develop swiftly into the onset of acute depression, propelling us to come up with absurd notions to break the cycle, such as attending evening classes or moving to Australia. Today I've settled upon a far less preposterous answer. I've decided to go to a gig every week for a year, to escape this repetitive strain injury of a life.

This feels like an especially poignant decision, seeing as six months ago I was unable to listen to music. Every album I owned felt too painful, too infused with memories of people, time, places and purpose. These albums were a map of my life, and my life had fallen apart. I was lost without my music; in fact, I was lost in every respect imaginable, until one afternoon last December, while transferring a handful of files over to my new laptop, I happened upon the contemporary gothic sounds of Anna von Hausswolff and Chelsea Wolfe, and everything changed. I emailed Joe, my musical encyclopaedia of a friend, asking for more gothic recommendations. It had to be dark, brooding, utterly bleak and miserable – these were my comforting sounds. I even contemplated becoming a Goth, but ultimately concluded that I would look too silly.

Thus sparked my musical rebirth and gave rise to this bold new idea of a year of gigging, perhaps the only solution capable of addressing my obsessive compulsion to fully absorb myself in music. It will start on my thirty third birthday and continue uninterrupted for twelve months henceforth. I will preach to others about my experiences, encouraging them to follow in my footsteps. Then I will cleanse the temple of merchants and money-changers, and I will turn water into wine, and I will ride a donkey, and I will turn some more water into wine, and then, after a bit of a rough patch, I will rise from the dead and everyone will be very impressed.

For that's what it's about, this musical expedition. Rising from the dead.

Muncie Girls, Dingwalls, London, Wednesday 8th June

- **Gig #1**
- **Musical birthdays:** Nancy Sinatra (1940), Bonnie Tyler (1953), Mick Hucknall (1960)[1]
- **Musical history:** The Beatles "Sgt Pepper's Lonely Hearts Club Band" goes to Number 1 in the UK; it will spend 27 weeks atop the charts (1967)
- **Non-musical history:** Muhammad, the founder of the world's second-largest religion, Islam, dies in Medina in the arms of his wife (632)

---

1 Kanye West (1977) is omitted owing to a lack of evidence linking him to anything resembling music.

I was compromised both mentally and physically going into my inaugural show. Mentally, due to an inexplicable cat illness. The vets haven't worked it out yet and I'm left just praying it's not kidney-related, as that would mean it's curtains for Mr. Kitten. Physically, because Emma and I decided to go out and get Prince tattoos directly before heading for our pre-gig drink, and it turns out that the inner bicep is five times more painful than the outer bicep.

I've known Emma since we were seventeen-year olds growing up in North Manchester. The daughter of a deliciously sardonic bookie and a benevolent hairdresser, Emma, like myself, had a thirst for live music and in her heady teenage years regularly spoke of throwing her undergarments at Chino Moreno of the Deftones or non-specific members of Less Than Jake. I remember lending her a book about Prince shortly after we became acquainted called "Slave to the Rhythm". I'm pretty sure that she's never given it back.

I hope that no more musical heroes of mine die before the year is out. The news of Prince's death reached us on the very evening that my friend Rhys and I were raising a glass in celebration of our Bowie tattoos. Seeing this as an omen, I've been repeatedly checking my phone ever since for news of any further musical catastrophes. Fortunately, at the time of writing the remaining real estate on my arms has been preserved.

As you've heard already, Prince and Bowie were amongst the most significant academics of my musical education. While I was fortunate enough to see Prince four times over the past decade, I never made it to a Bowie show due to a perennial lack of funds during my final year of university. Any money I had at the time was exclusively reserved for Jack Daniels, Miles Davis records and an improvised daily meal usually consisting of pasta shells and mayonnaise. My brother and sister, on the other hand, saw Bowie at the Manchester Arena. To this day I have held a grudge against them for their good fortune.

I find it frustrating when people complain about the elder statespeople of music who continue to perform well into their fifties, sixties, seventies and so on. After his heart operation and early live retirement, Bowie managed to avoid a lot of this disdain, but others haven't been so fortunate. McCartney, for example, comes in for a lot of criticism, despite regularly getting five-star reviews for his marathon three-hour sets. I saw Macca as recently as last year and we had a brilliant time. Neil Young shows have had their ups and downs over the years, but the high points have been inimitable. Leonard Cohen a few years ago released the best live album I've ever heard and he's about a hundred and thirty.[2] That's life – I'd still much rather see these people at seventy to eighty percent than miss out on them just because I wasn't a teenager in 1963. If it feels authentic and not just a weary, worn out cash cow of a show, then that's fine with me. Believe it or not, I saw and enjoyed Rod Stewart once, and his reputation has been mud for even longer than that of Phil Collins!

Anyway, I'm digressing; this was supposed to be a paragraph in tribute to Prince and Bowie and now I'm slagging off the man that brought us "In the Air Tonight" and "No Son of Mine". Lord Phil Almighty, I beg your forgiveness.

Muncie Girls was a peculiar gig with which to inaugurate my year of live music, namely because we were there to see the support band rather than the main act. We were also exceptionally unprepared. Neither Mel, Eleri, Philip or Emma had bothered to check out the bands, though in the case of Beach Slang, the headliner, this proved a blessing in disguise.

This sort of social unpreparedness leaves me ill at ease. I'm preoccupied by the irrational fear and pre-gig guilt that everyone might loathe the show I've suggested and come away feeling as though the evening was a complete waste of time. This is nonsensical; they're all adults perfectly capable of making their own decisions and with no rational reason to blame me for any poor choices suffered. Irrespective, I slightly resented my friends for their lack of preparation and may never forgive them.

---

2 Was. Sadly, the great man passed away during my year-long expedition.

To cut to the chase, the first band was mediocre and forgettable. Not bad, but not good (hence mediocre); forgettable, as evidenced by my inability to recall their name or what they sounded like. Muncie Girls, in contrast, were a band approaching a breath of fresh air. The set was too short, and the singer suffered from naive over-exuberance (so says I, the aged pedantic musician-critic) resulting in a few missed high notes. But the music is energetic and alive in that a way that's unique to female-fronted pop-punk bands. If guys try and make music like this, it comes off sounding like a novelty act (Blink-182) or just plain shit (Sum 41).[3] Since I first heard Hole's "Celebrity Skin" I've always had a soft spot for artists like Muncie Girls. Later in the evening we spotted their singer in the crowd watching Beach Slang who, as I alluded to earlier, were awful and not worthy of a write-up. I was persuaded by my friend Rhys, always rather more outgoing than I am, to go over and congratulate her on the band's performance. I did just that. She seemed very pleasant, albeit a bit on the shy side, which meant that the conversation was struggling for air within seconds. I asked her where the band hailed from. "Exeter," was her response. I said that I couldn't hear the accent in her singing voice. She seemed surprised. I panicked and began talking about the Wurzels. This topic continued for a good thirty seconds before I decided to cut my losses and abandon the affair. Thank goodness I'm not currently in the dating game – I'd have to shoot myself.

---

3 My editor wishes to let it be known that she wholeheartedly rejects any criticism of Sum 41. And, while the revelation has left me questioning her appointment, this footnote is designed to serve as a back-handed olive branch.

Neil Young & The Promise of the Real, The O2, London, Saturday 11ᵗʰ June

- **Gig #2**
- **Musical birthdays:** Nick Hallam (1960) and Robert Birch (1961), both members of Stereo MCs
- **Musical history:** Nelson Mandela's seventieth birthday tribute takes place at Wembley Stadium, featuring Whitney Houston, Phil Collins, Dire Straits, UB40 and others (1988)
- **Non-musical history:** Henry VIII marries Catherine of Aragon, whose only surviving child, Mary, will later reign as Queen of England for six years (1509)
- **Also:** Radio stations across Europe mistakenly announce the death of Roger Daltrey (1966)

My past few days have been absorbed by cat-related traumas and Mr. Kitten's eventual admittance to animal hospital on my birthday. It was possibly the worst birthday I've ever experienced, quite something given that my thirtieth birthday culminated in my then girlfriend breaking into my Facebook account, reading through half a decade of archived messages and having a go at me for things I'd sent other women years before I met her.

I was wearied and worn out by the time the weekend arrived, as well as tormented by the knowledge that, in going to The O2 for the night, we'd be missing England's Euro 2016 opener. However, this latest outing to see Neil Young, my fourth Young experience, was a Christmas present from my dad, booked well before the fixtures had been scheduled. Also, England are generally awful.

The last two Neil Young gigs I experienced were with Crazy Horse, a backing band that is significantly less crazy than the name suggests. These days they're more akin to a group of retired Navaho Indians resting on a reservation than roaming the plains hunting buffalo or warring with Apaches.[4]

---

4 It's possible that this sentence is an abomination of historical inaccuracy.

My prior Young gig had been a *difficult* set at Hyde Park comprising zero hits and at least four fifteen-minute-long tracks that I didn't recognise, supported by a Crazy Horse backbeat and rhythm section that chugged along at the pace of a Highlands steam engine beset by signalling problems. Yet, apart from the Icelandic ash cloud that once submerged Europe for a week, every cloud has a silver lining and my lacklustre Hyde Park experience prompted me to delve into the past and explore the great Canadian's back catalogue, thus ensuring that I would never again arrive unprepared at a Neil Young performance. By purchasing a further twenty Neil Young albums over the past twelve months, it's possible that I've gone slightly overboard, but then that's what we musical obsessives tend to do.

Oh then the irony of his set choices at The O2. Beginning with "After the Gold Rush", followed by "Heart of Gold", then "From Hank to Hendrix", this was quintessential Young that stretched at least eighty or ninety minutes before we arrived at the inevitable fifteen-minute electric epics. My diligence over the past year had paid off and I recognised all but two tracks, outdoing my dad who has had thirty years longer to listen to most of these records. This went some way to restoring my pride, having earlier lost an argument with him about the merits and pitfalls of driverless cars. I was in favour and my dad was against; his argument being that society appears hell-bent on using technology as a means of abdicating all forms of responsibility, and as this trend accelerates we are rendering ourselves redundant as a species. I backed down, not wishing to reveal that my own pro-driverless-car position stemmed from the fact that I still haven't plucked up the courage to learn how to drive. It would be interesting to know what Neil Young makes of driverless cars, given his lifelong enthusiasm for battered old gas-guzzling automobiles. A couple of years ago he even wrote an autobiographical account of every car he's ever owned, which I've read, and is far more interesting than it sounds.[5] Sadly, Young didn't mention cars

---

5 He even drove a hearse for a while, as it proved useful for transporting his band to shows.

once over the course of his two-hour performance, but despite this, it was a wonderful gig. I felt his iconic lead guitar playing was a little stiffer and less assured than in years gone by, perhaps no surprise for a seventy-year-old, but the quality of his voice more than made up for this; Young still sounds much the same as he did in 1971.

The band were also an upgrade on Crazy Horse (sacrilege I know), albeit with one glaring criticism – the inclusion of a bongo player whose contribution was utterly redundant. What were they thinking? Barely audible on the opening acoustic tracks, Mr. Bongo's presence diminished further and further as the gig progressed. By "Love and Only Love" and "Mansion on the Hill" he was completely inaudible, yet so overstated in his playing motions that he looked more like a member of Pan's People than a credible member of a legendary rock artist's backing band.

When Young and the group returned for a final encore of "Fucking Up", another track that did not in any way, shape or form, benefit from additional percussion, Mr. Bongo raised his arms in triumph, basking in the crowd's adulation. This irritated me – I felt as though there was a charlatan in our midst, contributing little, yet more than happy to bask in the mighty achievements of others.[6] My hope is that as the tour rolls on, one night, when he least expects it, his bongos will explode.

The Staves, Royal Festival Hall, London, Tuesday 14th June
- **Gig #3**
- **Musical birthdays:** George Alan O'Dowd aka Boy George (1961)
- **Musical history:** A bad day for musical deaths, as Echo and The Bunnymen drummer Pete De Freitas dies in a motorcycle accident (1989), legendary composer Henry Mancini dies age seventy (1994) and Rory Gallagher dies following a liver transplant (1995)

---

6 John Terry, #fullkitwanker.

- **Non-musical history:** Survivors of the mutiny on the HMS Bounty reach Timor in the East Indies after travelling nearly 4,000 miles in a small boat (1789)

Any post-Young euphoria was short-lived due to the pressures of preparing for an unbelievably stressful working week ahead. While I may present myself as a musical night owl and prematurely retired member of an unpopular indie band, I'm also a freelance marketing and communications consultant, a job I've held for all of six months, since the prospect of financial ruin forced me to abandon my search for a lofty PR agency role and go it alone. Do I like freelancing? Sure – it affords me plenty of space to frequent the local animal hospital and tend to my broken cat. It also allows me to take a fair amount of time off, either for travelling or simply to calm down a bit, a necessity given my ongoing mental troubles. The flip side of course is the lack of predictability. Sometimes working weeks are easy and straightforward; on other occasions, multiple projects collide and there's only myself to ensure that everything gets completed on time.

I was so stressed that I began my work on the Sunday to be sure of getting everything done. By Tuesday I was already exhausted and in need of a break – as ever, not the ideal backdrop for spending the night out at a concert. That said, at least this one would be a civilised affair, comfortably seated in the plush surroundings of the Royal Festival Hall, where one is generally guaranteed a great sound and an early finish.

When my friend Nick and I first saw The Staves, they were the unknown openers at the music streaming service Deezer's first-year anniversary party at the Hospital Club in central London. We were working together and on duty – Deezer was our new client and was already proving a challenge. Its main rival Spotify[7] took

---

7 This was pre-Apple Music, pre-Vinyl resurgence and pre-the resilient last stand of the mighty CD.

up high-profile sponsorships at major UK festivals and collaborated with mainstream publishers such as The Guardian. Deezer was more likely to be found at backwater Jazz and Improv festivals or sponsoring Pig Farmer's Gazette. Much of its summer awareness campaign that year was centred around a portable streaming disco that, when we investigated more closely, proved to be literally a wheelbarrow with speakers.

While our efforts to internationalise the Deezer brand were, unsurprisingly, a mixed affair, the discovery of The Staves made the whole endeavour worthwhile. The three sisters were a joy to watch even back then, just one EP in, and blew away the other two acts of the evening (Slow Club, and someone I can't remember) with a combination of insanely tight three-part harmonies, glorious folksy melodies and self-conscious, slightly awkward sibling humour. Not twelve-months later and they'd graduated to an opening spot on the Other Stage at Glastonbury, one of the few peaceful moments I enjoyed during an otherwise tumultuous five-day festival in which my other half attempted to beat me to death with our relationship. It's been three years since that unhappy outing and The Staves' debut tracks have stood the test of time. Since then they've released a more adventurous second album as well as a still more experimental new EP. What made this show – which was put on as part of the annual Meltdown festival – so special, was witnessing how much they've matured as musicians and songwriters, without losing any of their charm and down-to-earth Watford sibling likeableness. They spent at least five minutes of the gig engaged in a lengthy "pun off"[8] that felt more like a comedy panel show than an accomplished three-piece folk band.

This show was the perfect tonic for a horrible few days. In fact, there could've been a tsunami, alien invasion or unexpected

---

8 A back-and-forth exchange whereby, upon agreeing to a topic, participants take it in turns to discuss the chosen subject while attempting to inject an ever-increasing number of puns into their dialogue.

breakout of leprosy and The Staves would still have been the perfect tonic. Well, perhaps not perfect under those specific circumstances, but certainly a decent consolation before everyone inevitably died.

This was only week two of my year-long expedition into live music, but I left the Royal Festival Hall wondering if I was likely to enjoy any of the remaining fifty-plus shows quite as much as this one. They also took the time to mock Meltdown curator Guy Garvey's accent. Like myself, Garvey hails from Bury, Lancashire; in fact, two members of Elbow once showed up at my band The Angry Red Planets' performance at Manchester's iconic Star and Garter venue. I later found out they were there to see the band after us but had turned up early. I never found out what they thought, but I'm grateful at least that it wasn't one of the shows where I turned up dressed as a pirate or wearing flip flops and a feather boa.

Yumi Zouma, Moth Club, London, Tuesday 21st June

- **Gig #4**
- **Musical birthdays:** Ray Davies (1944), Brandon Flowers (1981), Lana Del Rey (1985), Marcella Detroit of Shakespeare's Sister (1959)
- **Musical history:** In the Big Apple, Columbia Records premieres a vinyl disc that plays at thirty-three and one third RPM (1948)
- **Non-musical history:** The last Viceroy, Lord Mountbatten resigns as Governor General of India (1948)

At the beginning of the week I saw Brett, my long-haired, long-bodied Australian and former housemate. We first met in 2006 at The Boogaloo on Archway Road, across the road from my lodgings at the time. He impressed us by being the only potential housemate to suggest going for a drink before looking over the flat itself, while he also reminded me of my former primary school teacher Mr. Taylor, another long-haired individual, a massive James fan and a formative influence upon my early years. The same, sadly cannot be said about Brett, despite his repeated attempts to get me into antipodean hair metal.

Having been to the same Neil Young concert ten days beforehand, Brett too was complaining about Mr. Bongo, the unwelcome addition to Neil's backing band, which left me feeling vindicated and wondering how many other of the eighteen thousand plus attendees were thinking the same thing. Brett and I watched England draw nil – nil against Slovakia while on the other screen Wales demolished Russia, thus guaranteeing that they'd top the Euro 2016 group at our expense. Most of the pub quickly turned on the England team and manager, relatively standard behaviour during a major international tournament, and I suspect I had one beer too many over the course of the evening for I awoke on gig day feeling distinctly under the weather. That said, I've felt awful on practically every show day since this expedition began, and it hasn't yet stopped me from having a great time.

The biggest challenge in attempting to go to a gig every single week is navigating fallow periods in the live concert calendar where the bands of note (that is, those with some sort of record deal) are less active, either holed up in the studio or busy on the European festival circuit. Who knows what I'll be able to conjure up during the week spanning Christmas and New Year, but I have the worrying feeling it'll involve a covers band attempting Slade, Wizzard and, God forbid, Band Aid. Summer has already proved similarly problematic. Hence in just week three, I found myself arriving in Hackney to meet Rhys and check out a totally unknown entity at a totally unknown venue called the Moth Club, a name that to my mind conjures up images of ancient wardrobes in lofts – like the one that plays such a prominent role in C.S. Lewis's classic tale of religious zealots and white supremacy.

I needn't have worried about venturing into the unknown, or about white supremacists. The Moth Club was great. It reminded me of Peter Kaye's legendary venue The Phoenix, albeit frequented by a considerably younger audience and no DJ Ray Von. With so many venues across the country being shut down, turned into luxury apartments or ruined by overbearing corporate sponsorships and Tuborg, we need to take what we can get, even if that means lauding what is essentially a 1970s working men's club cunningly disguised by the presence of craft lager.

I discovered Yumi Zouma a few days ago via a desperate Google search after my email out to friends requesting gig recommendations drew a mightily unimpressive zero responses. Bastards. Like any impulsive music fan, I heard one Yumi Zouma song at random on Bandcamp, proclaimed it fantastic and bought the album there and then. Despite the lack of any helpful input from my peers, I'm blessed to have friends like Rhys, who will go to absolutely anything, irrespective of whether he's heard of them or not. Nor does he seem to mind if they turn out to be diabolical. Rhys is a studio engineer and producer, not to mention a member of my semi-defunct band. He's been obsessive in his pursuit of a career in music production since I first met him almost ten years ago, and by rights should have a Grammy to his name for his engineering work on Uptown Funk but was unforgivably omitted from the list of production credits in the awards submission. One day I feel sure that he'll get the recognition he deserves, though sadly I doubt it'll be for our band's sophomore release, which has to date sold about a hundred and fifty copies to family, friends, and inevitably a handful of enemies also.

Yumi Zouma proved to be just a few steps short of delightful. They are from New Zealand, which is always good news (Bic Runga, The Naked and Famous, Crowded House),[9] and have hit upon a sound that rests somewhere between Beach House,

---

9 Also hailing from New Zealand are OMC of annoying 90s pop song 'How Bizarre' fame. I know this because my sister returned from her trip to the North Island last summer bearing the gift of a double CD of classic and contemporary New Zealand music. Never has the description "a mixed bag" felt more appropriate.

MGMT, Carly Rae Jepson, LIGHTS and Passion Pit. They had an enthusiastic on-stage demeanour and a stylish singer, a winning combo if ever there was one, though it should be noted that I am not generally regarded as an expert on style, so please do not take my word as gospel.[10]

Our conclusion was that Yumi Zouma were full of potential, with a great sound, but in urgent need of a live drummer. For all the ethereal electronic wooziness, sometimes you need a bit of bang-bang-bang (drums, not gunfire), to bring a show to life. It's also a dreadful name for a band, though I say that with some trepidation in case it turns out to be the singer's name. Still, I guess that's what deed poll is for.

As it turned out, the decision to invite Rhys made for a far more poignant affair than I was expecting. The day of the Yumi Zouma show marked the conclusion of Rhys's eight-year relationship; news which took me by surprise (and which probably would have taken the band by surprise too, had they known about it). Normally Rhys and I spend our time together naming our favourite Manic Street Preachers albums. I then alert Rhys to the existence of obscure silent Fritz Lang films or Rhys recalls to me an ancient episode of Dr. Who that was considered lost for decades before being found in a basement by a BBC cleaner or dragged out from under a bush by a dog.[11] At Yumi Zouma our conversations were far more reflective. Eight years is a long time, and certainly far longer than I've ever managed in a relationship, not counting my relationship with Mr. Kitten, who has just turned ten and is currently being fed through a tube in his neck after his recent brush with death and extended hospital excursion. I stayed out far too late considering that I had to be up

---

10 Nor am I religious.

11 I have since realised that I was thinking about the Jules Rimet World Cup Trophy, although on further investigation it turns out that seventeen years after the trophy was discovered in Upper Norwood by Pickles the dog, it was stolen a second time and is believed to have been melted down and sold.

early in the morning to catch a long-haul flight, but it was that sort of evening – full of contemplation about everything that had happened over the past decade and what on earth the future was likely to bring. For Rhys, freedom of sorts and potential happiness. For me, a hangover and a lengthy journey to Miami.

Weeks 4–8:
Everything All the Time

Are you being overloaded by information – via text, IM, desktop, laptop, tablet, digital billboard, wearable, etc.? And how much of that information is cat-related?

The internet is very cluttered, and mostly it's full of cats. Everywhere you go, everywhere you look, devices are out, and people are busy being entertained by cat content. In his speaking engagements Tim Berners-Lee tends to prioritise voicing concerns about privacy and civil liberties, but even he took time a few years back to cite his surprise at the proliferation of cats online. I raise this because it's boring. The internet is boring. Pictures and videos of cats on the internet are boring. Pictures of people's children are unbelievably boring. Pictures of people's children's birthday parties make me want to stab myself in the head. When I sit down on a train or at a bar and I observe person after person glued to their phone, I wonder if anyone else feels what I feel: bored.

I spend a worrying amount of my time feeling horribly bored while using my phone to convey the appearance of being engaged with something interesting. I have learnt to excel at this over the past year; it's an effective way of avoiding the gaze of others and thus lowers the likelihood of being drawn into conversations with strangers. My misanthropic inclinations were exacerbated twelve months ago when I found myself sitting on a train next to a dishevelled woman who told me she'd that morning been released from a women's prison in Kent and was on her way back to Manchester to be reunited with her boyfriend who lived in a tent near the cathedral. She then began telling me about her prior heroin addiction, estrangement from her two children and her arrest for shoplifting. At the start of the conversation she was reformed and trying to make a new start of things; by the time we pulled into Piccadilly Station she was blind drunk, hugging me repeatedly and using my phone to text her dealer. This, apparently, is what two hours on a train with me will do to a person.

Since that moment, I have endeavoured to keep my head firmly in my phone. Admittedly the likelihood of conversation with strangers is particularly severe on a train, but my general adherence to punctuality also places me in the high-risk category. I have a habit of arriving stupidly early to meet people who are invariably late.

To cope with the alone-time, I read the half-dozen websites that I follow regularly. Then I read them again. Nothing has changed on them in the two or three minutes since I last checked.

I log onto Facebook. I immediately get annoyed. It's like having a junk yard in the front garden that you feel repeatedly compelled to look out of the window at.

I go onto Twitter and I feel more bored than when I had gotten my smartphone out. This is pointlessness redefined for the digital age.

Occasionally I go on Instagram and check out what people have been having for lunch.

I was told recently that unexpected solar storms could temporarily knock out smartphones, satellites and cellular communications worldwide at any given moment. Science is not my strong point, nor is research, so I am lacking the basic tools required to confirm or rebut this claim, however it does raise alarming questions about just how many people would be left unable to function in the simple event of the sun deciding to misbehave, as well as the even more alarming question: would I be one of them?

One of my friends used to drive me to distraction with her over-reliance on Sat Nav to get around. She would switch it on for the drive to her parents, to go and see her friends, to go to the local supermarket just ten minutes away – a journey she made like clockwork once a fortnight. One week there were some roadworks nearby and the confounded technology ended up taking her completely the wrong way, a Pyrrhic victory for me, given I was her passenger.

Fast-forward twelve months and the tables were turned. I received a complaint from another source that I was suffering from smartphone reliance and addiction, ironically the exact criticism I was silently levelling at her. It is something I worry about a lot, including right now, as I'm writing this on my phone on a lazy Sunday afternoon. My hope is that in the aforementioned solar storm, I'd busy myself with my CDs and books, perhaps go for a walk and randomly knock on the door of one of my London friends (although literally no one does that in London and it tends to scare the hell out of people), while the wider world around me sits in stony silence, unable to comprehend existence in a meme-free society.

The situations I've referred to thus far involve downtime, but the sad truth is that at concerts these days I see a growing number of people spending the entire show on Facebook messenger or WhatsApp, shutting themselves off to the potentially life-defining special moments that come when you're up close and personal with the artists who most inspire you.

Cinemas do their level best to make people switch off their mobiles before the movie starts; the clear majority of us adhere to the code,[12] even if we know that the movie is going to be abysmal. At gigs, the artists are afforded no such privileges, and it's particularly depressing when I see singers replacing the old lighter-in-the-air moment during a ballad or schmaltz with the hold-your-phone-aloft routine, a spectacle that delivers approximately no emotional resonance (though in fairness, this could equally be blamed on the smoking ban). I'd support a mobiles-off gigging policy; maybe I'd support a mobiles-off life policy. I'm worried that no one is paying attention anymore.

---

12 Hello to Jason Isaacs.

Tebby, Pirate Republic, Nassau, Friday 1ˢᵗ July

- **Gig #5**
- **Musical birthdays:** Debbie Harry (1945), John Farnham (1949), Missy Elliott (1971)
- **Musical history:** Milli Vanilli score their first US No. 1 single with Baby Don't Forget My Number, which reaches Number sixteen in the UK (1989)
- **Non-musical history:** Hong Kong is returned to China after more than one hundred and fifty years under British occupation (1997)
- **Also:** The Chinese invent the first sunglasses (1200)
- Mr. Kitten is getting better! This is breaking news from the other side of the world, relayed to me via a series of amusing photos, courtesy of Philip. I know that I've just objected to the preponderance of cat pics on the web, but when it's your own cat and you are thousands of miles away I feel an exception ought to be made.

In other news, it turns out to be surprisingly hard to find live music when you're trapped in a Bahamian Hotel Island Resort with no discernible walkway to the mainland.

Before arriving in the Bahamas, I pre-emptively determined that hotel bar entertainment should be ineligible for "gig" status. Having now witnessed the entertainment first hand, I stand by this decree, writing as I am from Plato's Bar in our resort where two large Caribbean men are singing Karma Chameleon to an auto-accompaniment. I very much doubt this was part of Plato's grand design.

My girlfriend Laura and I journeyed here earlier in the week from Miami, having spent seven days holidaying in Coconut Grove, south of the city, a fabulous little hipster retreat where cocktails and craft lager can both be found in abundance. And as you may be gathering, it's *all* about craft lager these days. Unfortunately, Coconut Grove had the booze but not the muse(ic). Live performances were not to be uncovered for love nor money, though admittedly neither was exchanged in this pursuit. I refused to count the ten minutes of salsa-music that we could barely make out during a South American meal one evening, nor the two minutes spent watching a classical violinist busking to Beethoven to pay his way through college. Laura is more of a film, anime and video game buff than a music addict and can happily go an entire month without sticking a record on, let alone rocking up at a live music venue. It is surprising how tolerant she's being about my expedition, although it is not entirely impossible that she's bottling up deep-seated resentment and vitriol that will surface at some stage between now and next June.

These nearly-but-not-quite musical encounters left me facing a week without a show, a situation I couldn't possibly countenance so early into my year-long expedition. Hence, my insistence on a last-minute Bahamian backup plan. I wrote earlier about the challenges of finding good gigs in summer; this week has impressed on me the observation that, when one is thousands of miles from home, one cannot always afford to be too picky in one's choice of entertainment.

Enter Tebby, a young Bahamian singer songwriter scheduled to perform at the Pirate Republic bar on the Nassau waterfront. Here was my salvation, though sadly Nassau was a headache from the start. The afternoon began with me duped into buying a string bracelet off a street seller whom I mistakenly thought was providing tickets for the ferry between the hotel and the mainland. This is the Caribbean equivalent of travellers shoving a small flower wrapped in tin foil into your hands while you're walking from Leicester Square to Piccadilly Circus before trying to extract two pounds from you to complete the transaction.

Having avoided several more potential bracelet acquisitions while locating the ferry, we journeyed across this relatively narrow stretch of water in the blazing early afternoon sun to the accompaniment of a jaunty Bahamian regaling us with useless information about the celebrities who owned the various holiday homes on Paradise Island. Nassau was intense and over-crowded, a city struggling to cope with its status as a tourist hub, and it was a blessed relief on entering the Pirate Republic to find that we'd stumbled upon the one place that seemed to be frequented by locals rather than thirsty American sun-chasers. Neither of us had the faintest idea of what to expect from Tebby; my only hope was that it didn't sound anything like The Baha Men. She took to the stage around eight p.m. with her acoustic-guitar-playing sidekick, and for one fleeting moment my spirits soared. Nassau had been a disappointment – hugely claustrophobic and with little to actually do there – but perhaps Tebby was the region's true hidden gem. Perhaps we were about to witness a bona fide Rihanna in the making.[13] Then they began playing a cover of Maroon 5 (you know the song – the annoying one with the woah-oh-oh refrain) and my heart sank. Still, at least it wasn't selected from Maroon 5's recent repertoire, which has done to music what the protagonist of the late eighties Bon Jovi song did to love. Her Maroon 5 was followed by her take on Adele. It seems that Adele's wings have spread far and wide across the world and yet, like so many of her contemporary divas, has completely passed me by. I heard "Hello" for the first time in a taxi last week, though apparently it has been out for a year now. I still don't understand what Lionel Richie has to do with anything Adele-related, but maybe this is my own failure to grasp the zeitgeist, if indeed that is what one does with the zeitgeist.

Tebby could clearly sing and made the best of challenging circumstances, competing for the attention of a largely indifferent audience, distracted by an intense ongoing battle of Giant Jenga. Weirdly enough, I endured the same Jenga experience while performing at a gig of my own back in 2005. People should really stop bringing these novelty games into the live music arena.

A few songs into her show, Tebby announced that it was her birthday, distracting me from the performance as my mind wandered into contemplations of how old she might be, what she does

---

13 I don't like Rihanna, but off the top of my head I can't name any other Bahamian singer-songwriters. Except for The Baha Men.

for a day job, or whether she harbours any serious aspirations to make it as a singer and break out of the Nassau bar circuit.

Such thoughts took on a new significance as I returned to the moment and watched her perform two original numbers, entitled "Flashback" and "Lose Control". While not especially inspired, I saw Tebby's personality emerging in her own work. She was no longer channelling her favourite singers; she was channelling herself, and even the overwhelming smell of stale cinema (we were sitting next to an old-fashioned butter popcorn dispenser) didn't detract from the comforting sensation that we were at last watching a serious musician.

Regrettably, the feeling was short-lived, chased to the hills by an alleged '90s medley dedicated to *"all the '90s babies in the room"* – most of the crowd, it transpired. Not only did her pronouncement make me feel excessively old, but it led me, with some justification, to question whether a piece can be legitimately classed as a medley if it only includes two songs. I would argue that's a mash-up. It's certainly the absolute bare minimum number of songs a medley can contain. Also, while I concede that "Say My Name" was a late '90s hit, I'm almost certain that "Cry Me a River" was born of the noughties.

The medley was, in a word, shit.

This unfortunate descent pre-empted a far more unfortunate crowd singalong to not one but two Justin Bieber tracks that left me reconsidering my initial assessment of Tebby's abilities. As the microphone was passed around from youth to youth, audience member to audience member, it became evident that everyone in the Bahamas is a brilliant singer. And with that, Tebby's uniqueness dissipated, at which point we decided to call it a night, walking off in the direction of the boat while passing the world's noisiest nightclub en route. We could hear the DJ from half a mile away; by the time we arrived at the entrance, the noise emanating from the club was literally deafening, yet, when we peered in, it was deserted. At this juncture we realised that the DJ had in fact been able to see us across the street and was giving us a personal broadcast as we walked by. Like one of those Brixton evangelists with a loudhailer, he was attempting to induce us into joining him in his ear-splitting hell-hole. How this was possible I've no idea – he must have had a CCTV camera following us along the street. It's a deeply disturbing feeling being commentated on by an unknown third party as you go about your business; enough to make you go out and buy a loudhailer of your own in self-defence.

Band of Horses, Shepherd's Bush Empire, London, Wednesday 6ᵗʰ July

- **Gig #5**
- **Musical birthdays:** Bill Haley (1925), Curtis Jackson aka 50 Cent (1975), Kate Nash (1987)
- **Musical history:** John Lennon meets Paul McCartney for the first time and history is made (1957); David Bowie sings Starman on Top of The Pops and history is made (1972); East 17 are dropped by their record label as history attempts to unmake itself (1999)
- **Non-musical history:** At the height of the Black Death, Pope Clement VI issues a papal bull to defend the Jews against accusations that they are responsible for the disease (1348)[14]

I write from the depths and despair of the bitterest of hangovers. My holiday already feels like a distant memory, despite only landing back at Heathrow yesterday morning. A disaster of a journey back from Nassau to Miami (our plane didn't show up), followed by a lengthy wait in between flights at Newark, made for a gruelling thirty-six-hour trip. I don't tend to sleep well on planes – or anywhere, including my own bed for that matter – so long-haul journeys are made or broken by the quality of the movies and the quality of the wine. "Bridge of Spies" and merlot

---

14 I have no idea what became of the bull in question.

proved a winning combination; "Jurassic World", a glass of water and a headache made me wish I was extinct.

In short, I was in no fit state to spend an evening out beyond the last tube arguing about politics with Rhys, but I had been out of the country for the Brexit result and subsequent depression[15] so we had some catching up to do. I'm not sure how it became an argument, given that the two of us are on the same side, but it was generally good natured and respectful. Or at least I think that it was. I haven't heard from Rhys since so it's not wholly inconceivable that he's deleted me.

Our initial inclination to stay out had been triggered by a rapturous Band of Horses show that both reiterated the uniquely euphoric after-effects of great live music as well as reminding me of how much I like this band. I know nothing about Band of Horses, despite having been a fan of sorts for the best part of a decade. In fact, my total lack of knowledge about the band is probably indicative of the periodic disconnection from new music that I suffered throughout my twenties when life became too busy and too confusing to focus on delving and deep-diving into artists' histories. Save for the occasional birthday or Christmas present, new releases seldom appeared on my radar during this period, while I also lost the impetus to explore bands' back catalogues, breaking with the completest tendencies that had once driven me to temporary bankruptcy after I purchased every James recording ever released from Vinyl Exchange in Manchester.

To this day, I can own a record and love it, but never feel sufficiently motivated to listen to their complete oeuvre, a shameful habit that I've this year resolved to try and change.

While lying on a beach sipping sugary strawberry rum cocktails last week, I undertook a modicum of research to bring myself up to speed with Band of Horses. The latest record, "Why

---

15 I've avoided any detailed reference to Brexit because it's so wholly overwhelming. To cope with it, I'm replicating my attitude towards Kanye West and am pretending that it's not real.

Are You Okay?" has been heralded as a return to form, that rather hackneyed narrative that gets played out time and time again by a media, unwilling to admit when it hasn't been paying attention. It isn't a return to form because, having listened to the complete back catalogue over the past seven days, they didn't particularly lose form in the first place. What they did was begin to delve more into country and folksy Americana, which is perhaps not to everyone's taste. This was reflected in the reception that they received at Shepherd's Bush. The pop and rock hits went down a storm; the Americana tracks caused a doubling of the queues for the bar. For their encore, they returned with a wholly unexpected cover of Neil Young's "Powderfinger" and I began to see the band in a new light. After all, Neil Young has consistently discombobulated and wrong-footed his fans by veering off in one musical direction or another. I bought one of his eighties albums "Old Ways" this week. On my first listen it sounded awful. Band of Horses haven't done anything nearly so atrocious. They certainly haven't done a Sheryl Crow,[16] so I left the gig, resolved to follow them more closely in the future, for better or worse, in sickness and in health.

Whenyoung, The Shacklewell Arms, London, Wednesday 13ᵗʰ July

- **Gig #6**
- **Musical birthdays:** Roger McGuinn (1942)
- **Musical history:** Live Aid takes place, with Phil Collins managing to perform twice, on either side of the Atlantic, over the course of the day-long event (1985)
- **Non-musical history:** The Austrians conclude their investigation into the assassination of Archduke Franz Ferdinand, finding no evidence of Serbian Government culpability (1914)

---

16 A once promising artist with a strong country-rock debut album embarks on a journey into roots of American music and emerges with some of the most drab and mediocre recordings of the decade.

Since I returned from my holiday, my mood has taken a bit of a battering, perhaps as a delayed consequence of Brexit and the horror of contemplating a nation divided down the middle, or more likely because I'm still recovering from last year's traumas and suffering from decidedly ropey mental health – a fact that I sometimes forget or try and ignore. Shortly before the holiday I decided to self-medicate, or rather to self-non-medicate, going against medical guidance with the cessation of my daily anti-anxiety fix. Since then I've felt increasingly anxious, information which will doubtless come as no surprise to any GPs reading this. Motivating myself has become a challenge; keeping my spirits up an impossibility. I would not advise anyone to seek medical advice from me unless a mysterious virus has literally wiped out every other qualified medical professional on the planet. Even then, you're still better off looking on the internet.

On the plus side, my musical expedition continues. I've been to a different venue every single week, which is both impressive and unsustainable given the shortage of quality establishments playing host to regular live music, coupled with the fact that you won't catch me in New Cross, no matter how hard you look.

My latest venture was to the Shacklewell Arms in Dalston, a pub I'd visited just once previously with the intention of seeing Trust Fund, who I ended up bailing on due to exhaustion. The Shacklewell Arms has the sort of indie-hipster vibe that people will forever ascribe to me, irrespective of my countless efforts to reinvent myself. If I let my hair continue to grow, as I'm planning, there'll be no escaping such associations.

The night got off to a bad start when I walked into the ladies' toilets. The last time this happened was after a Twilight Singers gig in Camden. I was, as the Spanish would say, *un completo bastardo borracho*, and regretfully, my inebriation led me to venture through the wrong door, realise my mistake, attempt a swift exit, slip, fly into the air and land on my backside in a pool of dank and disgusting bathroom-floor-water in front of a gaggle of giggling female tourists.

My Shacklewell disaster was not a simple case of history repeating itself, but rather, short-sightedness (I'd forgotten my glasses) combined with poor signage. I wish venues would use clear and familiar symbols when directing customers to their facilities. When one is confronted with a choice between two peculiar painted creatures, one yellow, one pink, both adorned with writing scrawled in multi-coloured graffiti, one is forced into guesswork. Also, perhaps it's my age, but I confess I'm completely unable to read graffiti. As the signage left me no wiser about which door I should choose, I gambled, and I lost. Later in the evening I worked out that the graffiti read "Fellaz" and "Ladeez".

Idiots.

Such shortcomings aside, The Shacklewell Arms is a decent pub and a reasonably sized music venue for up and coming indie bands such as Whenyoung, a new venture by the former members of Sister. Being blunt, I had never heard of either, beyond a recommendation from Rhys who, given his current run-rate, may well in a year's time come to the unexpected realisation that he's also attended a gig every week.

It's sometimes hard to know how to approach these shows featuring unknown entities, shows where I lack the inside knowledge or background info to understand exactly what I'm seeing or why. I'm neither a journalist nor a hobbyist gig-reviewer, although I did enjoy a brief stint as the latter during my teens. I wrote under a mundane pseudonym for a short-lived local music website, using my anonymity for the purposes of evil, rather than journalistic impartiality, by taking the opportunity to stick the knife into every bitter rival of my own band The Angry Red Planets. Years later these reviews would resurface to haunt me after my pseudonym was exposed and the singer of Stone Fusion reminded me that I'd once described him as a "sex-mad buffoon".

Anyway, I'm of the view that putting down a detailed description of an unknown, unsigned band, outside a live review website constitutes a rather pointless exercise. Furthermore, in these half-hour performances the songs come and go in a flash, making it nigh on impossible to retain many details, unless a singular melody becomes etched upon the brain.

In the case of Whenyoung, I liked them, but I can no longer remember any of their songs. This is hardly a ringing endorsement, but nor should it be construed as criticism – it is reality, that's all.

I can tell you that they were a three-piece, female-fronted, a bit Sonic Youth, a bit post-punk, but with a lot more melody, and the less said about the drummer's hair the better, though of course, looking back through years of gig photos, the less said about my own hair the better.[17]

I can also tell you that I didn't enjoy the drumming, which felt too busy – too many kicks, too much snare and too many fills. Interestingly, when the drummer had to harmonise, he reverted to more conventional patterns and parts, to the benefit of the overall song. Sometimes men's inability to multitask can be a virtue.

By the time I walked back to the Overground station my earlier anxiety had given way to a sense of pleasure at my rekindled engagement with the unsigned music scene. Blink-182 are at the top of the charts this week and the majority of new major label artists seem remarkable only for how underwhelming they are. I'm happy that this expedition is shedding light on a world I'd hitherto ignored; ironic, given my many years of participation in it through various unsuccessful bands and side projects. The underground is alive, that's for sure, while the people selling shedloads of records and managing to make a living for themselves are the ones locked in drudgery and repetition. Except for Radiohead of course – their latest album is glorious – but one gets the feeling they're only releasing new material so that Thom Yorke can eventually save up enough to flee the planet.

---

17 As you may have noticed, I am obsessed with my hair.

Tired Lion, The Lexington, London, Thursday 14th July

- **Gig #7**
- **Musical birthdays:** Woody Guthrie (1912), Dan Smith of Bastille (1986)
- **Musical history:** Locals complain after it is unveiled that Sting has been approached to write an official anthem for Tuscany (2003)
- **Non-musical history:** The French Revolution begins with the fall of the Bastille (1789)[18]

My disconcertingly tall cousin Alex has been absent from my life of late due to a last-minute scramble to finish his PhD, an albatross around his giraffe-like neck these past eighteen months. It was a treat to find out, at ridiculously short notice, that our paths were to collide once more. Alex rarely responds to messages. Or voicemails. Or emails. I invite him to gigs and then immediately organise a back-up plan in case I don't hear from him. How he survives I don't know; I can't entertain such uncertainty and disorganisation in my life. Maybe things will improve once the PhD is completed, or maybe he'll move to Indonesia and become a hermit – I'd say it's 50/50 either way.

That being said, I couldn't knock Alex's enthusiasm on this occasion. He'd endeavoured to check out a Tired Lion song in advance, which is more than the rest of us (Rhys, Laura and myself) had achieved in the three weeks since the gig was booked. Tired Lion were another shot in the dark, a band with next to no online profile and a band name more likely to inspire narcolepsy than optimism. I had booked it just twenty-four hours before Rhys invited me to Whenyoung, meaning that technically this gig wasn't even needed. But that's hardly the point – we

---

18 I appear to have stumbled upon the rationale behind the naming of popular band Bastille, a delightful discovery, except for the fact that I don't like them.

were there to explore; to discover whether this latest unknown artist was destined for glory or destined to be buried in that tomb alongside the unknown soldier.

In an unexpected twist, Tired Lion turned out to be straight out of the '90s and very, very Australian.

I wonder what it was like being in Australia in the '90s. From the perspective of cultural exports, it strikes me that – for better or worse – the '90s was very much the Aussie heyday, with "Neighbours" and "Home and Away" at peak popularity, Natalie Imbruglia about to burst onto the music scene, Round the Twist leading the young people of the UK to assume that all Australians are insane and so on.

The only excuse I can offer up by way of explanation for my enjoyment of Tired Lion's performance is that, having grown up in the '90s, I'm the victim of cultural assimilation and thus utterly incapable of disliking their cheesy, out of date and sensationally uncool sounds. It fell somewhere between early Hole, which I don't like, Pearl Jam, who are awful, and Silverchair, who are worse. And yet it was impossible not to enjoy it – curse you Aussies for indoctrinating me over the course of my youth!

For the second night in a row I became totally preoccupied by the drumming. I heard it said once that Ringo never played the same drum fill from one song to the next. Tired Lion's drummer took this mantra to its most extreme conclusion. Every single section of every single song was totally different, as though he'd flicked a "product demonstration mode" switch and was henceforth automatically running through every part he was capable of playing. None of this suited the music or bore any relation to what the rest of the band was doing, but while in most circumstances this would be disastrous, for Tired Lion it was strangely effective.

Endeavouring to say something genuinely positive and without barb, it's been a long time since I saw a band so delighted, not to mention surprised, to be playing to a full room. Lord knows what the rest of the tour must've been like, as The Lexington isn't exactly large. As I watched their merry nonsense play out, I began to daydream once more, pontificating over the journey they'd been on to get to these shores, whether they had day jobs back in Oz and whose idea it had been to tour the UK. Did they have management, or were they just taking a chance, Field of Dreams-style?

Our band Silent Alliance, which ironically often gets misheard as "Silent Lions", once came close to touring Japan, but it was too hard for everyone to get time off work and we would have been forced to fund the trip ourselves. Perhaps we're all cut from the same cloth, except Tired Lion took the chance, sold off the family silver and are now slumming their way around UK pubs and clubs, earning £50 here and there for food and sleeping in their van.

By the time I emerged from these musings and returned from Oz, the band had finished, and I realised that I'd failed to pay any attention to half of the set, a worrying degree of absent mindedness that isn't without precedence. I did a similar thing while watching Suzanne Vega at Manchester Apollo in 1998. I also retreated into my own head for a full three hours during a performance of Benjamin Britten's operatic adaptation of "The Turn of the Screw", however this was deliberate and solely for the sake of my mental well-being, having never been confronted by such a mercilessly abominable racket.

Sun Kil Moon, Royal Festival Hall, London, Friday 22nd July

- **Gig #8**
- **Musical birthdays:** George Clinton (1941), Don Henley (1947), Rufus Wainwright (1973)
- **Musical history:** Aretha Franklin is arrested in Detroit following a disturbance in a parking lot; on leaving the police station, she promptly mows down a road sign (1969)
- **Non-musical history:** Wiley Post records the first solo flight around the world, posting a time of seven days and nineteen hours (1933)
- **Also:** Lightning kills 504 sheep in Wasatch National Park, Utah (1918)

I've been miserable and thoroughly not-myself all week; possibly not the ideal preparation for an artist who appears to specialise in pontificating on the hopeless futility of it all.

The peculiarly-named Sun Kil Moon, aka Mark Kozelek, has built up a reputation for doom and gloom, as well as for verbally abusing his audiences. Awkward and jarring audience interaction is one of the reasons I don't go to stand-up comedy. Thankfully, I don't generally have anything to worry about with live music, hence my perturbation as I arrived at the Royal Festival Hall wondering at what the evening might have in store for me.

It was strange being back in the Royal Festival Hall so soon after my last visit. If I ever get used to it, I'll know I've inadvertently risen in the British class system. If anything, it's a bit too civilised for someone like Sun Kil Moon. After about five minutes of the live show, I got the impression that he'd probably be happier in a redneck bar where the norm is for people to throw bottles as a signal of their discontent, and indeed their content.

Alex bought me the Sun Kil Moon album "Benji" for my birthday last year. I love it, but it is hard work, punctuated by unbelievably bleak, ponderous songs with high volumes of verses, very vague lyrical structures and various other oddities. A lot of the lyrics – which I'm assuming to be semi-autobiographical – are simultaneously disturbing and amusing. It's a unique piece of work, to say the least, but as I sat in partial terror watching him perform, I couldn't help thinking that his set was all a bit aimless. Too much meandering, not enough structure. One of the problems is that it's harder to hear the lyrics live, leaving some of the songs feeling very, very long. Over the duration of a two-and-a-half-hour performance, it made for a lot of bleakness and a lot of meandering.

Sun Kil Moon's songs could be broadly categorised into two camps, storytelling tracks, which I largely enjoyed, and topical tracks, which were to put it bluntly, rather blunt. Two of them, a song about the recent increase in mass shootings, and another about bereaved parents, sounded worryingly like misjudged charity singles – the sort that a bereaved parent might inflict upon the world, in honour of their deceased loved one, to raise a few thousand pounds for their new charitable foundation. I'm glad I didn't attempt to heckle him on this point. Kozelek's thunderous and acerbic wrath was plentiful. One unfortunate audience member was subject to a three-minute rant after he ill-advisedly shouted out, *"Mass shootings don't happen here mate."*

Kozelek tore him to shreds.

I'm being downbeat, I know – a reflection of my mood in general. I genuinely enjoyed most of the show and was impressed by Kozelek's voice throughout. There were numerous positives to take from the show, but they were obscured by the fact that I left the gig with the sense of having been through a considerable ordeal.

I guess it's a good experience to add to the mix, given that I'm doing an entire year of these gigs. If everything was rainbows, lollipops and unicorns, things might swiftly become dull. Although thinking about it, the above is a pretty accurate description of a Flaming Lips show.

Kone, The Sebright Arms, London, Friday 29th July

- **Gig #9**
- **Musical birthdays:** Brian Joseph Burton aka Danger Mouse (1977)
- **Musical history:** On the day of Charles and Diana's wedding, tribute records such as 'Lady D', by Typically Tropical and 'Diana', by Mike Berry, all fail to chart (1981)
- **Non-musical history:** English naval forces defeat the Spanish Armada, aided by a change in the direction of the wind (1588)

Not content with a band practice on Wednesday and a concert on Saturday, I snuck in an extra gig with Rhys this week so that he could find out whether the singer of Kone, with whom he'd done some recording eight years earlier, still recognised him or not.

She did.

Sadly, it was amongst the more underwhelming reunions that I've witnessed. As a firm believer in not speaking purely for the sake of it, I kept my post-gig contribution to a simple, "Well done." No doubt I made her evening.

Kone were, for want of a better word, "angular". To this day, I'm not entirely clear what the descriptor "angular" means or where it came from, but I'm relatively confident that it means Kone. We came out of the show confused and unsure whether we'd enjoyed ourselves or not.

The band that followed, Barricades, were less angular and far more enjoyable for their absence of corners – a blast of high energy garage rock with some Muse stylings thrown in for good measure. It was just a shame about the bassist, or should I say, the lack of one. I wish that the White Stripes had never existed, not because I dislike them, but because they made it cool to go out to the world with an unfinished band. When Prince made an artistic decision to cut the bass on "When Doves Cry" and "Kiss", it was cool. It's not cool to cut the bass because you can't be arsed finding a bassist. Rhys claimed that the guitar/ drum only combo is so popular because it's the easiest arrangement to arrive at. I pointed out that the easiest arrangement is not to bother at all.

Ultimately, this gig was most notable for a live-first, something I've never seen before and don't expect to see a lot of going forwards. It is the only time I've ever seen a confused attendee walk onto the stage mid-set, having taken the wrong route downstairs to the venue. One can imagine the shame and humility suffered by the poor young gent when he opened a door to find an entire room full of people staring back at him. I'll be surprised if he goes out in public again – it's not worth the risk.

Ludovico Einaudi, Royal Festival Hall, London, Saturday 30th July

- **Gig #10**
- **Musical birthdays:** Kate Bush (1958), Jyoti Mishra aka White Town (1966), Louise Wener (1968), Ian Watkins (1979)
- **Musical history:** Johnny Cash records 'Folsom Prison Blues' at Sun Studios in Memphis (1955)
- **Non-musical history:** There is much rejoicing (and presumably a lot of Folsom Prison Blues recitals) after a ban on steel-string guitars in prison cells is overturned following lobbying by Billy Bragg (2014)

Who the hell is Ludovico Einaudi and how did he get to be so popular? On arguably the greatest musical day of the calendar year,[19] this was my initial and admittedly harsh reaction to yet another night at the Royal Festival Hall. Admittedly I know precious little about classical music; however, it came as a genuine surprise to find a venue packed to the rafters as they witnessed a small, ageing Italian chap who played the entire show facing the rear of the stage. A belated birthday present for Laura, this was a not insignificant outlay for what proved to be two hours of watching the back of a man's bald head.

That said, I was in an obvious minority with such views. On arguably the worst musical day of the calendar year,[20] Einaudi received standing ovation after standing ovation from this adoring crowd, and it was difficult not to be swept along with their euphoria, despite my ever-active brain nagging at the question of why exactly everyone was so enamoured by the performance.

Einaudi specialises in what I'd describe as atmospheric film soundtrack music – like going to a concert by Angelo Badalamenti

---

19 Kate Bush's birthday.
20 Ian Watkins' birthday.

or something of that ilk. At times, it was very impressive, drawing me in with its wooziness and almost sending me to sleep at several points (due to relaxation, not boredom).[21] The concert also introduced Laura and I to the waterphone, a unique musical instrument the operation of which I couldn't quite fathom, despite having since been sent an explanatory diagram. The last time I felt that way was seeing Bjork at Hammersmith Apollo, an epic electronica show, during which, at no point, could I figure out what any of the musicians were doing.

Einaudi put on a strong performance, I can't deny it. Two and a half hours of absorbing, instrumental piano-led music with rousing strings, understated electronics and stirring waterphone. But as we took our leave, I still didn't understand the rapture – how he had managed to captivate so many people with his background soundtrack and bald bonce.

I guess that's the beauty of music, particularly in London. It's almost always possible to find an audience if you're talented, and the city is such a melting pot that it's possible to be exposed to types of music that you'd never normally come across. It makes me concerned about what might happen to the country given the current divergence of opinion about Europe and freedom of movement. I hope people of different backgrounds and cultures will continue to be welcomed here. People like Einaudi should be able to come and play for us at the drop of a hat (and my guess is that Einaudi has a large collection of exceptionally stylish Italian hats).

On a side note, I noticed that Einaudi's other tour dates were peculiar to say the least. Plymouth, Bournemouth, Birmingham and Glasgow. Maybe he wanted to enjoy a spot of sea-bathing

---

21 Back in 2002 I went one step further, succumbing to the comfort of the inviting Albert Hall seating and drifting off for several songs of a Lambchop gig. In my defence, I'd consumed two bottles of wine and it was during the "Is a Woman" tour, a record that gives a whole new meaning to the term "understated".

on our glorious south coast. Or possibly, he's looking to follow in the footsteps of other pensioners and retire there.

I'm being harsh. He didn't look that old.

Though my eye-sight is pretty bad.

Because I'm old.

Weeks 9–14:
Make a Scene

When I was growing up, I wanted to be an astronaut, followed by an airline pilot. Finally, any sort of explorer. I used to have a VHS documentary on the space race that I'd watch repeatedly, while my pre-bedtime TV would typically consist of Madhur Jaffrey's "Flavours of India" and "Holiday" with Jill Dando. I loved these glimpses into other worlds – from the gorgeous summer seaside resorts of Southern Europe, to the exotic otherness of India, to the less exotic, but extreme otherness of the Moon. I also had a VHS of "The Little Prince"[22], the rather bleak French tale of intergalactic exploration. Doubtless, my mum had bought it to try and advance within me what would ultimately prove a fruitless pursuit of bilingualism. It's also possible that she wished me to grow up, instilled with a profound understanding of the human condition within early 1940s French society. Either way, she failed, and it was the intergalactic element of the narrative that caught my attention from such an early age.

Unfortunately, in a cruel twist of fate that I'll put down to either the trauma of my parents' separation aged nine, or the discovery of beer aged thirteen, I forgot all about such grand career aspirations during my descent towards early adulthood. By the time I remembered them again, I had already commenced my professional life in an all-too-conventional office-based role.

---

22 I would later find out that the original novella, Le Petit Prince, is the fourth most-translated book in the world and was voted the best book of the 20th century in France. Who knew?

I'm calling my gig-a-week project an "expedition" because it taps into that innate love of exploration. I may have spent the bulk of my post-university years sitting behind a desk, but I always had an inkling (and now an inking) that perhaps there was more to life than a career in corporate communications, and that this greater meaning might be something worth exploring.

The use of the term "expedition" is also reflective of my idolisation of Michael Palin's travel documentaries. Racing around trying to meet deadlines and itineraries, Palin still always finds the time to chat to locals and explore his surroundings, whether bleak, bone-chilling or banal. He has the wonderful knack of making every stop feel like it's an essential addition to the globe-trotter's bucket list. Over the years, he's influenced my travel plans on innumerable occasions, most recently inducing me to book a winter excursion to Tromsø with Rhys to see in the New Year. Only Palin could've persuaded me to arrange a trip to the arctic circle, to a town of only seventy thousand inhabitants, at the coldest part of the year, when the sun doesn't manage to rise. Will there be live music in Tromsø? There'd better be, or my plans will be in tatters, with Rhys and I forced to steal some guitars and busk outside the Cathedral.

This might not be a bad idea, given the worrying anecdotes people have fed me about the price of pizzas in Norway.

My exploits may pale in comparison to the great explorers of this world, but after making it through the first five or six weeks of my minor musical expedition, I've started to feel a sense of purpose, excitement and above all duty, towards my mission. It's still early days but the prospect of achieving something meaningful, however small, is spurring me on from one week to the next. My weekly gig calendar is starting to fill up right the way into December and, so far, I haven't encountered too many hurdles in terms of finding bands who I'm at least half interested in seeing. Perhaps there's a parallel to travelling in this respect. You get excited about China, Brazil, Russia and New Zealand, but you're only stopping at Slovenia and Finland because they're on the way to somewhere else. It's not that these destinations are without merit or charm, it's just that you know far less about them and it's therefore harder to view them with the same eagerness. I have Steely Dan, Wilco and James waiting for me between now and Christmas. The trick is to make sure that Sunflower Bean and Clay are also afforded the attention and respect that they deserve.

As a general principle, I try to start with the assumption that all bands exist for a reason, and all have made the effort to go out and get shows because of some sort of underlying motivation, whatever that motivation may be. I've played in many bands since the age of thirteen, clocking up some abominable performances during that time, playing on out-of-tune instruments or with amps that have fallen apart mid-set, entertaining crowds of sub-10 people, and on one occasion at Mother Bar in Shoreditch, playing to an audience consisting solely of my sister. Had she lost a limb earlier in life then we would have literally experienced the sound of one hand clapping.

These were setbacks, to say the least, and I haven't even mentioned the time I accidentally snapped another band's guitar in half after falling off the stage at the Proud Galleries in Camden. I've kept going over the years because the buzz of a successful performance makes absolutely everything else worthwhile. It's highly addictive, and thus very hard to imagine any performance being your last, which is why I think it's understandable that you invariably find so many middle-aged women and men still playing regularly at local jam nights or pubs and wedding gigs. Many of these bands look and sound utterly ridiculous, more so if they take themselves too seriously, but there's a fundamental difference between seriousness and sincerity in music, and I'm of the view that if the bands are sincere – even if that means sincerely silly – then they must be afforded some respect. I've always hated Robbie Williams, a man who has more than a couple of decent tunes to his name, because he has always come across as being devoid of conviction towards either his craft or his audience. In contrast, James Blunt knows that he's middle of the road and not very good, but he does his best based on his abilities, and he seems happy if anyone decides to listen to it. I don't get the impression

Robbie Williams gives a damn about anything he does, providing it inflates his bank balance and fluffs his ego. He's the music industry equivalent of Boris Johnson.

It's out of my control, but ideally, I hope that my year-long expedition will manage to steer entirely clear of insincerity – there's enough of it already in this world. I don't mind if the bands I see are godawful, so long as they mean it.

Helpless, The Unicorn, London, Friday 5th August

- **Gig #11**
- **Musical birthdays:** Pete Burns (1959), Dan Hipgrave of Toploader (1975)[23]
- **Musical history:** Legendary country/rock singer David Crosby is sentenced to five years' jail-time for cocaine and firearms offences. The defence is not helped by Crosby sleeping his way through most of the trial (1983)
- **Non-musical history:** Plaid Cymru is formed, with the specific intention of rekindling the dying Welsh language (1925)

After another week spent suffering from low motivation and unpredictable mood swings, I was hit by a last-minute gigging disaster. We had intended to venture down to the Old Blue Last for the first time in years to see a promising sounding band called Future Love, however Rhys had been forced to bail, due to a forgotten prior commitment. Then at six p.m. on the day of the show, Nick called me up complaining of man flu.

The problem with suffering from low motivation is self-explanatory. Could I be bothered to head out to Shoreditch for a depressing evening on my lonesome? I could not. However, with plans already set in stone for the following two days, I had no option but to seek out an alternative show nearer to home.

---

23 A rotten day for music.

I decided to take a risk and head up the road to The Unicorn, a free venue that promises seven days of live metal every single week. That's an awful lot of metal. I'd been there once before to see my friend Dave's sensational noisefest Pist supporting the regrettably named Foetal Juice. This Friday night was "post hardcore" night. I knew not what this meant, but I held out little hope that post hardcore would prove more soothing and melodic than Foetal Juice's cacophonous dirge.

I arrived fifteen minutes before Helpless took to the stage, with low expectations given my previous experience at the venue. I felt rather helpless myself, given the eleventh-hour cancellations. One glimpse of the bassist's hair was enough to confirm that this was not going to be a quiet and laid-back affair. That said, I felt strangely at home in The Unicorn. The crowd was friendly and welcoming, much like the majority of the metal crowds I've encountered over the years. Metal has always struck me as one of the warmest and most sociable of music communities, perhaps because margins must be low, and much camaraderie must be needed to keep bands in business. I'm aware that there may have been the occasional murder exchanged between rival bands in the Scandinavian Black Metal scene, but I'm assuming that's just one of those regrettable minorities who give the rest of the Nordic Black Metallers a bad name.[24] And there was Dimebag Darrell of Pantera, who was shot and killed on stage by a former marine in Columbus, Ohio, in December 2004, but that seemed more a symptom of America's problematic gun culture than a reflection of troubles within the heavy metal scene. Dimebag Darrell was one of the true legends of metal, a colossus of the genre, as well

---

24 In 1993 tensions erupted between Black Metallers Euronymous and Vikernes, culminating in Vikernes and Snorre "Blackthorn" Ruch driving to Osla and fatally stabbing Euronymous. My further research has also revealed several dozen arson attacks on churches spanning the early 1990s; information which suggests that I probably shouldn't be letting this sub-genre off the hook so lightly.

as a legendary drinker[25] who modern metal bands are still trying (and mostly failing) to emulate. The last time I was at The Unicorn, one of the scheduled bands didn't play at all because they got too drunk and had to be taken home.

Helpless produced one of the noisiest and most dissonant soundscapes I've ever experienced. Constant screaming from the lead vocalist was supported by several backing screamers and underpinned by a raucous discord that ran unabated through every song. Remarkably, it was quite enjoyable, particularly the epic set-closer which stood out for its unbelievable intensity. I'm not sure I'd listen to it on record, for fear of my neighbours reporting me to the police, but it was an unexpected high in an evening that so very nearly derailed my entire expedition.

Elle Exxe, The Birthday Club, London, Thursday 11th August

- **Gig #12**
- **Musical birthdays:** Andy Bell of Ride (1970), Ben Gibbard of Death Cab for Cutie (1976)
- **Musical history:** Led Zeppelin play their last ever UK show at Knebworth (1979)
- **Non-musical history:** The last US ground forces withdraw from Vietnam (1972)
- **Also:** Karl Wiosna from Graig, Wales, has his stereo equipment destroyed by the authorities following complaints about the volume at which he was playing his Cher and U2 records (2008)

---

25 He is credited with creating the official drink for Pantera, the "Black Tooth Grin", containing a large shot of Seagrams Seven, a large shot of Crown Royal and a splash of coke. It is essentially a whiskey and coke, albeit a strong one.

When I began this journey, I pinpointed August as the potential problem month. Two weeks in, and my fears have already been borne out. Six days ago, I had to venture alone to listen to the near-nihilism of the post-hardcore scene. Tonight, we almost missed out entirely. Originally, I was going to see a band I'd never heard of called Toy, only to learn that I'd got the night of the gig wrong. Then I was going to see Gum, a Tame Impala-offshoot I'd also never heard of at the Moth Club. Rhys and I showed up with our free e-tickets, looking forward to seeing what this mysterious side project had to offer. As it turned out, we were offered only the street. Despite being ticketed, the bouncer took great pleasure in informing us that the gig was first come first served. Bouncers are generally about as receptive to questioning or counterpoints as they are to reason, logic or fair and equal treatment for all. I've argued with a few in my time, invariably resulting in my ejection from the venue in question. Hence, much though I wished to quiz him on the logic behind offering tickets for a show if the ticket provides zero guarantee of getting in, we decided instead to walk at a pace over from Hackney to Dalston in the hope of catching Elle Exxe – Plan C put into swift motion.

We arrived just moments before she took to the stage and her performance, it must be said, put paid to my complaints. Rhys was aware of Elle Exxe from a music production project he'd worked on a while back and described her to me on our walk over as "raunchy pop." I would've liked to have been in a raunchy pop band at some stage in my career but alas, the opportunity has never presented itself and, as I'm now underway with my thirty-third year, one suspects that the raunchy boat may have passed me by. Rhys was correct though – it was rather raunchy, especially for a prude such as myself. I'm not a fan of T-shirts that feature depictions of the naked female form, less so ones that provide a marker pen outline of the wearer's actual bosoms. To me, that's more weird than raunchy, as well as being extremely distracting. I'm also not sure why a serious musician would want to wilfully encourage half the audience to stare at their chest, but then, I know nothing of fashion, little of contemporary art, and not a great deal about chests.

Anyway, sound and beats and vocals quickly took over and I began to get into the Elle Exxe groove. It turns out that Elle is Scottish, and I can honestly say I've never heard a Scottish person make raunchy music before. In fact, the only artists I can think of that could claim to be in the raunchy ballpark are Rod Stewart and Sheena Easton, and both require quite a stretch of the imagination.

A bit Beyoncé, a bit Amy Winehouse, a bit Kesha,[26] we were treated to forty-five minutes of upbeat, bombastic R&B and dance-infused pop music from a woman with excessively large hair and an excessively large stage presence. Elle Exxe is clearly still trying to make her way up the ladder and the venue was far from jam-packed, however she received a rapturous response from those in the know and even managed to elicit call and response audience participation. A huge risk for an unknown artist, the call and response, if unsuccessfully executed, can induce an audience-wide cringe and kill the gig. I once saw Placebo bomb at V Festival after Brian Molko attempted to get everyone to sing along to "Slave to the Wage". For whatever reason, the audience couldn't grasp what he was beseeching them to undertake, until he became so pissed off he aborted the attempt and brought the song to a halt. The rest of the gig was lacklustre, and I haven't been back to see Placebo since because of the awkwardness. That was fifteen years ago.

---

26 In honesty, I have no idea who this is, what she sounds like or why she sometimes appears with a dollar sign in her name, however my enlightened editor has since made me aware of the abuse she suffered while carving out her career in music, so I doff my cap to her for her achievements and hope that one day the music industry will shift its arse out of the Stone Age.

Clay, Hoxton Square Bar & Kitchen, London, Friday 12ᵗʰ August

- **Gig #13**
- **Musical birthdays:** Mark Knopfler (1949), Ron Mael of Sparks (1950), August Darnell of Kid Creole and The Coconuts (1951), Sir Mix-A-Lot (1963)
- **Musical history:** To close the LA Olympic Games, Lionel Richie performs "All Night Long" to an estimated global television audience of 2.6 billion people (1984)
- **Non-musical history:** Queen Cleopatra VII commits suicide in Egypt (30 BC)
- **Also:** The two-day Moscow Music Peace Festival, featuring performances from Motley Crue, Ozzy Osbourne and Bon Jovi, marks the first time that an audience can stand up and dance at a concert in the Soviet Union (1989)

Clay was supposed to be a calculated risk. I would enjoy a credible rock artist (Gum) on my Thursday night, leaving Friday free for an unknown Yorkshire youth pop act that I had felt increasingly dubious about ever since I saw a picture of them.[27] Then of course, I ended up seeing Elle Exxe last night, in doing so, receiving my pop fix for the week. Hence there was no point to Clay, no reason for my being there. I almost suggested to my friend Eleri that we go for a meal or do something else entirely, however we had paid for the tickets and so it seemed daft not to at least check them out. Hailing from South Wales and spending many blissful days of her youth helping her dad run the bars for gigantic Welsh music and sporting events (think Tom Jones or anything relating to rugby), Eleri is my gigging soul sister and she's always held a special place in my heart since she turned up on her lonesome to see one of my band's shows. Unfortunately,

---

27 They were in possession of what can only be described as "suspicious hair".

I wasn't wearing my glasses at the time and so I didn't recognise her; I've spent the subsequent decade trying to atone for this.

As it was, our attendance served as charity to these young whippersnappers. Crowd numbers were low, and every additional audience member went just that little bit further towards sparing the bands blushes, which were made more pronounced by their extensive lighting rig and illuminated Clay logo. Bands that have labels and financing behind them aren't supposed to be playing to empty rooms and it's always awkward as hell when a promoter misjudges their popularity.[28]

Eleri and I were meat in the room and almost totally indifferent to the band's output, but given they all looked about twelve years old we didn't want to knock their confidence by walking out after two songs. The music was so poppy it could've been produced by a boy band and boy bands aren't especially popular in Shoreditch right now. Perhaps they will improve with time and maturity, but the music industry can be brutal and short-termist. I see a one-way-ticket back to Yorkshire looming, unless of course they're being bankrolled by a rich aunt or a former member of Toploader, the band they most resembled. Harsh, but fair.

Laurel, The Social, London, Tuesday 17th August

- **Gig #14**
- **Musical birthdays:** Kevin Rowlands (1953), Belinda Carlisle (1958), Maria McKee (1964), Donnie Wahlberg (1969), Claire Richards of Steps (1977)
- **Musical history:** Paul Williams, former singer in The Temptations, shoots himself in his car, leaving behind $80,000 in unpaid taxes and a failed celebrity boutique business (1973)

---

28 For a similar example, see East 17, who in 2015 played a gig in Dublin to just thirty fans after demand was severely over-estimated.

- **Non-musical history:** John White, North Carolinian Governor of Roanoke Island colony, returns from England to find everyone in his colony has vanished (1590), while 355 years later, Korea is divided into North and South (1945)
- **Also:** Glasgow council introduces a city-wide policy of mandatory bathing caps for anyone sporting a Beatle-cut due to excessive volumes of hair clogging local swimming pool filters (1964)

Since when did The Heavenly Social get rebranded as The Social? Not that I'd ever been there before – I have no right to care. This was my first venture to this tucked away and tiny venue near Oxford Circus. I remember Heavenly Records from the days when buying CD singles was central to my very being, and I would read every single line of text on the sleeve to discern who wrote the track, where it was recorded, and of course, which label had the pleasure and privilege of the artist's company. My first Heavenly single was "From a Window" by Northern Uproar, a classic slice of northern Britpop from a band whose career was sadly cut short by a total lack of interest from anyone other than me and the small contingent of Mancunians who would listen to anything and everything that sounded remotely Oasis-like. We even used to eat in the Oasis Café near Afflecks Palace, despite it being underwhelming, overpriced and having nothing whatsoever to do with the band.

I saw Northern Uproar play at Burnley Mechanics in either late 1995 or early 1996, making it my second or third gig. It was my first standing show (there are no seats at Burnley Mechanics) and to describe it as a baptism of fire would be putting it mildly. They were supported by The Cornerstones, a band who never made it as far as Northern Uproar but whose debut EP I still have to this day, proudly signed by all the band, who we met while wandering around the bar in the vague hope that someone might buy us a pint (they didn't). During The Cornerstones' set, we discovered that the crowd were very much alive to the phenomenon of pogoing, a concept with which I was unfamiliar at the time. I emerged forty-five minutes later battered, bruised and lamenting the fact that everyone else in the venue was a clear foot taller than I was. After a short period of recuperation, I pushed my way back to the front and did it all over again.

Returning from this brief sojourn down memory lane, sadly we weren't at The Social to witness the spectacle of a reformed, rejuvenated Northern Uproar, but to check out a singer-songwriter called Laurel, of whom neither Alex nor myself had heard. It was the day after Alex's viva and the completion of a long-awaited PhD, so this was a gig-based celebration to follow his official, more conventional celebration the previous evening. My night had been derailed first by having to break for my therapy session after several pints,[29] and second by getting stuck next to a drunken philosopher who took issue with everything I said. I am used to such objections when, from time to time, I make an ill-judged dive into their philosophical pond; last night, however, my conversational contributions were about Neil Young, Audrey Hepburn and Woody Allen. My major learning: "real" Jews don't like Woody's work. It would appear I'm not a real Jew.

Anyway, Dr. Alex was all apologies for his friend's behaviour, a normal and expected occurrence after alcohol has been consumed by the young gent, and so the matter was put to bed. We made our way into The Social, a tight squeeze of a venue and arguably better suited to unpopular artists than acts like Laurel. Heavenly seems to be pretty invested in her, perhaps because she sounds more than a little like Lana Del Rey, and ever so slightly like Adele. That said, Laurel was better when she veered away from such mimicry; Lana because she's too unique to ape effectively, Adele because she's far too ubiquitous.

Laurel's songs had a haunting quality, enhanced by her distorted and disjointed guitar accompaniment. But as we were leaving the venue, those songs were already fading from my mind,

---

29 I am not sure that you're supposed to drink before therapy.

leaving me to fear that she was destined to become another artist, like Northern Uproar, lost in the sands of time. Laurel was also quite the potty-mouth, which further detracted from my enjoyment. I don't like swearing in music. It's my Victorian side coming to the fore, a repression borne of never swearing around my parents, nor being sworn to, which means I am embarrassed to this day if anyone swears in the presence of my mother. I have no idea why this discomfort extends to song lyrics, but I guess that's just how the cards are dealt.

Bugeye, The Sebright Arms, London, Saturday 27th August

- **Gig #15**
- **Musical birthdays:** Malcolm Allured of Showaddywaddy (1945), Glen Matlock (1956)
- **Musical history:** Beatles manager Brian Epstein is found dead at his London home after a suspected overdose of sleeping pills (1967)
- **Non-musical history:** Krakatoa erupts with a force of 1,300 megatons, killing 40,000 people (1883)
- **Also:** Miley Cyrus popularises the twerk in front of a global audience at MTV's Video Music Awards (2013)

After two successive underwhelming shows in a mostly underwhelming month of gigging, not to mention weeks of battling ongoing mental health challenges, low motivation and lack of energy, this week brought with it another hasty and regrettable last-minute gig rearrangement. I had been planning to go to an obscure Welsh language music festival in Cardigan, however my enthusiasm waned when I saw where Cardigan was on the map (it is the opposite of nearby), before disintegrating entirely on receiving the news that Eleri had rowed with her father and the offer of a caravan had been subsequently withdrawn. Rhys, the boldest of the three of us, as well as the only fluent Welsh speaker, decided to go on his own. From his later description of the weekend, it sounded as though the event resembled more of a school fete than a major music festival.

Anyway, it meant I was yet again short of my weekly gig quota, hence a return visit to the Sebright Arms with Eleri to see yet another hitherto unknown act called Bugeye. I made things tricky for myself by walking more than thirty miles in the preceding thirty-six hours (half the Central Line) meaning that I turned up to the Sebright Arms barely capable of movement. After falling down the stairs into the venue, I propped myself up against the wall and waited for Bugeye, a three-piece comprising two prim and proper looking women in flowery dresses, along with the obligatory geeky drummer. Despite appearances, they were loud and raucous, recalling Courtney Love back before she lost the ability to sing, play the guitar or string a coherent sentence together. They also had a cowbell, one of the most ridiculous yet joyous percussive instruments of all time – a welcome first for my expedition.

Bugeye were great. The only bum note was their new single, which was dissonant, bordering on unlistenable. Why they chose it as a focus track is beyond me, but that said, the song, like the gig, was over in a flash, leaving me to cause a small pile up in the corridor as I attempted, slowly and painfully, to climb the stairs and get myself home to a much-needed ice bath.

Red Sun Revival, Zigfrid Von Underbelly, London, Friday 2nd September

- **Gig #16**
- **Musical birthdays:** Billy Preston (1946)
- **Musical history:** Thieves break into Bjork's London home while she's asleep and steal her recording equipment (2002)
- **Non-musical history:** Eighty percent of London is destroyed after The Great Fire of London begins at two a.m. on Pudding Lane (1666)

I always used to think Goth music was very silly. And, largely, it is, however the darkening of my mood over the past twelve months seems to have invoked within me a greater appreciation for the genre. As I write, I'm listening to Sisters of Mercy, who are daft as a brush, and yet rather brilliant at the same time.

This was my first Goth show of the expedition and, suitably timed to coincide with the end of summer, we were heading out to watch Red Sun Revival, a band I was only aware of because the violinist is my siblings' former babysitter. As she was never my babysitter, I can't claim to know her all that well, hence when I heard about the show I was apprehensive. I hate seeing acquaintances play live, just in case they're rubbish, and I have to lie to them about it afterwards. Alex has taken this to a whole other level; on the rare occasions he plays solo shows, he has a tendency either not to promote them to anyone, or worse, to actively discourage people from attending and appearing visibly irritated if they show up irrespective. For me, I experienced a truly painful moment a few years ago when I was sent a whole arsenal of demos by a distant friend asking for some constructive feedback. I listened to the first song and it was shit. I listened to the second song and it was shit. The third song was of a similar standard to the first two. I had nine more to go. By the final track I swore that going forwards I'd avoid any situation that required me to give musical feedback to someone I knew. I also swore that, if an opportunity presented itself, I'd break my friend's fingers in the hope of bringing his musical career to a premature end.

As it happened, Red Sun Revival were fantastic. There was too much reliance on their backing track, while the band was also carrying their second guitarist, who barely played and looked suspiciously like a younger Meatloaf, but nevertheless it was an accomplished performance driven by the lead singer's lovely Marr-meets-Sumner-esque guitars and an atmospheric electric violin. There is something very epic about Goth music. While I can understand why some people might hate it or see it as too self-important, grandiose or overblown, I quite like the melodrama and over-blown sense of sincerity. Red Sun Revival played as though every line and every note really *mattered*, giving the performance greater warmth and emotional power than much of what I had seen during the previous month.

I was quick to congratulate Christina at the end of the show. It seems she is just as bad at taking compliments about her music as I am, and I reduced her to embarrassed silence with my effusion about the performance. Most awkwardly, I remarked that she is clearly as competent a musician as she is a babysitter, a unique combination which, given the age of her bandmates, could potentially bode well for any extensive touring commitments. Paul and Linda McCartney famously took their children on every Wings tour during the 70s, and except for their aborted final tour of Japan,[30] the ill-effects of a life on the road appeared few and far between.

Sophie Ellis Bextor, Bush Hall, London, Thursday 8th September

- **Gig #17**
- **Musical birthdays:** Jimmie Rodgers (1897), Patsy Cline (1932), Aimee Mann (1960), Alicia Moore aka Pink (1979)
- **Musical history:** Bruce Dickinson of Iron Maiden makes an unexpected career change as a chartered airline pilot, starting work as a first officer with Gatwick-based airline Astraeus and flying holiday-makers to Southern Europe and North Africa (2002)
- **Non-musical history:** In Florence, Michelangelo's statue of David is first unveiled, giving considerable delight to lovers of fine art everywhere (1504)
- **Also:** Star Trek is first broadcast, giving considerable delight to lovers of sci-fi and fine acting everywhere (1966)

---

30 Macca was arrested on arrival and spent a week in jail ingratiating himself to fellow inmates with some impromptu a cappella performances through the bars of his cell.

I've always prided myself on my musical eclecticism,[31] hence I took some satisfaction in the knowledge that, one week after a brief gothic interlude, the next stop of my expeditions landed me in the peculiar realm of the former pop icon. That's the beauty of music – you like what you like and damn the eyes of any naysayers.

Rick and I have always loved Sophie Ellis Bextor. During the summer of 2002, shortly after we celebrated our nineteenth birthdays, my mum and my siblings left me solo in the family home for a fortnight. Rick would turn up every night with a crate of beer, accompanied by a random bunch of acquaintances – different friends, foes, waifs and strays every night – and we'd watch music TV for hours with a VHS permanently armed to record every gem that we came across. The aim was to create the most incredible pop video compilation, a one-off treasure that could be enjoyed time and again for years to come. DVDs killed that dream but there's no doubt that we chose a great summer for our pop immersion. The big singles were Vanessa Carlton's "A Thousand Miles", Avril Lavigne's "Complicated" and Amy Studt, who warned us in "Just a Little Girl", *"Don't ever underestimate what I can do."* Unfortunately, her rather short lived musical career suggests that she was anything but underestimated.

Sophie Ellis Bextor had arrived the previous summer with "Groovejet", "Take Me Home" and "Murder on the Dancefloor", the combination of which induced me see one of her earliest solo shows, a clunky performance at Shepherds Bush Empire that somehow managed to become an official live DVD further down the line. Undeterred, I journeyed to Nottingham to see her again with Rick and enjoyed a far more accomplished performance, along with a moment of worrying precognition about life to come, when she covered Talking Heads' "Once in a Lifetime" and I realised that I was the only one in the crowd old enough to have a clue what it was.

---

31 The only genre I refuse to countenance is hip hop, which I see as the musical equivalent of a failed state.

Her big single in the summer of 2002 was "Get Over You", not a particularly fine track but a video in which she looked undeniably fantastic. We had quite the crush on her; fast forward fourteen years and it's comforting to find that some things never change.

Sophie is thirty-seven and has spent the last few years collaborating with Ed Harcourt, one of my favourite singer songwriters. Rick and I both observed the last tour in Manchester and delighted the social media world when we had our photo taken with Sophie afterwards. She seemed impressed when I told her that we had first seen her performing in a band called The Audience, supporting James at Manchester Apollo in 1998. I neglected to mention that I'd also once had breakfast with her mum.[32]

While we went home elated that night, resolute and determined to attend her next show as and when it materialised, I was now a bit apprehensive. After all, the Ed Harcourt co-written album Wanderlust was a one off, masking an uninspiring ten years beforehand.

I shouldn't have worried. The lights went down, the band took to the stage, and Ed was there. It turned out they'd co-written a second, equally charming pop record that was played, note-perfect, in its entirety. Afterwards we queued again for another autographed CD and the chance for a second picture with her, at which point Rick embarrassed us by coming over a little too gushing, before compounding his error by accidentally walking off with her phone.

I love gigs that randomly connect past with present, and despite the scorn and bewilderment that has often greeted my self-professed love of Sophie Ellis Bextor,[33] she connects me with an important summer in my life, coming out of my first relationship,

---

32 Janet Ellis, of Blue Peter fame. It was purely professional, I promise. I'm not that guy. I don't entirely know what I mean by that.

33 When I emailed my friend Dana to invite her along to the show, her response was: *"Ah, you're kidding me ... You are kidding, right?"*

reconnecting with absent friends following my first year away at university, learning about who I was and discovering my love of pop music for the first time as an adult.

She also connects me with Rick, one of my three longest-standing friends, reminding me of how much we've experienced together and how many great stories[34] we share of that time. The gig was another triumph for Sophie and a definite triumph of an evening for me — a reminder that even when mental health is difficult to manage, the love of music endures and the most beautiful of times can still be experienced.

---

34 By "great", I mean "reprehensible."

Weeks 15–19:
Into the Diamond Sun

Where were you on the day following the Brexit vote? Did you have a soundtrack to your own personal Brexit? I was in Coconut Grove at the time, twenty minutes south of Miami and a stone's throw from Biscayne Bay, immortalised in mid-70s Steely Dan's track "Doctor Wu," the standout selection from Katy Lied. Katy Lied is famous for the band's notorious "revolving door" approach to their musicians, challenging the very notion of the term "band" by employing no less than seven different guitarists for a ten-track album. I spent most of the Brexit aftermath lying by the hotel pool listening to The Dan while attempting to recover from a night of minimal rest, nothing out of the ordinary for an insomniac such as myself, but an affliction that I was for once able to blame a hundred percent on David Cameron, for forcing me to stay up and witness the full consequences of his weeks of scaremongering and party-political madness.

Where were you when you found out about the death of David Bowie? I was at my old flat in Camden, unemployed, rapidly running out of money and thoroughly lacking in motivation when I awoke at eight a.m. to a text from my mum alerting me to the awful truth. I spent the day trying to apply for jobs while Sky News blared out hastily compiled tributes on repeat in the background, punctuated only by clips taken from the haunting Lazarus video. In the evening, I took a wander into the centre of London and observed well-judged digital tributes, courtesy of the BT Tower and the National Theatre. I'd bought Blackstar on its release date just a few days earlier, but I couldn't bring myself to put it on that day – the incessant Sky reporting was already inducing me to tears.

If you've made music a meaningful part of your life then you'll always find an association, however tenuous, between your musical world and the events unfolding around you every day. Going back two decades, I'll never forget the day Princess Diana died, not because I'm one of those weirdos who stood outside Buckingham Palace for a week claiming a deep personal connection with and to the people's princess, but because of the bizarre musical footnote that began my morning. I had a paper round at the time and walked into the newsagent early on the Sunday in question to find huge discrepancies in the front pages that faced me. *"Diana is in a car accident,"* according to some; *"Dodi is dead, Diana is in critical condition,"* according to others; *"Diana is dead,"* according to the most recent editions to arrive in north Manchester. Yet the one that's etched into my memory is the front page of the News of the World, which had gone to print before the news broke of Diana's demise and instead featured a grainy image of Noel Gallagher mooning the paparazzi from his summer holiday home. "Be Here Now" had been released ten days previous at the height of Oasis's domestic popularity and, if you're to believe the acclaimed "Live Forever" documentary, the album was to mark the zenith of Britpop, for all of two weeks before the death of Diana triggered the conclusion of this blissful but brief period in sociocultural history.

Oasis were everywhere back then and while it's nevertheless hard to understand how Noel Gallagher's arse constituted news, I've never been the editor of a major UK tabloid newspaper. One week later, Oasis couldn't have made it onto the front page if they'd tried. Mother Theresa couldn't manage to make a splash, despite dying, which is usually a guaranteed headline-grabbing act. The people's princess was to dominate the headlines for an entire month, or, in the case of the Daily Express, for a further fifteen years.

We all remember the most significant moments in our own personal histories, and for me – and surely many others – music is totally embedded within my memory. Diana makes me think of Noel Gallagher, while my paper round makes me think of

Jess Wright, a girl whose kitchen floor I was once sick on after overdoing it at a party. Getting up to do my paper round the following morning was one of the most painful moments of my life. I have absolutely no idea when the party took place or what happened prior to my humiliation, but for some reason, as clear as day, I can remember Green Day's "Time of Your Life" being played in the front room midway through the evening.

This is what my memory is like.

I've no idea what date Diana died or what I did that day – I just have Noel's arse to go on. There are scores of days, experiences, moments, even *people*, that appear to have been erased from my mind. Yet for all of the memories I've lost, I can tell you with certainty that in 1997 at Manchester Arena, Radiohead played just two tracks off Pablo Honey, "Creep" and "Lurgee", and midway through "Creep" Jonny Greenwood hit the wrong pedal by mistake.

Every day of this expedition has its own history – macro and micro, musical and non-musical. It's become my way of exploring the world, with music connecting the dots between time, place and memory, as I seek to compile my own minor musical footnote.

Sunflower Bean, Scala, London, Thursday 15th September

- **Gig #18**
- **Musical birthdays:** KG of MN8 (1976)[35]
- **Musical history:** For the first time, Abba tributes leapfrog Elvis impersonators to become Britain's most popular cover- acts (2003)
- **Non-musical history:** An attempt to assassinate Benito Mussolini by anarchist Gino Lucetti fails after his homemade bomb bounces off the dictator's car and explodes on the nearby pavement (1926)

---

35 Slim pickings today.

Four years ago, I introduced Rhys to my friend Abi and history was made. The London Olympic Torch finale in Hyde Park was without question one of the best days of my life, although every single one of the live bands was truly awful, with Dizzee Rascal proving himself a strong contender for worst artist I've ever had the misfortune to see perform. Boris Johnson was also present, basking in the glory of his predecessor's successful Olympic bid, but the buffoon couldn't spoil our fun. Magical things happen when you're least expecting them – in this instance, the randomness of our surroundings, the randomness of the people I'd brought together, the hilarity of watching shite pop act after shite pop act, the copious volumes of Tuborg[36]. Everything came together perfectly, and when we parted company that night, I felt sure that we'd stumbled upon a rich and enduring gigging combo.

Since that fateful day in June 2012, the three of us have been to approximately no gigs together. I felt compelled to change this, hence, having already arranged the rendezvous with Abi, I invited Rhys along as an eleventh-hour surprise guest. I am quite the hypocrite when it comes to surprises. I delight in making these mischievous plans to confound and bemuse my friends, but woe betide the sorry individual who tries to spring the unexpected upon me. In addition to randomly matchmaking my friends on these nights out, I have at times tried to cultivate an enigmatic aura by disappearing midway through an evening – sometimes for good, sometimes to reappear hours later. I have a feeling however, that this is perceived by others as more annoying than enigmatic.

Fortunately, on this occasion my plans paid off.

Abi seemed delighted by this Rhys-driven turn of events and the three of us quickly picked up where we'd collectively left off. Tonight, we were heading to Kings Cross to watch Sunflower Bean, yet another unknown quantity. From the name, I inferred

---

36 A mini-festival wouldn't be complete without an unbelievably bland, low-strength lager.

pleasant US indie rock, the sort that your alternative hipster friend buys for you, you play it five times, put to one side, and never listen to it again because you can no longer remember who the hell they are. There are countless artists in my CD collection that have suffered this fate, although I can't refer you to them at this juncture, as I'm unable to recall any of their names. The generic indie rock support band gave further credence to my theory. They were undeniably pleasant, but so unmemorable that I'd forgotten them before they'd walked off stage.

I like to think of myself as a person who is rarely wrong. Unfortunately, however, this assessment is wrong. I completely misjudged Sunflower Bean, a classic case of making a snap judgment based on no evidence whatsoever. The band were prog-tastic, psychedelic seventies throwbacks fronted by a bleach blonde frontperson, who crowdsurfed to practically every song while continuing to play her bass. Admittedly, she didn't play it particularly well during those moments, but one must admire such commitment to rock. Much to my eternal shame and regret, I've never crowdsurfed and I suspect that my ongoing back complaints mean that I probably never will. Back in our early teens, when we would emerge from every gig bloodied and bruised because we were half the size of everyone else in the crowd, I'd routinely lie to my friends about my crowdsurfing endeavours. Truth be told, I was so criminally shy I couldn't bring myself to ask anyone around me for a leg up. I did however once aid a young child in achieving their first ever crowdsurfing experience. Back at Glastonbury 2002, said whippersnapper approached me at the start of a surprisingly entertaining Nelly Furtado set and asked me if I could put him on my shoulders to compensate for his lack of height. Setting aside any questions about where his parents were, I willingly obliged. Five songs later I asked if he wouldn't mind getting down, as my back was starting to ache. He refused. Two further songs later I asked again. He refused again. Being at the front of a festival crowd is something everyone should try at least once; however, it does leave you with rather restricted mobility and crouching down to remove a disobedient young boy from your torso is far easier said than done. Hence, after a final unsuccessful request for him to dismount, I lifted him off my shoulders and threw him out into the crowd. My assumption is that he a) survived and b) appreciated my actions, at least in retrospect.

Returning to Sunflower Bean, it's worth noting that for crowd surfing to be truly successful, you really do need a substantial crowd; without a sturdy audience, it starts to resemble some sort of weird coffinless pallbearer procession. This show was packed beyond the rafters, to the point of irritation, as scores of young indie kids and Hackney hipsters constantly pushed past us to get closer to the action. Like Einaudi a few weeks ago, I was left wondering how on earth this band managed to become so popular without my noticing. I felt strangely dislocated from proceedings – here was a band with real buzz, that much was clear, yet by picking them out at random, arriving late and standing near the back, we had made ourselves the uninvited guests at their otherwise uproarious party.

Francis Lung, The Lexington, London, Wednesday 21st September

- **Gig #19**
- **Musical birthdays:** Leonard Cohen (1934), Don Felder (1947), Faith Hill (1967), Liam Gallagher (1972)
- **Musical history:** Status Quo cement their status as legends by making it into the Guinness Book Of Records as the only band to appear live in four UK cities within a single day: Sheffield, Glasgow, Birmingham and London (1991)
- **Non-musical history:** The People's Republic of China is proclaimed by the country's communist leaders (1949)

- **Also:** The Blackpool Illuminations are switched on for the very first time, making the seaside town the first in the world to have any form of electric street lighting (1879)[37]

Going to gigs isn't supposed to make you nervous. Normally, my only source of pre-show concern is an irrational fear that the singer's voice will fail to last the duration of the set, a bizarre paranoia which I can only attribute to the fact that so many of my favourite artists are over fifty and have, at various points in their past, overdone it a touch. Bob Dylan is a case in point. In the past twenty-four months the music world has witnessed a miraculous resurgence in his vocal capabilities, however before this he spent the nineties sounding as though he had a frog permanently lodged in his throat, followed by a further fifteen years sounding like a crazed wolf.

Francis Lung is not Dylan. Nor is he over fifty. He is the younger brother of an ex-girlfriend who I haven't seen since an explosive final argument on the platform of Market Street Metrolink station in central Manchester. I needed a gig to go to, but I was hugely circumspect about the idea of turning up at a Francis Lung show, to the extent that I pre-emptively tried to smooth things over by extending an olive branch to my ex, in the form of a short note apologising for the unhappiness our derelict shanty town of a relationship had caused her and wishing her well in her future endeavours. Within twenty-four hours she had blocked me on Facebook.

This didn't bode well; I had visions of being slighted, slated and slammed, or worse still, slandered on stage. *"Thank you for coming. This next song is dedicated to all of you except for Tom*

---

37 Unfortunately, as anyone who has been to Blackpool in recent times will likely attest, the seaside town does not appear to have been given a lick of paint in the intervening one hundred and forty years, and until its planned regeneration project is complete, it is arguably better left unilluminated.

Kirkham, who is nothing more than a knave, a vagabond, a miscreant and a true scoundrel."

Actually, I quite like that description. My brother, a friend of Francis Lung, planned to attend the show, as did trusty Rhys and Eleri who kindly offered to make me a disguise for the evening using a paper plate, colouring crayons and pipe cleaners. I decided against this on the combined grounds of personal pride and laziness.

The support act, Half Loon, were a band that looked too cool for school, but ended up sounding altogether too boring for school. And as I recall, school was not especially interesting. The last time I observed a performance so totally spiritless and dead was Teenage Fanclub supporting Radiohead in 1997, making Half Loon the most boring band I've seen for nineteen years. I have created more interesting songs while singing in the shower, something I typically only do as a way of reminding myself not to forget mundane household chores: *"Phone the gas company … la, la, la, la, la … don't forget to phone the gas company … do, do, do … they'll cut you off if you don't phone them soon …"*

Francis Lung began his music career as the guitarist in one-album-wonder Wu Lyn, their five minutes of fame provoking wild jealousy within my household after they reached the giddy heights of performing live on David Letterman. I've been playing in bands for about a decade longer than Lung, and I've never so much as busked in the US. However, such petty bitterness has long been consigned to the past. The Francis Lung solo catalogue is a very different and far more enjoyable beast, embracing joyous, uplifting sixties West Coast pop sounds that are much needed in this pig of a year. His six-piece act were tight and accomplished, the drummer demonstrating an exuberant, geeky genius, while Lung's understated stage demeanour created a calming aura akin to listening to Pet Sounds while being given a shoulder massage.

Post-set opportunities to chat to everyone were limited. The band had to head straight back to Manchester so that the keyboardist could resume her role as a secondary school teacher. According to Francis Lung's bassist, around half of the UK teaching workforce currently comprises touring musicians. As for my dreaded personal reception, Mr. Lung spotted me relatively early in the evening, shook my hand, and engaged me in conversation for a couple of minutes post-set, though it was hard to get a word in edgeways, due to Eleri's star-struck and effusive (and quite possibly drunken) praise for his performance. She spent a good ten minutes thereafter beating herself up for concluding the conversation with that most erudite of compliments, *"Good job."* However, Francis Lung seemed delighted with the compliments, proof if proof be needed that a bit of ego massaging outweighs family loyalty every time.

11 Paranoias and Luminous Bodies, The Unicorn, London, Friday 30th September

- **Gig #20**
- **Musical birthdays:** Johnny Mathis (1935), Marc Bolan (1947)
- **Musical history:** BBC Radio 1, the UK's national pop music station, is launched, with former pirate radio DJ Tony Blackburn the first presenter to take to the airwaves (1967)
- **Non-musical history:** Suleiman the Magnificent takes over from his father as Sultan of the Ottoman Empire (1520)
- **Also:** Police are forced to break up a fight between a Blue Oyster Cult and a Lynyrd Skynyrd roadie at a joint concert after the latter accuses the former of turning his band's sound off midway through their set (1974)

This was the week the gig almost died. Laura and I were supposed to be seeing a band called Phoria, friends from her teenage years growing up in Salisbury, when they used to hang out around the cathedral and cause trouble for passing tourists.[38] However, after

---

38 This is my assumption of what youths in Salisbury get up to, and not necessarily a factually accurate account of Laura's teendom.

passing out in a Lille hotel room the previous evening, before extensive vomiting on the Eurostar somewhere underneath the English Channel, I was in no state to do anything other than lie in bed lamenting my decision to consume several pints of a beer I couldn't pronounce followed by a sizeable portion of steak tartare.

The upshot of this unhappy episode was that by Friday I still hadn't been to see anything, leaving me once again resigned to another visit to local metal hub The Unicorn. This proved to be an ill-advised choice, not just for me and my expedition but also for my housemate and close friend Philip, whose grandmother had just died and who could've done without such an utterly unbearable racket prior to his early flight to Sweden the next morning. Philip has always been Swedish and has always spoken better English than I've ever been able to muster. He's one of the world's leading experts on the portrayal of inter-faith issues within the media, and the only person I know who owns a Star Trek uniform, all of which combines to make him a truly unique character.

Wishing to emerge from the evening with our ears intact, we only stayed for two of the four bands. Luminous Bodies offered us half an hour of relentless monosyllabic screaming. 11 Paranoias started off as what can only be described as a twenty-first century hardcore take on Frank Zappa, before compounding an already challenging musical experience by introducing relentless monosyllabic screaming. I left the venue wondering whether The Unicorn is not perhaps north London's home of live metal, as it claims, but rather, whether it might better be described as the North London Home for Bad Metal, a homeless shelter for the city's most uninspired and ungifted riffers and rockers. That would certainly explain why you never have to pay to get in; there appears to be zero restrictions on who they'll allow to grace the stage.

This is the regrettable side of the metal world. There are many geniuses to be found, for sure, but there are also too many artists lacking imagination or basic songwriting skills. At times it feels like a world in which, if you've got a distortion pedal and a beard, that's enough to get you a gig. Tonight's bands were little more than noise.[39] If other people want to listen to noise, that's fine, but I'd argue there are plenty of other metal bands over the decades that have shown it's possible to do more: to combine a great riff, interesting lyrics and screaming vocals in perfect, demented harmony.

This was by a mile the worst gig I've been to, with none of the bands offering anything remotely new, different, interesting or relevant. Like the metal equivalent of a Gary Barlow solo show.

No gig (week 18)

Alas, this was the week that the gig *did* die, leaving me mortified, inconsolable; royally fucked off, to put it bluntly. My failure has arrived barely one third of the way into my expedition. Last week was already a catastrophe, a cesspit of vomit causing me to miss the Phoria gig and forcing me back to a metal hellhole for my weekly fill of live music. This week, the flu struck me down – not man flu, but Real Flu[40], the sort that knocks you out for seven days and leaves you unable to move for more than ten minutes without feeling as though you're about to collapse. I was supposed to be seeing a Welsh artist whose name I couldn't pronounce. I had listened to his debut album and didn't like it, but that mattered little – a gig was a gig, to be enjoyed, experienced or endured, as part of an altogether grander endeavour.

After realising that my destiny was to be bedridden, I began frantically searching for an alternative plan to land a show before the week was out. Had I been a fifteenth century English monarch, I'd have willingly parted with my kingdom for a gig, or, failing that, a horse to take me to a gig. Unfortunately, my state of incapacitation bore the hallmarks of a Shakespearean tragedy rather than a largely inaccurate historical epic. As much as it pained me to admit it, my quest for a weekly live fix began to

---

39 Yes, I'm showing my age. But even noise was better in my day.
40 Like Real Ale, or Real Tennis.

look more and more impossible, unless of course I resorted to impersonating a dying child in the hope of inducing Coldplay to perform by my bedside.

It's heart-breaking to be in this situation, but what can be done in the event of the totally unprecedented? It has been six years since illness last knocked me out for more than forty-eight hours. The day before the flu hit me I'd been in France again enjoying twenty-seven-degree heat, editing my gig notes while relishing the weeks and months ahead. Such is life, and when one falls from the horse, one must simply strive to get straight back on the horse.[41]

Stealing Sheep, Moses, The Voyeurs and Is Tropical, multiple venues, London, Saturday 15ᵗʰ October

- **Gig #21**
- **Musical birthdays:** Richard Carpenter (1946), Chris De Burgh (1947), Tito Jackson (1953), Shayne Ward (1984)
- **Musical history:** "La Mer", seminal work of composer Claude Debussy, receives its national premiere in Paris (1905)
- **Non-musical history:** Eleven-year-old Grace Greenwood Bedell Billings unwittingly changes the course of US history by writing to soon-to-be-President Abraham Lincoln, urging him to grow a beard to improve his appearance (1860)
- **Also:** Lieutenant Pigeon tops the UK singles chart with "Mouldy Old Dough", the only mother and son act ever to land a UK number one (1972)

After a fortnight in the wilderness without a show to my name, we returned to the weird semi-festival that is Hackney Wonderland

---

41 Richard III may have failed, but he certainly had the right idea.

with a view to consuming as much music as we could possibly stomach within a four-hour period.

The first venue of our evening, Oval Space, brought back strange and poignant memories of an office party I'd attended in the same establishment a few years ago which fell on the very day my resignation was announced to my peers. Rhys and I arrived just in time to watch Stealing Sheep, whose debut album I mysteriously owned.[42] I was a fan of their low-key electro noodling. Alas, after two songs, a group of a dozen inebriated locals pushed in front of us, obscuring our view, and proceeded to take selfies and hug one another for the remainder of the set. This is not an uncommon occurrence at gigs in Hackney. One day I'll write a guide to gigging etiquette, print copies and hand them out to these reprobates as and when they inevitably waver into non-conformance. This will almost certainly be the day that I die.

Stealing Sheep may not have the songs for a full set at this moment, but they have the look and the vibe. Three women in matching outfits and shades, bass, keys and electronic drums – like an electro version of The Staves.

Ah, The Staves! Were they my favourite live act of the expedition to date? Quite possibly. They are also just about the only thing on Facebook that I enjoy following. I wish they were my friends, and as the Stealing Sheep set came to an end, my mind was bizarrely preoccupied with the idea of wandering around Watford in the hope of bumping into them.[43]

---

42 This happens to me all the time these days – a combination of an ever-growing music library and an increasingly erratic memory.

43 I'm aware that it's unlikely they still live in Watford, and still more unlikely that, in their downtime from touring, they go everywhere as a threesome. But these are the demented ravings of a madman who has on more than on one occasion wandered aimlessly around Primrose Hill in the hope of running into Liam Gallagher. I don't have much luck when it comes to celeb-spotting. Emma Watson did however once walk past me while I was standing outside the Nellie Dean in Soho. Completely star-struck, I spent the following weekend rewatching the Harry Potter films.

Then disaster struck.

Having lost his bike to opportunistic thieves three days earlier, Rhys was apprehensive about our location and we briefly left the venue to check on his replacement vessel,[44] haplessly unaware of the Oval Space's one-in-one-out policy. Alas, Mystery Jets fans had by this stage flooded the area, leaving us to face the sad reality that it'd be a good three hours before we got back in. The prospect of seeing Eel Pie Island's finest was swiftly abandoned, and we headed to the comfort of the Sebright Arms to catch Moses (nondescript but energetic indie-rock) and The Voyeurs (awful but rescued by a brilliantly inventive and utterly hammered lead guitarist).

The evening felt less like a festival and more like a pub crawl, as we concluded our festivities by venturing further east to the London Fields Brewhouse to see Is Tropical, the archetypical trendy East London band that, unfortunately, has been consistently trendy for more than a decade without managing to convert coolness to tangible popularity. Fronted by a compelling female singer with ridiculously long hair, Is Tropical could've been fabulous were it not for the two ageing rockers who flanked her and were too keen to hog the limelight. They have decided to employ a female singer, so they need to use her, rather than reserving the lead vocals for themselves. She's not Dave Gahan, she can't get away with just dancing through every other song.[45]

---

44 Almost certainly not an appropriate term for a bicycle.
45 Perennially under-used Depeche Mode singer often reduced to spinning around on stage with his arms outstretched in a manner not dissimilar to the rotating blades of a helicopter.

Weeks 20–23:
Night Time

The oldest music ever discovered is a three-thousand-four-hundred-year-old cult Sumerian folk song, recorded on a tablet in the Hurrian language and unearthed several centuries ago in the ancient Syrian city of Ugarit.

It's awful.

That said, I respect the Sumerians' attempt to try something new, and it's certainly more listenable than portions of Lou Reed's back catalogue.

There is a time in everyone's gig-going life when they start to feel distinctly Sumerian in age. For me this moment arrived at Reading Festival 2006, a misjudged attempt to repeat the glorious past of six years' previous, only to find that I was a twenty-three-year-old surrounded by drunken, irrepressible teenagers intent on staying up all night singing, banging drums and falling over other peoples' tents. Just as I had been back in 2000, in fact.

The difference was that I didn't spend the final night of my festival staggering around offering people free hugs or setting toilets on fire.[46] Festivals are an acquired taste at the best of times, but I noticed that in the months following Reading 2006, my tolerance for antisocial, disruptive and occasional inexplicable behaviour at shows dwindled and I became more easily frustrated;

---

46 In contrast, I spent my final evening of Reading 2000 sitting in the mud behind a burger stand, inarticulately declaring my love for a seventeen-year-old Berkshire girl I'd met on AOL Instant Messenger a few years earlier.

more likely to voice my dissatisfaction at those breaking with gig etiquette and ruining it for those around them.

Here then follows the ultimate evidence of my descent into middle-aged gigging: my own, non-comprehensive and highly subjective guide to appropriate in-venue decorum.

1. Don't speak. At least, not all the time. Those surrounding you haven't paid £20 to listen to the story of your day or the issues you've been having at work. Nor have they paid for the pleasure of hearing you wax lyrical about the band you're supposed to be watching. You're not a character from High Fidelity, and your opinions are most likely dreadful.

2. Don't be tall. This is admittedly a challenge if you are tall, as I am. Try and be mindful of the fact that you're almost certainly standing in front of the shortest person in the venue. Also, no Chewbacca costumes, or similar. Save those for the cricket.

3. Don't push your way forwards. We all want to gain a better vantage point, but there are easier ways to get to the front without steamrolling your way through the middle, infuriating everyone in your path. Go to the left or right side of the venue and proceed – it's quieter there and you'll find less resistance to your efforts. Then you can move sideways into the centre of the crowd. It's still a nuisance, but at least people can see you coming and move their bags, beers and children out of the way.

4. Don't pour beer over everyone around you, unless they specifically request it.

5. Don't heckle incessantly. I tried to shout something at Ed Harcourt once at Madame JoJo's and committed the cardinal sin of making an unfunny heckle. Had there been any tumbleweed in the venue, other members of the audience would have piled it into a makeshift bonfire and burnt me at the stake. Since then I have forever held my peace and, unless you're Jimmy Carr, I'd advise you to do the same. And pay your taxes.[47]

---

47 Not strictly gig etiquette, but a good way of avoiding resentment and unpopularity (unless you're at a Gary Barlow show).

6. Don't video every song. YouTube clips of gigs are a wonderful thing; holding your phone aloft for ninety minutes, obstructing the view of those behind you, is not. These days some people start complaining if their camera is nudged or the people around them are singing too noisily and impinging upon the quality of their recording. Artists already struggle to make ends meet, so go buy the live DVD, rather than moonlighting as an amateur filmmaker.

7. Don't urinate into plastic cups. And certainly, don't throw the cups out into the crowd. Earlier this year, for the first time in my life, I was hit by pigeon excrement as I walked down the road towards my house. I received this unwanted gift with weary resignation. Everyone gets hit once during their lives, I'd survived the indignation for more than thirty years and, after I'd cleaned myself up, my mood brightened in the knowledge that I was now safe to live out the rest of my days free from further incident. Thus far, my trust in such matters of fate has served me well. However, the incident did impress upon me just how deeply upsetting it can be when unknown and dubious substances are unexpectedly dispersed over your person. At an Oasis gig in 2009 the gentleman next to me, a copious drinker and, I suspect, a rather shady character, appeared to take great pleasure in repeatedly employing his bladder into his empty pint glasses before sending them airborne into the mosh pit. This is antisocial.

8. Don't attack those around you. There's always a degree of pushing and shoving at the front of gigs, particularly when watching the more boisterous and rowdy performers. However, an inadvertent shove should not serve as an excuse to turn around and headbutt the perceived culprit in the face. This happened to my brother while we were at an Oasis show in 2008 at Wembley Arena, just a few hundred metres away from the Stadium where the later pissing incident occurred. Other incidents at Oasis gigs I've attended include several youths in the crowd openly snorting cocaine in front of my mother, my ex-girlfriend falling out with me after I looked up to

see a girl on my neighbour's shoulders exposing her breasts at Liam Gallagher's request, and a friend who shall remain anonymous defecating in his trousers after taking a suspicious looking unmarked pill given to him by a passing drug dealer.

9. Do not try and order a cocktail at the bar. It is a gig, not a corporate soirée, and there are thousands of people to serve.

10. Finally, play nice. Live music is euphoric and blissful; the best live shows are timeless and stay with you forever. Be respectful, courteous and civilised, so that your peers remember the show for the music, rather than as the night that their friend accidentally shat themselves.

Steely Dan, Beacon Theatre, New York City, Wednesday 19th October

- **Gig #22**
- **Musical birthdays:** Keith Reid of Procol Harum (1946)
- **Musical history:** Oasis is born, as the band play their first gig with Noel Gallagher as a member at legendary Manchester venue The Boardwalk (1991)
- **Non-musical history:** University of California scientists discover evidence that life on earth may be three hundred million years older than first realised (2015)

Going to seated gigs on your own is always a slightly awkward experience. When you're standing, it's far harder for anyone to tell that you have no friends, particularly if you keep looking around expectantly, or pretending to talk to the person next to you at moments when the music is particularly loud so that no one realises you're not actually saying anything.

Seated shows become harder still when you're overseas in a huge city, in an area of New York City you don't know at all, having attempted to walk to the venue but having had to abandon your efforts several miles in after realising it was far too far and you were going to be late, having then hopped on a subway but overshot the venue by fifteen blocks, forcing you to run the remaining distance to the venue, thus arriving at the venue a giant, sweaty mess.

I'd like to claim that I don't make a habit of doing this, but my love of walking borders on maniacal and, as I don't use maps, many of my excursions take on an inherent unpredictability; especially when I'm unencumbered by arrangements with friends. Still, after walking at a pace from Wall Street to Penn Station, I felt as though I'd done some decent exercise, and ultimately, it was only the elderly gentleman sitting next to me who was likely to judge my dishevelled appearance and discombobulated demeanour.

If you're in need of chillaxation, Steely Dan ought to feature in your plans. This was the first of two trips to The Dan Who Knew Too Much tour and I was eagerly anticipating a performance billed enigmatically as "Steely Dan: By Popular Demand." Whose demand, exactly? I was not consulted on the setlist and I'm confident the OAP to my right was also left out of the loop, given his dour and stony face. As my friend Jeremy once remarked after a comment of his was misinterpreted by a client, the gentleman … *"looked as though I'd just taken a shit on his mother."* Indeed, the chap looked so displeased that at one point I wondered whether he'd turned up at the wrong concert. Perhaps he thought that he was off to see Jersey Boys or the Spiderman Musical. Donald Fagen and Walter Becker of Steely Dan were unlikely to be swinging around the stage or leaping across the scenery; they're in their late sixties and both have piled on the pounds since last I saw them. It's also possible he was hoping to catch the "By Unpopular Demand" show.

As it was, the performance was more hits-oriented and less unexpected than I'd hoped for. Furthermore, Walter Becker's choice of white trainers and jogger-bottoms, combined with a loose-fitting sweatshirt, unshaven white beard and scraggly greying hair, rendered him more akin to a hobo than a jazz-rock legend. His frame is today so expansive that he rather waddled on and off stage. I became so preoccupied by his appearance that I paid unduly close attention to what he was playing, which led me next to the realisation that he didn't seem to be trying particularly hard. To his right was their session guitarist, a virtuoso musician who seemed to be tonally in sync throughout – everything he played, scripted or improvised, was spot on. Becker in comparison, was meandering aimlessly through much of the set, as though the other members had all rehearsed to perfection together before telling him, *"Just do what you like over the top of it."* It felt like a sad decline for one of the true songwriting geniuses of the past fifty years.

I've written an entire paragraph criticising Becker, much of it for his weight (and who knows, he might have some sort of medical condition), which is problematic. There was no need to fixate upon this – it was my own weird brain distracting me and I should have endeavoured to resist it. This is certainly proof of how the brain can do funny things, how the best band is not always the most enjoyable gig, how being in the company of others perhaps positively affects enjoyment of events in ways that we don't always consciously realise, and how even seemingly tolerant and accepting people can suddenly venture forth on sizeist rants.[48]

Okkervil River, Webster Hall, New York City, Thursday 20th October

- **Gig #23**
- **Musical birthdays:** Tom Petty (1950), Mark King of Level 42 (1958), Dannii Minogue (1971), Snoop Dogg (1971)
- **Musical history:** Tragedy strikes the music world when Ronnie Van Zant, Steve Gaines and Cassie

---

48 Walter Becker passed away unexpectedly in September 2017. It was touching to see the vast and diverse range of tributes paid to him from across the entire music world. Today, I feel like the world's biggest philistine and musical fucktard for writing this cack-handed gig entry, but I've kept it in because they were my sentiments at the time, however misguided, and I deserve to own them.

Gaines from Lynyrd Skynyrd are all killed after their plane runs out of fuel and crashes into a Mississippi swamp (1977)

- **Non-musical history:** Legendary Norwegian explorer Ronald Amundsen sets out to the South Pole in a race that will ultimately have disastrous consequences for rival Scott of the Antarctic (1911)

The late Steely Dan finish was followed by an early start in the office, which quickly spiralled into yet another relentless day in the Big Apple. The city doesn't sleep, or so I've been told, and boy I wish it would at times. New York is fabulous but the amount of energy expended walking around it tops every other major city I've visited. Thanks to a combination of endless Walk/Don't Walk, hold ups and continual dashing and darting around the merciless passage of pedestrians, I've arrived at every destination on this trip so far sweating profusely and wishing humankind had mastered how to fly.

Relentless though my working world had been, I managed to make it out promptly at five thirty p.m. to meet my brother Lew on his first full day in the US. It was great seeing him in town. He seemed to have adapted to the city instantly. As he explained it, because New York is so integral to our cultural lives – in music, movies, art etc. – he immediately felt as though he'd been here before. I have a sneaking suspicion this owes much to his love of Sex in the City.

The evening was going swimmingly, pints of local ale knocked back in a craft beer tavern, metro back to the hotel, delicious pizza in a chic Italian place on Third Avenue, another beer in the Pour House Sports Bar and an amusing conversation with a waitress who was losing her voice and struggled to make out our Mancunian twang, before finally heading over the road to Webster Hall for Okkervil River.

I have conflicting emotions towards Okkervil River, following a couple of underwhelming records that left me with the impression that the band had lost their mojo. It was therefore a welcome surprise to find Will Sheff and co. back at their joyous best, exuding a palpable wave of positivity I could feel as I traversed the crowd. This was an amazing feat in itself, given that there was an obscenely loud dance club downstairs forever impinging on the sound. The gig was another reminder, like Band of Horses many moons ago, of why I started my expedition in the first place – to see bands that I might normally miss, despite my relative fandom, or to try and give myself more diverse experiences. These are the advantages of forcing oneself to keep up appearances in the concert-going world.

Unfortunately, however, *the city that never sleeps* is a mentality with problematic consequences for gig etiquette. We arrived at the venue around nine p.m. Okkervil River did not take to the stage until ten forty-five p.m. In London, this would be fifteen minutes before curfew. In fact, in every city I've visited previously it would be far too late. People usually boo Madonna, Justin Bieber and Guns 'n Roses when they arrive on stage late.[49] As I had to be up at six a.m. the following morning for a work event, the late starting time forced me to miss the last twenty minutes of the show, which I gather from Lew included a guest appearance by someone from Neutral Milk Hotel. I don't particularly like Neutral Milk Hotel, but that's beside the point.

There are all manner of good reasons for having a curfew on school nights, not least that huge portions of the gig-going public have jobs with relatively traditional working hours. Dylan knows how to do it – he takes the stage at seven forty-five p.m. and plays for two hours. No more, no less, with everyone returned home to their beds by eleven p.m. Lord knows he needs his beauty sleep.

---

49 I'm firmly of the opinion that people should boo Guns 'n Roses irrespective of their punctuality.

Steely Dan, Beacon Theatre, New York City, Saturday 22nd October

- **Gig #24**
- **Musical birthdays:** Orville Richard Burrell aka Shaggy (1968), Zachary Walker Hanson (1985)
- **Musical history:** Songwriter Elliot Smith commits suicide aged just 34 by stabbing himself in the heart with a kitchen knife. To this day, conspiracy theorists argue that his death ought to be treated as murder, or at the very least, suspicious (2003)[50]
- **Non-musical history:** At the International Meridian Conference in Washington, D.C., Greenwich Mean Time is formally adopted worldwide (1884)
- **Also:** Paul McCartney is forced to publicly deny claims that he is dead after a Michigan Daily journalist begins a rumour that will prove enduring for the following half century (1969)

Following several high-octane days of working and partying relatively hard, we arrived at the zenith, our raison d'etre, at least as far as this New York outing was concerned: Steely Dan playing their classic 1980 album Gaucho in full. What had been a crazy pipe dream of an idea back in the Summer slowly morphed into a reality as pub chats led to rough plans, tickets were booked, hotels were cancelled and rearranged at the last minute and finally, many months down the line, we were there together at the Beacon Theatre. This gave our evening a surrealist edge; could it really be that we were here, about to witness the stuff of our dreams?[51] The title track Gaucho is a song I've always been des-

---

50 Smith's lyrics, though admittedly brilliant, err rather upon the bleak side, one of the many reasons I take issue with the conspiracy theorists. He did not seem like a particularly happy individual.

51 It is almost certain that these dreams are not shared by the majority of thirty-three-year-old Londoners.

perate to witness on the live stage. Lew thought we saw them play it at Hammersmith Apollo a decade earlier, but alas, he has a rich history of re-imagining gigs in his mind. At one stage, a few years ago I was forced to trawl through the extensive R.E.M. gig archive to prove that we had never seen them play "Leave," a lesser known song from the 1995 album "New Adventures in Hi-Fi". These errors are, I suspect, the impact of prolonged and excessive drinking at concerts.

Our evening began with an entertaining discussion about where in Middle Earth we would choose to live. Lew opted for Hobbiton so that he could spend time in an allotment. I had to be talked out of Minas Tirith (due to security concerns) so I plumped for Isengaard, a lonely habitat to be sure, but one with an undeniably brilliant view. The night ended with us discussing mental illness and my various ailments in another Third Avenue bar, before we returned to the more comfortable geekdom of Lord of the Rings. Had I made it to Mount Doom, would I have destroyed the one ring? These questions will plague me until the end of my days.

The gig itself was arguably a little top-heavy, as the Gaucho performance that opened the show was so perfect that nothing could follow it. The first forty-five minutes were spent in heavenly reverie; the second forty-five were entertaining, but we were back on this mortal coil, possibly already contemplating the loss that came with knowing we'd never be able to relive the moment. Some of the best excursions arrive on a whim or an unpredictable impulse, and this week felt like the perfect realisation of crazy beer banter becoming blissful reality. I will be forever grateful to The Dan for delivering the inspiration to form this crazy plan, and it'll be hard to return to comparative mundanity when the trip is at an end. I can but take comfort in the knowledge that the Brexit-inflicted exchange rate would've bankrupted me had I stayed on much longer.

Field Music, Shepherd's Bush Empire, London, Wednesday 26th October

- **Gig #25**
- **Musical birthdays:** Bootsy Collins (1951), Natalie Merchant (1963), Judge Jules (1965), Keith Urban (1967)
- **Musical history:** Who on earth riots at a Bill Haley and His Comets gig? Germans, evidently, after the band play Germany's first ever rock 'n' roll show, only to find 7,000 attendees tearing up the venue (1958)
- **Non-musical history:** Catholic churches in San Juan, Puerto Rico, stage one of the most ineffectual protests of all time, when they request that residents tie black ribbons to trees to demonstrate their discontent at a Madonna concert (1993)

I took a useful mental note from tonight's show. It's not a good idea to book concert tickets for the day you arrive back home after a long-haul overnight flight from New York. My body clock has fallen out with me due to this poor decision-making, and though it's fair to say we were never close, I could do with some form of reconciliation before the next working week arrives, as at the time of writing I don't feel as though I'm awake.

Nevertheless, the decision was made, for better or worse, and so, on just a couple of hours' sleep Laura and I made our way across London to see a band she'd never heard of and that I'd obliquely described as "very difficult pop".

I never fully understood the criticism of Field Music when they arrived on the music scene. They were berated for having more positive reviews than they had fans, the implication being that they were a bit too clever and knowing for their own good. They were the darlings of the media yet were haunted by the allegation that normal music fans didn't give a damn about them. Annoyingly, this viewpoint was then perpetuated by the media. I'm overly influenced by music reviews, much to my chagrin;

though I disagree with many journalists, their words still ring and reverberate around my head. This of course influences my perception of the records I'm trying to explore, meaning that in recent years I've tried to hold off reading reviews until I'm already settled on my own opinion.

Fortunately, in the case of Field Music, any sense that they might be too calculated to invoke emotional resonance disapparated[52] the moment I first saw them perform back in 2007. For starters, the venue was full, evidence enough that they did have some fans. More pertinently, I was struck by their warmth and humour, a bunch of deadpan Sunderlanders (I am unsure of the official collective term) who bantered ceaselessly with each other on stage, involved the audience in the experience from start to finish, and generally didn't take themselves too seriously. When listening to the records in this context, I was then able to hear this collective personality within the music. Somehow, the hooks, refrains and lyrical passages all seemed interlaced with sardonic, subtle humour.

The two brothers at the heart of Field Music are insanely competent singers, guitarists and drummers. It makes me sick, but mostly in a good way. They alternate instruments throughout the set, and it's hard to pick a favourite between the two of them (as well as being a totally pointless exercise). They're also the only band I'm aware of that have side projects – School of Language and The Week That Was – featuring the exact same members of the main band.

I've seen Field Music twice already and School of Language once, so I knew what to expect when we arrived in Shepherd's Bush. However, as they took to the stage my spirits rose, for the core group of musicians was supported for the first time by both strings and brass accompaniment. I didn't catch the name of the string quartet, but they jokingly referred to the brass section as the Quincey Jones Review. Sadly, these part-time

---

52 I assume that JK Rowling's international success means this is now part of the accepted lexicon.

musicians – presumably friends of the band – did not chance an attempt at any Michael Jackson brass refrains.

This was a fabulous performance, the most accomplished and confident I'd ever heard from the band. Unfortunately, the jetlag became so overwhelming that we had to leave before the end – a worrying habit that I seem to have developed over the past fortnight, and while mitigating circumstances may have been to blame, I can't allow this premature gig ejaculation to continue. I refuse to become a blasé Londoner who no longer gives a damn who they're seeing, what time they show up or how long they stay for, and who talk their entire way through the gig. Earlier in the year, at a James gig, I temporarily lost my rag with two gents displaying utter indifference towards the band and the audience around them. When I politely asked them to stand at the back to continue their conversation, I was told that, *"The gig doesn't matter – we've seen them loads of times already."* The mind boggles. You can have a conversation in a pub without having to pay £45 for a ticket. My somewhat hopeful assumption is that, due to the volume at which they conversed, they lost their voices and were unable to attend work the following day, forcing them to miss major corporate presentations and thus lose their jobs, leaving them unable to make rent and reduced to busking through feeble cover versions of James songs on the streets of Brixton to unsympathetic passers-by.

Killing Joke, Brixton Academy, London, Friday 4th November

- **Gig #26**
- **Musical birthdays:** Sonny Bono of Sonny & Cher (1935), Tracy Morrow aka Ice-T (1959)
- **Musical history:** Members of Emerson, Lake & Palmer are arrested in Salt Lake City after skinny dipping in a hotel pool (1974)
- **Non-musical history:** The first tube station at Stockwell is opened by the Prince of Wales; more than a hundred and twenty years later, people are still searching for a reason to visit Stockwell (1890)

Oh my poor, sweet ears. Brixton Academy has a reputation for veering towards the cavernous, murky side of sound deskery, and I can't remember the last time I experienced tinnitus quite as extreme as the cacophony currently ongoing within my head. I ought to consider a visit to the doctor, but for the short-term I'm opting to continue the head-in-the-sand policy that has served me adequately over the past few decades. Both Phil Collins and Pete Townshend have complained of severe hearing difficulties and earlier in 2016 Brian Johnson famously had to retire from AC/DC after experts warned him that he would go deaf if he attempted to tour again. The late genius that was Sir George Martin was essentially deaf in his later years, and he came from a classical background and didn't even play live. And I haven't mentioned Beethoven yet. Is this the fate that awaits me? The binary question, *"Would you rather be deaf than blind?"* feels particularly pertinent this morning; one of the great pantheon of stupid hypothetical conundrums. I've always instinctively answered affirmative to the loss of sight despite my every behaviour signposting the alternate fate. Close friends of mine wear earplugs to concerts; I find it destroys the live experience, which to me is about noise and energy and euphoria. We all experience moments of quiet euphoria in our lives, but I'm not sure we should go looking for them in music.

When I began to put together my expedition itinerary, Killing Joke was one of the events I flagged as a potential highlight. I'm a comparatively recent convert; perhaps that was part of the reason for being so excited about the prospect of seeing a band whose heyday was some thirty years ago. Often, I will hear artists that I quite like and over time, they'll grow on me incrementally until I find I've become quite fond of them. With Killing Joke, the opposite occurred, a random moment of discovery during which I unearthed, in a single revelatory moment, the genius of Jaz Coleman and co., hitting me with the full force of a late eighties Peter Gabriel track.[53]

---

53 Funnily enough, I saw Gabriel back in 2004 and not only was he brilliant, but he also performed several songs whilst standing upside down on the ceiling of the arena. I bet even Lionel Richie never did that.

I met up with my friend Jonathan in the Trinity Arms in Brixton, a favourite pre-Academy haunt of mine that is tucked away in a leafy and quiet square around the corner from the high street, meaning it tends to be frequented only by those in the know, rather than the alarming crew of Brixton trendies with their daft clothes and predilection for cocktails served out of jam jars, flower pots and vases.

One thing I always forget about Jonathan is that he drinks at a pace, and I tend to reciprocate. When Joe and Philip turned up, I was already feeling a little foggy. Jonathan compounded the issue by purchasing our pre-performance beers in two-pint cups, ridiculous devices that were – to the best of my knowledge – invented by the Academy as the only means of curbing the abominably lengthy bar queues endured at the venue.

By the time Killing Joke took to the stage, I was stuck in a daze, and my ability to recall specific moments from the performance is rather limited. I remember it being insanely loud from the off, impossible to hear individual guitar notes through a wall of distortion, though Coleman's voice was surprisingly clear in the mix which at least made it possible to discern one song from another. About four tracks in, two scantily clad ladies appeared on the stage with tourniquets of fire and danced around, much to the delight of the predominantly middle-aged male audience.

Sadly, the rest of the gig is a blur, while two songs from the end, I took leave of my senses entirely. Joe, Jonathan, Philip and myself had been separated, for reasons I cannot explain (i.e. I can't remember), and I found myself in the toilets in the ninety second respite between main set and encore. At this juncture, I decided I would retreat to the rear of the venue, sneak out before the mass exodus and call Eleri in the vague hope of relaying an impassioned, motivational speech that was forming in my head, designed to provoke her out of the recent discontent and malaise that I knew to be afflicting her.

This wasn't an altogether inexplicable thing to do. Events relayed to me by Eleri earlier in the week had left me worried about her continued relationship friction. As I've mentioned before, I also have a track record of randomly disappearing whilst drunk, abandoning the company around me to pursue seemingly inexplicable devices. This was a common occurrence in my early twenties; I was forever sneaking away from house parties to wander the streets for hours on my own, or unexpectedly parting ways with friends by leaping from the tube a stop early, to avoid otherwise preordained plans that I wasn't wholly invested in. These immature behaviours were triggered by my severe social anxiety, and one can only imagine what those around me made of my unpredictability and penchant for chaos.

The plan to rendezvous with Eleri was now a necessity in my mind, however things went awry from the off, a consequence of her neglecting to pick up the phone. I decided to make my way over to her South Brixton home. Technically there was no benefit whatsoever to this course of action, as I couldn't remember which house it was, and I certainly had no intention of randomly ringing doorbells. Hence, my hastily-conceived Eleri intervention ended up with me staggering up and down a random side street for ten minutes while placing missed calls to her phone, before cutting my losses and heading back to Brixton tube. I have since sent her an apologetic note, attributing my behaviour to alcohol and Killing Joke, while silently reflecting on this, the least successful intervention since Owen Smith's leadership challenge to Jeremy Corbyn.

Aliens, Royal Albert Hall, London, Sunday 6th November

- **Gig #27**
- **Musical birthdays:** Glenn Frey of The Eagles (1948)
- **Musical history:** Aerosmith perform their first ever show at Nipmuc Regional High School in Mendon, Massachusetts. They will go on to sell more than a hundred and fifty million records (1970)[54]

---

54 This makes them America's biggest selling rock band ever.

- **Non-musical history:** The Russian Revolution begins as Bolshevik forces attack the Winter Palace in Petrograd (1917)
- **Also:** The Monkees endure a box office disaster and destroy their squeaky-clean image in the process, by releasing feature film Head, a dark, satirical adventure about the group's manipulation at the hands of the entertainment industry, interspersed with scenes of Vietnam War atrocities (1968)

Should orchestras count within the framework of my expedition?

That was the question I posed to myself (and to Laura, who was not especially invested in the question, but was gracious enough to indulge me) as I wandered around South Kensington in the rain, desperately searching for a pub with a spare seat to watch the Leicester versus West Brom Premier League clash while I waited for Rick to arrive from Manchester. For the record, Laura felt that watching an orchestra perform a film score *did* count as a legitimate live music performance, despite it not being the primary motivation.

I've been to one of these film/orchestra tie-ups before, a showing of David Lean's A Brief Encounter at the Royal Festival Hall, which featured an entire performance of Rachmaninov's second piano concerto, followed by the orchestra-backed screening of the film itself. On this occasion, I couldn't remember the plot of Aliens, let alone the score, and I hadn't been given any choice in the proceedings, as Rick booked the event without my knowledge or consent before insisting vociferously that I had to attend. When, five minutes before the show began, he announced that the tickets were £65 each, I felt like strangling him. This is relatively normal with Rick.

Leicester versus West Brom amounted to a copper-bottomed keg of shit, if such an expression exists, so it was a relief when Rick showed up and we made our way over to the Royal Albert Hall, probably the classiest venue I'm likely to attend all year. Three and a half hours later, we both emerged, myself tipsy, Rick off his face, engaged in an absorbing discussion about how un-imaginably difficult scoring an action thriller must be.

I've tried my hand at a fair few musical genres over the years, but I've never done any proper soundtracking, mainly because it seemed like it would be too difficult. Several years ago, my friend Vanessa asked me if I could lend her some of my music to accompany a short film she was working on. I duly obliged, lead-ing to minor uproar further down the line, when Alex discov-ered that I'd handed over one of his tracks to the film without bothering to consult him. The movie, complete with an Alex-penned track that he didn't like, went on to be shown at a range of UK and US film festivals. Since then, none of my film-mak-er friends (all two of them), have asked me for any further assis-tance and in honesty I'm not sure I'd be able to do it.

In the case of the Aliens score, Rick and I were astonished by the number of lengthy passages that relied almost entirely on snare rolls and subtle, understated Tuba snarls, not to mention the concentration levels required by both conductor and orchestra to precisely land the quiet-quiet-bang moments that arrived out of the blue. Admittedly, the conductor was supported by a vid-eo screen with visual cues, but it was nevertheless the first time I've ever had any sense or understanding of what the hell a con-ductor does, other than standing at the front looking silly, con-tributing little and then taking credit for absolutely everything at the close of each act.

I like the film-orchestra tie-up, no matter how gimmicky it is, and I left with a huge sense of regret at having missed Amadeus in the same venue a few weeks earlier. But I couldn't dwell upon my regret for too long, as Rick required my attention. He was a mess, albeit a surprisingly cogent one, and his condition made for rather an inauspicious end to our big night out as I led him down a side street off Charing Cross Road to be sick. He then insisted on a trip to Chicken Cottage, before promptly being sick again. If he'd told me earlier that he hadn't eaten for twen-ty-four hours, then I wouldn't have bought the second bottle of wine. At Royal Albert Hall prices, wine really needs to be kept down, or at least, as cats sometimes indulge in, regurgitated and reconsumed.

We returned home, and I put Rick to bed, consigning myself to a sleeping bag on the sofa. He awoke me at four a.m. inexplicably boiling the kettle. Again, I wanted to strangle him. Mr. Kitten then started attacking my sleeping bag, and dread began to flood my mind about the prospect of venturing out yet again the following evening for another gig.

The Japanese House, Heaven, London, Monday 7th November

- **Gig #28**
- **Musical birthdays:** Johnny Rivers (1942), Joni Mitchell (1943), Sharleen Spiteri (1967), Neil Hannon of The Divine Comedy (1970), Patrick Chukwuemeka Okogwu aka Tinie Tempah (1988), Ella Yelich-O'Connor aka Lorde (1996)
- **Musical history:** Leonard Cohen dies at his LA home (2016)[55]
- **Non-musical history:** The oldest meteorite with a known date of impact, Ensisheim, hits an Alsace wheat field (1492)
- **Also:** The world record for guitar string plucking is set by Steve Anderson, who plays continuously for a hundred and fourteen hours and seventeen minutes (1975)

Monday's show at Heaven, a venue I'd never previously frequented, and which smelled suspiciously of vomit (an unwelcome throwback to the previous evening with Rick) was already notable for being the first time I'd successfully managed to move my therapy session forwards to accommodate an evening plan. I

---

55 This latest musical tragedy occurs while I'm out watching The Japanese House. Leonard, your quiet genius and majesty will live on always.

rarely feel particularly sociable after therapy, so it's lucky that to-night's gigging partner was Rhys, one of the people I tend to feel most at ease with irrespective of the circumstances. He doesn't ask how therapy has gone, for starters. This always helps; otherwise it tends to become a second therapy session but with a less qualified participant.

My post-therapy decompressing began alone in the Mulberry Bush, a medium-sized establishment set back from the South Bank that has always occupied a special place in my heart after a series of unexpectedly satisfying evenings spent there over the years. The last such evening began on the day Bowie died when Eleri turned up drunk at eight p.m. having earlier drowned her sorrows at the Thin White Duke's passing on the train over from Windsor. We chatted at length about the great man's genius before heading along to the impromptu vigil at the Brixton Bowie mural, narrowly missing Rhys who was also busy paying his respects, before dancing the rest of the night away (to Bowie of course) at another excellent pub, The Effra, which, despite the protestations of several bar staff refused to close until Bowie's greatest hits had been replayed three or four times. At two a.m. I took a discombobulated Eleri back to her house, before getting on a night bus, getting stuck at Oxford Circus where they were busy disassembling the Christmas lights, walking most of the way back to my house and finally making it to bed at four a.m. Fortunately my self-employed career had not blossomed at this early stage in the year and I was afforded the quintessential lie in of the drunken unemployed. That night I had been given no reason to go to bed or be sensible, so I did neither.

My stint at the Mulberry Bush this time around was confined to a solitary pint before I felt obliged to dash over to Charing Cross and search out the location of Heaven. I had no idea where the venue was, and, as we've established, I'm one of those stubborn digital dinosaurs who refuses to use Google Maps unless necessary, so I wandered aimlessly until I came across a previously undiscovered street and a previously undiscovered pub called the Sherlock Holmes, which sold both a Holmes house ale and a Dr.

Watson's golden ale. I chose something else entirely, working to the logic that neither individuals were, to the best of my knowledge, renowned for their brewing prowess. They are also fictional.

Rhys arrived shortly thereafter, and we headed over to Heaven, which by a happy coincidence turned out to be next to the pub. Despite reeking of vomit, Heaven is a great venue (and a place on earth), especially if you accidentally wander up to the balcony in search of some working toilets. It's a fabulous vantage point, made more enjoyable by the fact that most of the patrons don't seem to know it exists. As for The Japanese House, it turns out it's not really a band but a twenty-year-old called Amber Bain. And she's unbelievable. She was note perfect throughout, her vocals fed through some sort of vocoder to create weird and alien-like harmonies (appropriate given last night's film), combined with electronica and some Prince-esque guitar licks delivered on an upside-down Stratocaster. She also appears to be cultivating a huge fanbase, despite being just three EPs into her career. The venue was rammed, the audience utterly attentive throughout and people were willing to shut up during the quieter moments, a rarity at a London show.

We were blown away; it was one of the best shows I've been to since my merry adventure began and, if she plays again, I'll be there in the front row. By front row, I do of course mean back row – being at the front is a pain in the arse.

Weeks 24–26:
The Whole Love

My journey back into music began at the point in my life when everything went wrong, and it's hard to avoid traversing these unhappy shores once again, when considering the events of the past week and the outpouring of misery and anger being unleashed on both sides of the Atlantic, following the US election result.

When everything in my world fell apart, I had no idea what would come next – whether each subsequent morning would bring the faintest cause for optimism or whether it would heap further misery at my door. In my own uncertain existence, music gave me a mooring; irrespective of life's twists and turns, music was still available and within my grasp.

The election appears to have fuelled a collective global anxiety that everything imaginable has gone wrong. My favourite Facebook post: *"Went to bed thinking Hilary was a shoo-in. Damn my social media bubble!"* My favourite Tweet: *"Mayans admit to four-year margin of error in their predictions."* This sums up the tone of the debate currently raging around my daily life.

And yet, for the moment at least, we are all still living and breathing. We can't pretend to know the unknown or predict and pre-empt the outcome of the inherently unpredictable. This is not to belittle the fears of many millions of people with genuine reasons for anguish over what their future may hold, following the most unexpected presidential election result in history. But I hope that as a society, we manage to avoid being consumed by our unhappiness and our anxiety; we must continue to influence what we can and seize upon what remains in our grasp.

I'm reflecting upon this because the week also marked the one-year anniversary of the Paris terror attacks in which scores of concert-goers at the Bataclan lost their lives, simply through being in the wrong place at the wrong time. The resounding, defiant response of Parisians in the aftermath of the attacks was to continue living, to show their attackers that no one could bring basic existence to a halt. Three days after the attacks, we went to see New Order in Brixton and there was palpable tension in the air. Security was high, getting into the venue took an age, and by the time the band went on, everyone indulged in a much-needed collective outpouring of emotion. Bernard Summer and the others performed against a backdrop of the French flag and we joined in our own minor stand of defiance. People lost their lives in the pursuit of music, but the only possible response from the music world in the aftermath was to carry on.

One year later, and in a crazy, topsy-turvy world of great uncertainty and great apprehension, we must do the same. We may not like the world that we live in right now, but it is our world all the same and we can only strive to carry on and do whatever we can, however small, to make it work for ourselves and everyone around us. Fear gets us nowhere, and music has certainly helped me get through the moments that I've been most afraid, whether as motivation, distraction, as an outlet for anger and discontent or simply a means of instilling some calm amidst an otherwise turbulent landscape.

On a different note, one aspect of the US election that struck me was how lacklustre the Rock the Vote movement seemed, compared with years gone by. Is The Boss losing his touch? Has Katy Perry passed her sell-by date? From my distant vantage point, I observed a public that appeared thoroughly unengaged by the efforts of the artistic community to sway the undecideds and rally the maybe-voters. People in 2016 have certainly shown themselves to be fed up with the status quo,[56] so maybe this was part

---

56 The popularity of Status Quo, on the other hand, continues to endure, despite the band's decision earlier this year to quit playing electric shows because they're now physically incapable of playing their own hits fast enough.

of the same backlash, a rebellion against the inevitability of the creative world saying the same old things (Democrats = Good, Republicans = Evil) in an election that in every other respect, defied conventional wisdom.

Maybe if it had been Bono against Trump he'd have had more success than Hilary. Pitting the world's most divisive rock star against the world's most divisive celebrity businessman would've made for undeniably compelling viewing. I think I'd sooner have backed Courtney Love, everyone's favourite middle-aged singer-cum-nutcase, for victory. I will be sure to lobby Love extensively over the next three years before the madness ensues once more.

Assuming we're not engulfed by nuclear war in the meantime, let's all keep going, let's keep listening to music and let's keep being nice to one another – sometimes there's not much more that can be done.

Wilco, Brixton Academy, London, Saturday 19th November

- **Gig #29**
- **Musical birthdays:** Jason Pierce of Spiritualised (1965)
- **Musical history:** Michael Jackson dangles his baby over the edge of a Berlin balcony (2002); one year to the day, a warrant is issued for Jackson's arrest following sexual abuse claims (2003)
- **Non-musical history:** Lincoln delivers the Gettysburg Address (1863)
- **Also:** Milli Vanilli are stripped of their Grammy Award after the truth emerges that the duo did not sing on their debut album (1990)

My mum and her best friend Janet were supposed to be seeing Wilco in Manchester last night.

I caught up with Janet at the Francis Lung gig back at the end of September. She seemed in good spirits, having recovered from a recent health scare, and we had a lovely chat about Neil Young, as well as laughing at the ridiculousness of having to book Wilco tickets thirteen months in advance, which is what we'd both had to do in preparation for this tour.

I won't see Janet again. She died earlier this week, twenty-one days after being admitted to hospital following the discovery of several new, previously undetected cancers, along with a rogue tumour that would ultimately cause her body to poison itself, destroy her kidneys and ensure that there was no prospect of a recovery. I've never in my life observed anyone transformed and distorted by illness so swiftly, so thoroughly, and in such hostile, relentless fashion. I don't have the words to describe the deep unfairness of it all.

Wilco are a good band to see if you're in need of a lift. They remind me of R.E.M., a band that released fantastic albums, were consistently great live, always intelligent, never too showy, an inspirational frontperson and so on. The last two Wilco albums haven't been vintage but, having seen them five times, I knew to expect a career-spanning set. They were fabulous as ever – I never doubted them – and it was a shame that I spent too much of the performance lamenting the state of Brixton Academy. Grumpy old man that I'm becoming, the venue strikes me as blatantly over-capacity. It's perpetually rammed, it takes an age to get to the bar, it takes hours to get out of the venue afterwards because it's so badly designed and, if you're anywhere near the men's toilets, it reeks of urine, a staple entry in my top five least favourite smells.[57]

Given the extent of the overcrowding, I tried to lift up my sister Fran at one stage to afford her a better view. She was extremely unhappy, as well as being heavier than I'd have expected for a vegan. Not especially heavy, of course, but I'd always assumed that vegans would be so light as to make them vulnerable to over-balancing or being swept away by the faintest breeze.

---

57 In no particular order: Urine, excrement, vomit (the holy trinity of unpleasant smells), fish markets and fear.

Rhys and I wandered down to Stockwell after the show to try and find a pub. He was returning from a trip to the Bataclan and two nights of Pete Doherty shows where he'd been semi-working alongside his new girlfriend, Pete's violinist. Apparently, Doherty was the first act booked in for the venue's reopening, but then Sting turned up a day earlier and stole his thunder. Bastard. Not that I like Pete Doherty, but for some reason Sting's position within the rock aristocracy grates with me. I look at Dave Gilmour, Bryan Ferry, Kate Bush, Bryan May, Elton John, even Tom Jones and Rod Stewart, and Sting feels like a charlatan in their midst, the guy that has snuck into the dinner party uninvited and is scoffing canapés as he tries to avoid the host's gaze. In case you're wondering, Paul McCartney is the host, and if he spots Sting there'll be an almighty fracas – a bit like the debacle with the photographer underneath David Blaine's Tower Bridge pod[58] that led Macca to fire his publicist. The publicist, Geoff Baker, was quoted following the incident as saying, *"I'm available for parties … and pole dancing."*

Remarkably, that was thirteen years ago, and it should be said that, for all the macro- and micro-trauma in the world today, the fact that David Blaine isn't being forced into lives on an ongoing basis is a true blessing. I've just Googled him. It turns out that two days ago he was hospitalised after shooting himself in the throat while trying to perform the legendary "bullet catch" magic trick. The man is a moron.

Jack Cheshire, The Finsbury, London, Tuesday 22nd November
- **Gig #30**
- **Musical birthdays:** Steven Van Zandt (1950), Karen O (1978)

---

58 Sadly, David Blaine was left unscathed by the McCartney/photographer fracas.

- **Musical history:** Michael Hutchence of INXS is found dead in his Sydney hotel, hanging naked behind the door to his room (1997)
- **Non-musical history:** Rich pickings today, as Vasco da Gama makes his way around the Cape of Good Hope on the first voyage from Europe to India (1497); more than four hundred and fifty years later, JFK is assassinated (1963)
- **Also:** Alice Cooper rescues Patrick and Dee Ann Kelly from the threat of home repossession after they paint his face on the house to help sell the property (1991)[59]

*"What's the difference between a musician and a twelve-inch pizza? …
A twelve-inch pizza can feed a family of four."*

This was the first of Jack Cheshire's two jokes. The second one involved mocking his ego-centric band name as he introduced the other members of his ensemble. Both were quietly effective, though alarm bells tend to start ringing when you reflect on a performance and realise that the singer's sense of humour is more memorable than his songs.

As I've touched upon already, our world today is a deeply uncertain and foreboding place, one in which people are finding it hard to prevent their anxieties and frustrations from bubbling to the surface. Alex, Brett and myself began a heated discussion about US politics an hour before the show, and we were still hard at it when Jack Cheshire took to the stage. We still hadn't finished two and half hours later, stood outside Manor House tube station finally, on the verge of heading home. Brett was particularly animated, perhaps understandable given his start-up business went under last week due to the inexplicable decision-making of

---

59 It is unclear exactly why they thought that a depiction of Alice Cooper's face on the side of their house would boost its value. Indeed, if this were true, surely everyone would do it.

an out-of-touch billionaire investor. Alex was more measured, though one suspects a lot must be going on under the surface. He's going to be bringing a child into the world come next spring (well, his girlfriend is), a fact currently unknown to most of our friendship group. I can only imagine what it must feel like to be introducing a new life into this catastrophic mess of a Western world. I've considered emigrating many times over the past five years, though the cons have generally ensured a victory for head over heart. Language barriers, loneliness, the difficulty securing employment/visas, the basic question of where the hell to go.

Maybe it's still an option though, the *"Fuck this, I'm outta here!"* approach, if Western society continues to autopilot towards hell. Perhaps I'll ask Laura if she's ever thought about moving to the Far East and see if we can arrive at a consensus.

I don't have an awful lot to say about Jack Cheshire and his Nick Drake-meets-jazzy musings repertoire. It was infinitely more accomplished than the average pub band but was ultimately an overlong and forgettable set and – given the climate I've been describing – felt completely insignificant. The most poignant moment in the gig was an unexpected solo Leonard Cohen cover, by far the best track of the evening; which served to remind us that a true legend left the stage recently, one whom few contemporary artists can ever hope to emulate.

It was my first visit to The Finsbury, a venue that has just been entirely revamped in a belated bid to bring it into the twenty first century. Inexplicably, said revamp included the installation of a dry ice machine in the roof of the venue. Dry ice behaves in unpredictable ways when unleashed from above instead of below within a confined space and Alex, from his vantage point to the far left of the stage, found himself repeatedly submerged in fog over the course of the hour-long performance. We tried to photograph his discontent, but alas, the resultant image was a hazy blur, in which one can just about identify an unhappy figure raising their middle finger to the camera.

The sight of dry ice emanating randomly from a ceiling, mid-song, was truly baffling and provoked understandable mirth within the venue, much to the vexation of Mr. Cheshire and his outfit. The Finsbury should probably rethink its special effects setup, as musicians don't tend to enjoy being laughed at as they're pouring their hearts out. The incident took me back years to an old Angry Red Planets performance at the Flying Shuttle in Bury. This was in the days when it was a rough, old-fashioned boozer, prior to its conversion into a gay bar called The Sailor.[60] Our bassist Johnny arrived with a dry ice machine borrowed from the Summerseat Players amateur dramatic society, regrettably sans instructions. We took to the stage with Dave, our enigmatic but slightly unreliable singer opting to trigger the device immediately, which set off in earnest but then would not switch off again. As we began playing, the venue quickly became cloaked by a pea-souper, totally obscuring our performance from the audience and restricting on-stage visibility to the extent that we could no longer see our instruments, thus leading to many rudimentary errors, as well as Dave coughing incessantly throughout our opening track. After the plug socket for the rogue device was located, it took a further fifteen minutes and several error-strewn cover versions before visibility was restored.

Now that I recall, The Flying Shuttle was a particularly unlucky venue for The Angry Red Planets. On another occasion, we were heckled for forty-five minutes straight by a middle-aged bald bloke repeatedly insisting that we play some Oasis. When we eventually obliged, he promptly took to the stage and exposed his genitals to the crowd.

---

60 I'm not a hundred percent sure that this is true and have yet to find any evidence online to substantiate the memory, however as we are now living in a post-truth world, I feel comfortable presenting this information as a cast-iron fact.

Airborne, Electric Ballroom, London, Wednesday 30th November

- Gig #31
- **Musical birthdays:** William Broad aka Billy Idol (1955), Des'ree (1968)
- **Musical history:** Michael Jackson releases Thriller, which will spend an unprecedented one hundred and ninety weeks in the UK album charts (1982)
- **Non-musical history:** Mexico declares war on France in what will become known as the pastry war, a conflict that arises following the looting of a French pastry chef's shop by Mexicans (1838)
- **Also:** The Boy Scout Association criticises Elton John for performing at the Albert Hall with six male stripping dancers dressed as Boy Scouts (1999)

Fresh from a brief sojourn to the surprisingly beautiful Bulgarian capital of Sofia, I decided to ramp things up a notch and take on five gigs in a fortnight. Laura and I had not been served encouraging reports about Sofia. The word 'dump' was bandied about a lot, and dump is a word that no one particularly wants to see, in any context. However, such reports were wide of the mark, and my second visit to Eastern Europe proved just as delightful as my trip to Crimea eleven years earlier. The centre of Sofia was beautiful, full of impressive architecture and archaeology (a two thousand-year-old settlement was recently unearthed bang in the middle of town during the construction of a new metro station), the people were lovely, and the food was universally excellent, despite their predilection for putting cream cheese into absolutely everything. Without wishing to court controversy, I applaud this idea and hope it catches on at home.

Like most holidays, the trip felt like a distant memory after just hours back on UK soil. Still, what better way to get back into the gigging habit than with Airborne, the silliest band I have seen since my expedition began six months ago. There is no other way of putting it – this band *is* AC/DC. All that was missing was a giant bell, some cannons and an enormous inflatable hooker. Singing songs entitled "Rivalry" and "Going Down on You", writing tribute tracks to Lemmy, playing the entire set topless, partaking in mesmeric head banging and suchlike, Airborne were completely and utterly ridiculous, and an absolute joy for it. Hailing from a small town near Melbourne, they went about their business without a hint of irony, thus differentiating them from their cousins The Darkness. They indulged in good old fashion rock 'n' roll, which also included swearing a lot and, most notably, the singer repeatedly smacking cans of beer against his head until they exploded everywhere, a feat he undertook at least a dozen times during the show. There is nothing clever about any of this, but then music doesn't always have to be clever. Sometimes being fun is more than enough. I've always loved DC for precisely this reason. They only have one chord sequence, but it's a belter, and playing it repeatedly creates an exuberance that's surprisingly hard to beat.

At the end of the gig, Airborne's singer, one of the daftest frontmen I've ever come across, made the following proclamation to the packed-out venue:

"As long as we are alive,
As long as you are alive,
Rock and roll will never ever die."

This is perhaps not the most profound statement ever made, though it could potentially be the most profound statement made by an Australian.[61] In these uncomfortable times, his words felt strangely comforting.

---

61 Sledging

**The Julie Ruin, Koko, London,
Friday 2nd December**

- **Gig #32**
- **Musical birthdays:** Nelly Furtado (1978), Britney Spears (1981)
- **Musical history:** Cindy Birdsong of The Supremes is kidnapped at knifepoint by a maintenance man working in her building. She will thankfully escape unharmed (1969)
- **Non-musical history:** Fidel Castro assumes presidency of Cuba (1976)
- **Also:** The first day of the photo shoot for Pink Floyd's iconic Animals album takes place at Battersea Power Station. The following day, the giant inflatable pig will break free from its moorings and float to Kent, where a farmer will complain that it has alarmed his cows (1976)

The story of my week could be summarised as Three Gigs, Two Trips and a Funeral, though this is taking a bit of a liberty by describing an hour-long audience with Michael Palin as a gig. Which it wasn't. As incredible as it was to see this legendary comic, intrepid explorer, poignant author and personal hero of mine in the flesh, he didn't pick up an instrument or so much as hum a single tune during his Q&A session at Waterstones Piccadilly.

The Julie Ruin had a lot to live up to, falling just twenty-four hours after Palin and seventy-two hours after possibly the most unexpectedly enjoyable gig of my expedition to date. Not only that, but in the past twenty-four hours I had made a whistle stop visit to Manchester for Janet's funeral, which was incredibly moving and exceptionally carried-off. As I dashed down to Koko in Camden to meet my friend Caitlin,[62] I was emotionally

---

62 Caitlin is also the editor of *Pop Life: The Story of a Minor Musical Expedition*; however, she was unaware of this information at the time of the gig.

and physically drained and sporting a brand new cold sore as evidence of the extent to which I'd run myself into the ground. I was not in gigging mood, but as with so many of these evenings over the past few months, music won me over. The Julie Ruin is a longstanding project from Kathleen Hanna, who previously brought the world Bikini Kill and Le Tigre. I knew nothing about either of these bands or about Hanna, one of Caitlin's all-time heroes. After just minutes on stage I could see why. Hanna was like a cartoon superhero with a squeaky speaking voice, a small and diminutive frame and a repertoire of eccentric and outlandish dance moves. Yet as a singer, her voice was capable of triggering earthquakes and avalanches (in a good way), and her eagerness to experiment with unorthodox melodies and to stretch her vocal range to the max reminded me a little of Kate Bush. She was unbelievably likeable, to the extent which, at various points in the set, I was so transfixed by her presence that I forget to pay attention to whether the songs were any good or not.

Hanna was a compulsive talker who uses band-audience interaction as a form of therapy, sharing the burden of her insecurities, traumas and political and social fears. I like bands that talk to the crowd, and although different in tone, this show made me hark back to The Staves five months ago and their unique way of engaging the audience, making us feel as though the band is a friend and compadre in life. Palin has this ability too; when you hear him speak it's as though you're listening to an uncle you've known for decades. The Julie Ruin have carved out their own variant on this formula. For the ninety minutes they were on stage, only about half of which were taken up by playing songs, we were made to feel like a member of their movement, a glorious resistance against the intolerance, prejudice and cruelty that too often goes unchallenged within society. It felt empowering, and the crowd responded with warmth and enthusiasm. By the final song we were bouncing up and down to an ancient Bikini Kill micro-hit, a rare experience in these days of enhanced security and indifferent middle-class London audiences who spend their gigging time complaining about the volume, or the fact that their view is being obstructed, or the appalling state of the toilets. Gigs should not be sanitised; for every Royal Festival Hall performance, there needs to be a show at The Boston Arms.[63] I think that The Julie Ruin would appreciate this sentiment.

---

63 A shithole.

Weeks 27–30:
Sleeper

It's Christmas time and there's no need to be afraid.

Except that I am afraid. Not of Band Aid – they're harmless enough, despite their misguided and rather patronising plans to try and fix Africa. I'm afraid because this time of year is my Achilles heel, a consistent vulnerability exposed every twelve months, as society around me swings in one direction and I swing in quite the other. My mood declines, my behaviour becomes erratic. Problems spring up out of nowhere and the impact of every such problem is magnified ten-fold in my mind. I fear the ghosts of Christmas past, a haunting that begins with the year my ex-girlfriend and I – just two weeks following our break-up – were forced to spend the entire winter holiday together with my family, after she was unable to secure an earlier flight home to her native Washington state. Awkward, or "totes awks", as the youth of today would put it.

This unhappy memory is well over a decade old, not to mention being a problem entirely of my own making, yet the incident somehow triggered a series of unfortunate events that, over the intervening years, slowly began to turn my festive experience into an endurance test rather than a period of celebration. Fast forward to the present day and, despite my best efforts, I find myself alienated by the merriment going on around me, dislocated from the community spirit and coming-together-ness, and ultimately unable to bask in the fuzzy warm glow of mulled wine, mince pies and preposterous jumpers.

Even when things are all going smoothly, I still find myself grumbling with far greater regularity through the month of

December. This year, I've decided to take issue with the UK's in-fatuation with German Christmas markets, which seem to have grown exponentially over the past decade. Why would anyone in their right mind want to flock to an over-crowded town centre in the middle of winter, to purchase ornate wooden ducks, eat over-priced pretzels and stand in the freezing cold to watch mis-guided locals attempt Schuhplattler dancing?[64] Like St. Patrick's Day, an event that seems to be observed more by the English than the Irish, the German markets have become yet another excuse for local yobs, reprobates, boozehounds, bartenders and thieves to behave like drunken morons in public, free from ad-monishment or reprisal. It's apparently permissible to be com-pletely pissed and staggering about in a town centre at two p.m. provided you're at a Christmas market.

I've been to local markets in Berlin and Frankfurt and at nei-ther did I find the townsfolk exhibiting similar characteristics. What must the Germans make of this misappropriation of their festive traditions?

It's surely no coincidence that the Germans repay our an-nual dalliance in their culture by sitting down once a year and watching a peculiar black and white British comedy skit from the 60s called Dinner for One, in which a butler gets drunk for the amusement of the Lady of the House.[65] We think of our

---

64 If you're unfamiliar with Schuhplattler dancing, it is a bizarre and anti-quated thigh-slapping ritual practiced by ageing men (and possibly wom-en) in the Alpine regions of Southern Germany and Austria. According to Wikipedia, Schuhplattler dancing is becoming increasingly popular with young people, however, having seen it, I find this extremely hard to be-lieve and suspect it to be a modern myth, like the second coming of vinyl, or the resurgence of the Welsh language.

65 I'm not making this up – it is a widely-held German tradition, as well as in many other non-English speaking countries, to watch Dinner for One every New Year's Eve. For some reason however, it hasn't caught on over here, hence on British television we must make do with Jools Holland's Hootenanny, which I recently found out is pre-recorded, thus meaning that they all must fake the New Year's countdown.

European neighbours as crazed sausage-eaters dancing around in Lederhosen. They think of us as absurd drunkards staggering around in our stately homes.

I'm conducting this rant from my workspace in Goodge Street, where I'm sitting in an over-priced café-bar area, trying to avoid making eye contact with a gawkish, doe-eyed waitress, whom one could easily mistake for a Zooey Deschanel character. She's taken over the jukebox and remarkably, in the past twenty minutes, every single track she's chosen has been a band I've seen live. Earlier, I attempted to engage her in conversation about my expedition after she randomly selected the recent James single "Nothing but Love," however the conversation broke down after she mistook my polite banter for flirtation. She has since done everything in her power to avoid further interaction, while I made the situation more intense by admonishing her for putting on Little Drummer Boy, a song I have thankfully never seen live, as it's a pile of crap.

This is the halfway point in my expedition; like Palin in "Pole to Pole", I've reached the Equator and there is now as much live music behind me as lies ahead. If live music were water, it would drain neither clockwise nor counter-clockwise.[66] It hasn't flown by, but nor has it dragged its feet. In the past six months, I've discovered musical worlds that were hitherto unknown to me; I've rekindled my love for unknown talent, dingy venues, taking a chance on artists and attempting to suspend non-musical judgements, so that each band gets assessed only on the essentials. I've gained my inaugural tattoos – both of which are musical tributes, grown my hair long for the first time in a decade, and retaught myself the valuable lesson that the way you dress for a night out is far less important than the company with whom you spend it.

It pains me to think that I could ever have forgotten such a basic truth, but then, much pains me about the way in which the

---

66 Live music is, regrettably, not water, with the possible exception of the Water Phone, as memorably featured in Ludovico Eunaudi's band.

last few years have panned out. In this sense, the expedition feels as though it has gone some way to restoring my sense of self, allowing me to try and be the person I want to be, rather than the person I think I need to be. There is still a vast distance separating the Equator from the South Pole, but there is still life in the tank, providing I can make it through the frost, the snow and the pools of mulled wine vomit staining our city streets.

Pete Doherty, The Forum, London, Tuesday 6th December

- Gig #33
- **Musical birthdays:** Jonathan King (1944), Peter Buck of R.E.M. (1956)
- **Musical history:** Seminal blues artist Leadbelly dies. He was once jailed for shooting a man after they had argued about a woman (enough to give anyone the blues) (1949)
- **Non-musical history:** Jews are officially excluded from Barcelona, after Don Alfonso V of Aragon grants the city this permission (1424)[67]
- **Also:** Elton John and Rolling Stones records are burned in Tallahassee, Florida due to their sinfulness, after a local survey reveals that nine hundred and eighty-four of one thousand local unmarried mothers want have sex to them (1975)

I never thought that I'd see the day I went to see Pete Doherty live. The man I've come to regard as the older music fan's Justin Bieber released a new album recently, and announced a handful

---

67 The people who point to the Jews as the most persecuted race in history may be onto something. As I've ploughed through the archives for daily facts of historical significance, it has become apparent to me that an act of persecution against the Jewish people has been committed on practically every single day of the year.

of European shows, culminating in nights at two moderately sized London and Manchester venues. I'm not a fan, I've never been a fan, I didn't like The Libertines, I don't condone burglary[68] and I'm automatically jealous of anyone that has claimed a close acquaintance with Kate Moss. On the other hand, a few months ago, Rhys started dating his violinist and, in a successful bid to make a positive first impression, she offered Eleri, Philip and me free tickets.

I had no idea what to expect, other than a vague Live 8 influenced notion that large sections of the show might be out of tune. I bet Elton hasn't forgotten the humiliation – he seems so well-presented most of the time. I gather that Pete blamed Elton's band for the shambolic rendition of "Children of the Revolution" in Hyde Park that day, referring to them as *"a bunch of fucking wankers. What a bunch of sausage sucking, session, slaphead, ponytailed p*****, you know?"*[69]

Laura was unfamiliar with Pete and messaged me midway through the performance to tell me that she'd found him on Wikipedia and she wasn't sure why I was there. Nor was I. This was not for me; a man whose talents appear destined to forever escape me. The first half of the gig was pedestrian; the second half was a bit of a mess. Pete, to my mind, has become a charmless Morrissey[70], ambling around the stage delivering forgettable melodies against a mundane and unremarkable musical backdrop. Miki's violin was a ray of light in this two-hour drudge, but she was regularly forced to play second fiddle[71] to Carl Barat,

---

68 That said, I did once remove and make off with an entire set of bathroom cabinet handles at a house party after an altercation with the host.

69 I've transcribed this quote from an article in The Sun which blanked out the offensive terms, however I've had to leave one of the expletives censored as I'm not entirely sure what it is! It is most likely "pricks", but it could also be "pussies."

70 Admittedly, he faces quite a lot of competition from Morrissey himself in this regard.

71 Not literally.

a man whose outfit was more impressive than his ad hoc musical contributions.

I could go on and talk at great length about Pete's shambolic guitar playing, his tendency to throw mic stands and other heavy and dangerous objects at the crowd, and an encore that was one of the worst things I've ever seen in live music and which culminated in the ritualistic massacring of Leonard Cohen's Hallelujah, but it hardly seems worth it. Clearly Pete's endless party is not one to which I've been invited, and I'll be happy if I never hear from him again.

Frightened Rabbit, The Roundhouse, London, Wednesday 7ᵗʰ December

- **Gig #34**
- **Musical birthdays:** Tom Waits (1949), Damien Rice (1973), Nicole Appleton (1974), Aaron Carter (1987)
- **Musical history:** The first Sony Minidisc is released in the US, an MTV Unplugged EP from Mariah Carey and surely an omen for the format's fate (1992)
- **Non-musical history:** The Japanese Navy attacks Pearl Harbor, possibly because of a premonition about the Mariah Carey minidisc (1941)
- **Also:** Shock-jock Howard Stern successfully talks a caller out of throwing himself off the George Washington bridge, live on air (1994)

It was a mistake to stay up dancing in my front room with Philip and Eleri until three-thirty a.m. this morning. Dancing to my own band, no less. Last night I was an ego-driven mess; when I awoke, I was the anti-ego, quickly descending into a pit of shame. The day was a total write-off, such was the severity of my hangover, and I spent most of it asleep in bed. Thank goodness for self-employment – no doubt my self-employed brethren occasionally submit to this type of colossal stupidity too. We lack job security or benefits, but we have the happy ability to stay up late and get shit-faced on a weekday.

Around mid-afternoon, I realised I was supposed to be at another gig that evening. Other weeks I may have abandoned the plans, but on this occasion, I was keen to wash away the stains of Doherty and get back to seeing music that made me feel alive. Frightened Rabbit were the perfect tonic. In many ways, they're my ideal band – musically intelligent, lyrically foreboding, wry humour infused in catchy melody, unafraid to go for a big chorus if one presents itself. That said, I'd seen them twice before and they were underwhelming on both occasions, unable to capture the intricacy of their records in the live arena.

Thankfully, this performance put paid to that notion. Laura and I trundled along to the nearby Roundhouse, fortified by a little mulled wine (the Christmas Bloody Mary) and were treated to a fabulous spectacle. Their latest record, Painting of a Panic Attack, isn't my favourite, but it has spurred Frightened Rabbit into more dynamic and energetic live performances. Furthermore, the singer, who impressed me last time out by introducing one track with the immortal line, *"This is a song about being eaten by a shark,"* was on glorious form. He charmed the crowd with random anecdotes about Ken Bruce, made us giggle with his declaration that the first Frightened Rabbit album is a waste of money (thank goodness, as it's the only one I don't yet own) and appeared genuinely humbled by the rapturous reception afforded to the band, to the extent that he questioned both the sobriety and sanity of the audience.[72]

This was just what I needed after last night – a reminder of why I continue with my expedition week-in week-out. There's nothing more satisfying than being surrounded by a crowd of people who are appreciating a band just as much as you are. It creates a perfectly-formed community, intent on making those on stage feel like the princes and princesses of the universe for an hour or two, at which point we go our separate ways, forever connected in time and place by the live experience.

---

72 Both things that I question about myself each and every day.

One day I might meet someone who was at that show and we can reminisce fondly, just as Laura and I did when it transpired we went to the same Mew show (also at The Roundhouse) a good seven months before we hooked up. Weirdly, in one of my old companies a few years back, I met a colleague about eighteen months my senior who had been to the same Manic Street Preachers, Kula Shaker and Ocean Colour Scene gigs at Manchester Apollo in the mid-nineties. All three shows were excellent, from memory, though when you see posters for contemporary London festivals advertising Ocean Colour Scene as your headliner, it's not hard to understand why so many promoters in 2016 are battling against insolvency. Some parts of the nineties are better left where they are, TFI Friday being case in point. Besides, as Hanna from The Julie Ruin noted the other week, *"Unfortunately, the 90s resurgence has been ended by Trump, and now we're all living in hell."*

James and The Charlatans, Liverpool Echo Arena, Liverpool, Saturday 10th December

- **Gig #35**
- **Musical birthdays:** Brian Molko (1972), Meg White (1974)
- **Musical history:** Frank Zappa is pushed off the stage of The Rainbow in London by the jealous boyfriend of an audience member and suffers fractures, head trauma and injuries to his back, leg, and neck, as well as a crushed larynx (1971)
- **Non-musical history:** Red Cross founder Jean Henri Dunant and peace activist Frederic Passy are awarded the first ever Nobel Peace Prize (1901)

Twelve years have passed since I last set foot in Liverpool – one of the UK's most marvellous musical cities – for a live music experience. Back in 2004, I skipped a week of university to follow The Twilight Singers around the UK, a tour which culminated in a tiny Liverpool University show for about a hundred lucky fans, during which the singer Greg Dulli flirted with my friend Louise and I felt inexplicably jealous.

This time, the outing was to see James, supported by Manchester indie veterans The Charlatans. The quintessential Britpop lads' night out, with hopefully no further band flirtations on the cards. Liverpool was in full-on Christmas mode from the moment we arrived. Every shop bustling, every restaurant rammed, every pub packed to the rafters. Regrettably, the one bar we found with some spare seats turned out to have no beer available on tap due to an issue with the pipes – the third time this has happened to me in as many months, which is a little bizarre. As far as I'm concerned, if you can't serve draft beer, you might as well shut up shop and go home. A pub without a pint is like Bono without The Edge – unbelievably irritating.

Despite several months of planning, the weekend didn't get off to the best start due to eleventh hour revelations that a) we had a spare ticket to shift and b) the hotel I had booked for us turned out to be in a completely different town, resulting in a £64 estimated taxi fare to Widnes. The next setback was seeing The Charlatans. It's the cruellest of descriptions, but they were past it. In recent years there have been goodness knows how many examples of ageing artists defying the odds, not to mention their juniors, to produce game-changing music and life-defining live performances. When Leonard Cohen released his "Live at The O2" album in 2008, one of the reviews led with the headline, *"Old aged pensioner unexpectedly makes greatest live album of all time."* Come to think of it, Rick Astley, of all people, managed to make a comeback this year.

Unfortunately, The Charlatans have not followed suit, and what they gave us for this one-off Christmas show was an hour-long exposé into why people don't listen to early nineties, dance-infused indie-pop anymore. Their hits have not aged well, and with little to make the band stand out on stage, save for Tim Burgess's truly appalling blond bob, they best resembled a dad-rock pub band several years' past the possibility of rekindling their former glories. The music held little merit in 2016, other than provoking a vague sense of longing for a bygone era, while any feeling of legitimate nostalgia was diminished by the crowd around us, a motley mix of mid- to late-forties drunken men dancing badly, knocking other people's beer over and spending the downtime between acts singing The Verve at the top of their voices, a bittersweet symphony if ever there was one.

I was nervous about the prospect of including a James gig within my year of live music. Part of me wishes they had taken some time off, allowing me to skip over them during this expedition. The basic challenge is that I don't really have the words to express what their songs mean to me or why I continue to love them so much. They are so intertwined with my life these days, that it's almost irrelevant whether they're still making good music or performing well. They play, and I go and see them – that's how it works.

Starting in March 1997 at Manchester Apollo I've been to see them somewhere in the region of thirty-five to forty times, although no one can quite work out the exact number. I cannot be objective, other than to say that of the people I've taken to James shows over the years, very few have come away disappointed. As ever, they were resplendent, and that's all I can currently contribute.

At the end of the show, my friend Brendan and I decided to seek out the legendary Cavern Club which, by some miracle, we managed to find immediately. Brendan is one my oldest friends; we met at school some twenty years ago, formed a band together, played video games together, went camping together, attempted and failed to impress girls together, laughed and cried together. Times like this are far rarer these days. When we do manage to hook up it's as though we've never been apart, with the prospect of an enlivened political debate/brutal argument always just around the corner. Brendan is what one might call a "salt of the earth" character, a description that might well annoy him, which is precisely why I'm including it. Longstanding Mancunian friends take great delight in winding one another up, and I wouldn't have it any other way.

Growing up, Brendan's dad ran Summerseat Liberal Club, a rather unsavoury and often deserted haunt that had an upstairs function room with a small stage, perfect for our band to practice in for hours on end and annoy the few patrons below. The sheer amount of time spent at the club may well be the reason why the two of us have always gravitated towards old man pubs or out-and-out dives in favour of anything fancy. We whiled away the rest of the night watching a mediocre covers band invite random tourists from as far away as Argentina onstage to butcher Ramones, Oasis and Beatles classics. One of the world's most iconic music venues, The Cavern is today an unabashed tourist trap – Hard Rock Café in a claustrophobic basement. We emerged at two a.m. to a classic Christmas street brawl, ordered our extortionate taxi and retreated to the inappropriately named Best Western Hotel, the corridors of which were adorned with vomit due to a raucous Christmas party that continued long into the morning. I felt weary; the rigours of three shows in a week taking their toll on mind and body. This was week twenty-seven, the first week beyond the halfway point in my expedition, but as I lay there, listening to a jilted office lover sobbing onto a colleague's shoulder outside our bedroom door, it felt like I still had an awfully long way to go.

Our Girl, The Shacklewell Arms, London, Tuesday 13th December

- **Gig #36**
- **Musical birthdays:** Tom Verlaine of Television (1949), Tom Delonge of Blink-182 (1975), Amy Lee of Evanescence (1981),[73] Taylor Swift (1989)
- **Musical history:** After seventy-four years, Melody Maker announces its closure (2000)

---

73 Clearly the most significant day in musical history.

- **Non-musical history:** Saint Celestine V abdicates the papacy in a bid to return to his previous life as an ascetic hermit (1294)[74]
- **Also:** Music Choice analyses Christmas No. 1 singles from the past thirty years to highlight common criteria that determine their success, including the use of sleigh bells, children singing, church bells harmony and references to love. They conclude that "Mistletoe and Wine" is therefore the ultimate Christmas song (2002)

After a truly horrific day in the office on Monday, which had itself followed a disaster of a train journey back from Liverpool, surrounded by an inebriated chorus of die-hard West Ham fans on the Sunday night, I needed my Tuesday to give me a lift.

I hate December – it's dark and miserable and damp and it has played host to far more of my life's disasters than any other month I can think of. I'm also not a fan of Christmas, which tends to mean I spend most of December feeling simultaneously guilty and unpopular. Furthermore, the third week of my misery month began with the double blow that Ian McCaskill, smiley Scottish weather forecaster from the golden age of BBC meteorology, had died, and over in the US Donald Trump had appointed the head of ExxonMobil as the latest member of his Suicide Squad. A quick look at our domestic political news proved similarly discomforting, being dominated as it was by an ongoing discussion about the cost of our prime minister's leather trousers. Bob Dylan released an understated acoustic covers album in the early 90s entitled "World Gone Wrong;" now feels an apt time to revisit it.

About thirty minutes into the Our Girl set I found myself drifting at last into serenity, the pains and perils of our crazy planet evaporating before me as I succumbed to a peculiarly mesmeric

---

74 I have no idea what this means, but it sounds like the sort of thing I might like.

soundscape conjured up by yet another newcomer on the London indie scene. This was a million miles away from my last shot in the dark – the world of Jack Cheshire and his uneventful Nick Drake musings. Our Girl have energy, life and vivacity, as well as possibly being siblings. Alex and I spent some time contemplating this possibility, eventually concluding that they probably were cut from the same cloth. I can't bring myself to Wikipedia them for fear that we may be completely wrong. The guitarist and bassist had the same chin, if that's evidence enough? It was harder to tell with the drummer, who looked about ten and was thus very fortunate to be admitted to the venue in the first place,[75] but it's certainly possible that she was their younger sister. In this sense, they reminded me of Hanson; thankfully in every other sense, they did not.

It was a great show and I was struck, not for the first time, by the attentiveness of the Shacklewell Arms crowd. The venue appears to be frequented by similarly minded people that, as rare as it sounds today, go to gigs to watch bands perform rather than to take endless selfies and to WhatsApp their friends. As an added advantage, it's rare to see anyone staggering around the venue singing Verve songs. As Our Girl closed their set in a beautiful cacophony of distortion, I glanced around the packed room, wondering to myself whether anyone was currently undertaking a similar expedition to myself. Perhaps at some stage I'll get wind of a bona fide lunatic doing a gig a day for a month or,

---

75 I hold that rarest of accolades: being ejected from my own gig. In fact, it's happened to me twice, the first occasion being The Angry Red Planets' performance at The Antelope Lounge in 1998 when I was thrown out due to the strict over eighteens policy as soon as we'd finished our set, leaving me to spend three hours wandering the streets of Kearsley, before my mum arrived to pick me up. The second was The Waterside in 2000, on this occasion the landlord turfing us out of the venue on musical grounds after we made the ill-judged decision to play an extensive medley of comedy Travis covers midway through our two-hour set. While understandably furious at the time, in retrospect I have a feeling the landlord made the right call.

more perilous still, for a whole year. I have absolutely no doubt that this would kill me, or at the very least I'd go one better than Van Gogh and cut off both my ears at the end of the final show. Maybe that wouldn't be so bad – I could follow in the unstable genius's footsteps and gift them to my lady-friends.

Fields of the Nephilim, Shepherd's Bush Empire, London, Wednesday 21st December

- **Gig #37**
- **Musical birthdays:** Frank Zappa (1940)
- **Musical history:** The infamous Elvis/Nixon meeting takes place at the White House, with the two men discussing, amongst other things, the US's ongoing fight against narcotics (1970)
- **Non-musical history:** In the North West of England, the Rochdale Pioneers start up their business and get the Cooperative movement underway (1844)
- **Also:** "Gangnam Style" becomes the first YouTube video to reach a billion views (2012)

So, this is Christmas. Almost. It's certainly my final gig before the holiday season is officially underway and thank goodness for that.

The sooner Christmas is over and done with, the better. I am a Grinch, as we've already established, and what better way to mark the conclusion of my working year than by raising my middle finger to Mariah Carey, Tony Bennett, Bing Crosby, and the countless other purveyors of festive cheer in musical form, and instead venturing out to see a dark and miserable Goth band who were about as likely to play a Christmas song as they were to burst into a cover of the national anthem.

Having concluded my final business meeting of the year, I spent my afternoon wandering aimlessly around Shepherd's Bush, taking conference calls by constantly flitting between mute and unmute due to the ever-growing number of motorcycles that fill the streets of London these days. I blame Just Eat.

The exertions of the past two weeks had left me half dead, running on empty, craving my bed, craving some peace and quiet. But the show had to go on, so I sat myself in the excellently named Defector's Weld and spent a good few hours chatting to Philip about the Goth movement, the misappropriation of gothic clothing, and whether Nine Inch Nails and Marilyn Manson could legitimately claim to be Goth music. The reason for this inane but harmless banter was Fields of the Nephilim, the Gothiest of Goth bands, a band who have perfected the art of wearing large hats on stage, making music that sounds akin to an evil U2 with Darth Vader as a frontman. It was a peculiar set that seemed to frustrate some of the die-hards I spoke to at the bar, but it was well-performed, and Philip was able to satisfy his inner Goth. On the return home, we talked about our housing arrangements post-New Year – serious stuff and a conversation I'd put off for a couple of months. With consensus quickly reached (we are going nowhere imminently), we moved on to discussing Christmas songs, argued about Mariah Carey, poured out some vodka and lamented the recent break-up of Swedish indie band Kent, possibly the greatest band who no one has ever heard of in this country.

Neither of us can remember going to bed, yet when I awoke this morning the room was peculiarly well-organised, which reassured me that I hadn't repeated the nonsensical over-indulgence of the Pete Doherty night. These memory lapses worry me though – I know I'm overdoing it, and I'm not entirely sure how to stop. I need to find a way to be less busy, but I find the restless and relentless London lifestyle addictive and, being self-employed, it's so easy to have one more drink and push the alarm clock back another half an hour. This freelance existence affords me insufficient structure at times, essentially allowing me to run amok and succumb to every dangerous whim and compulsion. Next week I'm off to Norway, and I'm hoping it'll serve as a marker of some kind. New Year's Resolutions can be formed; perhaps action can be taken. A gig every week is one thing, but I need to be able to get through it without sustaining irreparable damage, and right now, as I reflect on a gig just last night' that I can barely remember, I know that I've got to tone things down.

Svein and Birkir, Jernbanestasjon, Tromsø, Thursday 29th December

- **Gig #38**
- **Musical birthdays:** Ray Thomas of The Moody Blues (1941), Marianne Faithfull (1946), Bryan Holland of The Offspring (1966)
- **Musical history:** Band Aid top the UK singles charts with "Do They Know It's Christmas?"; over in the US the altogether more satisfying Madonna classic "Like a Virgin" sits at the summit of the Billboard Hot 100 (1984)
- **Non-musical history:** Emma Snodgrass, a lesser-known member of the women's rights movement, is arrested in Boston for wearing trousers. Proclaimed by local media as an "unfeminine freak", Emma will suffer an astonishing number of arrests over the course of a single year before disappearing without trace (1852)[76]
- **Also:** Barbra Streisand makes her first recording, putting down a vocal for "You'll Never Know" at the tender young age of thirteen (1955)

At the beginning of the month I checked in with my doctor to ascertain how long she felt I ought to continue taking my anti-depressants. Her recommendation was unequivocal – they don't ever suggest that people come off these drugs during the winter months, as the short days, long nights and general lack of sunlight tends to play havoc with people's moods. It was at this juncture that I mentioned my forthcoming trip to Tromsø and

---

76 This bizarre story of persistent cross-dressing and Emma's refusal to bend to the will of local law enforcement is well worthy of further investigation.

the arctic circle. She laughed and said, *"Well that's a no then — you'd better keep taking them."* Lo and behold, I arrived in Tromsø to find I'd forgotten to pack the damn things. Lord knows what impact this is likely to have on my body, mind and mood over the next few days, but for now I'm doing just fine in one of the strangest environments I've ever set foot in.

Daylight hours in Tromsø, if you can call it daylight, are between eleven a.m. and two p.m. Everything else is just varying degrees of darkness, which plays tricks on your mind, not to mention making you feel like going to the pub at three p.m. Fortunately, Norway is outrageously expensive and so lengthy stints of boozing are nigh on impossible without risking insolvency. This morning we paid £10 for a baguette; the less said about the price of crisps the better. However, these are minor quibbles in the grand scheme of things, for Tromsø and its surroundings are nothing short of extraordinary. We're surrounded by huge, snow-covered mountains, vast lakes flanked by pine trees, this unadulterated landscape punctuated only by the occasional boat or red wooden house elevated on stilts, presumably to avoid rising water levels when the snow melts in the spring. It's a terrain that feels simultaneously breath-taking yet foreboding, tranquil and calm yet also barren and desolate. Positively *Shining-esque*. The eerie twilight of the hours either side of midday add to the otherworldliness. It's genuinely as though we've travelled out to the very edge of the planet; I have a feeling we're on the perimeter of the Arctic tree line, or at least we would be, were it not for the Gulf Stream, which means the weather isn't quite as deathly cold as elsewhere in the Arctic Circle. Our receptionist at the hotel told us she had lived all her life in the town and still hadn't got used to this time of year. *"I hate it — it sucks. It's so friggin' miserable. Oh and by the way, in the summer it's sunny twenty-four hours a day for a month. That sucks too."*

I think our receptionist should accompany us to Tromsø Jernbanestasjon before we conclude our trip — it sounds as though she could do with cheering up. Purporting to be Tromsø's most popular bar, TJ (as I'm going to abbreviate it from here on in) played host last night to a two-hour cover show from a middle-aged Icelandic duo called Svein and Birkir. We'd been on the verge of retiring for the evening, exhausted after a seven-mile snow-trek and a couple of strong Mack Bayers, the decidedly punchy local beer which, despite being brewed approximately five hundred metres from the bar, costs £9.50 per pint. Of course, that's still cheaper than a baguette. However, we opted to stay for one song on the off-chance that the fading rocker with blond-grey hair and his suit-clad accomplice might be half-decent. Remarkably, they did not disappoint, opening with "Life on Mars", into "Brown-Eyed Girl", followed by a Johnny Cash combo of "Ring of Fire" and their version of his epic take on NiN's "Hurt". Comedic mispronunciations gave us the impression that Svein's command of English was not much better than our command of Norwegian, but the dude possessed a fine set of pipes. Hence, our decision to stay an extra ten minutes quickly turned into three hours and the accumulation of an £80 bar bill (four drinks each). The piano/electric guitar duo entertained us throughout, taking on Orbison, Rea, U2, The Byrds and countless others to an increasingly vociferous local crowd who boogied, slow-danced, grabbed the microphone for the choruses and occasionally regaled the rest of us with a rendition of the town song, the lyrics to which went *"Tromsø, Tromsøooooo, ahh, ahh."*

This was a glorious live treat and a reminder that covers bands can often command an adulation and euphoria that even the biggest artists sometimes struggle to attain. While waiting for Rhys to purchase an £8 hot dog from the Seven Eleven, I began contemplating the best and worst cover bands I'd ever seen. Svein and Birkir have made it into my top ten. As for the worst, that unfortunate accolade must go to the German Credence Clearwater Revival tribute act I saw thirteen years ago in a small village on the outskirts of Frankfurt. They were beyond awful; indeed, if John Fogerty ever discovered their existence he'd probably try and sue for defamation.[77] And yet, the next day I still went along to a tiny local record store and purchased the Best of Creedence. Such is the mysterious power of the covers band.

The Fat Rats, Bastard Bar, Tromsø, Saturday 31st December

- Gig #39
- **Musical birthdays:** Henry John Deutschendorf aka John Denver (1943), Donna Summer (1948), Danny McNamara of Embrace (1970), Park Jae-Sang aka PSY (1977)
- **Musical history:** An incredible day for live debuts, New Year's Eve sees the first ever performances by The Beach Boys (1961), The Kinks (1963) and AC/DC (1973)
- **Non-musical history:** Ottawa is chosen by reigning British monarch Queen Victoria to be the new capital of Canada (1857)
- **Also:** Def Leppard drummer Rick Allen loses his left arm in a car crash after being goaded by an aggressive Jaguar driver into overtaking on an unpredictable stretch of road (1984)

I'm thrilled that, over the course of 2016, I've been able to experience music venues with such brilliant names as Pirate Republic and Bastard Bar. It is no surprise that they're overseas; in the UK, it would likely be The O2 Bastard Bar.

Tromsø's premier rock 'n' roll bar (as opposed to its most popular bar, TJ, which was about 100 metres away) did not disappoint. It was as old school as they come, bartenders donning white suits

---

77 I am not for one second suggesting that Mr. Fogerty is some sort of petty spoilsport who goes around firing off legal action at anyone who – irrespective of purpose or intent – attempts to appropriate his musical legacy. But the band were *diabolically* bad.

and bowties to add to the atmosphere, and it offered a far cheaper pint than anywhere else in town (a mere £7 per drink). This was a page torn straight from my masterplan for the winter holiday period – get away to a remote part of the world where one could avoid as much of one's usual routine as possible, see some sights, meet some locals, and spend New Year's Eve boozing it up to some good old-fashioned rock 'n' roll. Everything had been going swimmingly during the holiday up until the morning of December 31st. We'd been on a drive twenty-four hours earlier that was possibly the most spectacular landscape I've ever seen, we'd caught the excellent acoustic Icelanders and we'd been to the world's most northerly botanical gardens, my reservations about which were proved completely correct (snow tends to subsume most plant life), but which still could not topple our enjoyment of the wild and shimmering scenery.

Then, on our drive back, Rhys was struck down, not by an archaic Norse God, but by his glands, which grew ever more swollen and painful by the hour. By the early evening I was out watching football on my own in a bar as he tried to sleep off the sickness. Alas, it was to no avail – he lasted approximately ninety minutes in the Bastard Bar before it all became too much, and he was forced to retire, leaving me to face the highly unanticipated scenario of welcoming in the New Year on my own for the first time since 2003.

I remember that night very clearly; my ex-girlfriend and I, having been forced to spend the whole of Christmas with my family up in Manchester, decided to occupy the evening watching a Beatles tribute act in a local pub, The Waterside, an establishment that made national news just twelve months ago when it collapsed and fell into the River Irwell during the winter flooding. The tribute band in question, Just John and Paul, were sensational, to the extent that Vanessa and I were temporarily able to banish the true horror we'd experienced over the previous seven days and enjoy a pleasant evening together. When we exited the pub at eleven-thirty p.m. we were greeted by a wonderland, snow cloaking the roads, pavements and terraced Summerseat houses, and continuing to flutter lightly down as we began the walk back to my mum's house. At that point, I fell victim to a momentary lapse of reason and attempted one of the enigmatic[78] disappearing acts I've described previously, dashing off into a nearby alleyway and running as fast as I could in the vague direction of Greenmount Cricket Club.

I didn't get far.

Fate, rightly concluding that it was fundamentally wrong to be deserting Vanessa so close to midnight, took matters into its own hands and I promptly slipped on a hidden patch of ice, smacked my head on the pavement and was forced to bring in the New Year alone, lying on my back in agony in the snow.

That incident in 2003 is a memory worth clinging to as it serves to remind me of what an appalling person I had become at that point in my life, exhibiting a series of behaviours I have no wish to replicate ever again. How strange that this memory should return to me thirteen years later, standing on my own watching the Fat Rats on the eve of 2017 in a strange underground bar on the seventieth parallel north. Yet for a swift half hour, I was transported back through time and space to an earlier version of myself. When the Fat Rats finished their first set, I made for the exit, congratulating the band on their performance on the way (for I had no intention of returning), only to be confronted by a mild blizzard, just as when I had been outside The Waterside. And, just as in 2003, my instinct told me to move at pace away from humanity, to flee the town and create a moment of solitude from which to explore the passing of one year and the birth of another. So that's what I did, walking directly into the snowy wind and blundering my way past couples, families and groups of friends all making their way in the opposite direction, presumably to hit the harbour in time for the midnight fireworks display.

Within minutes I had left the town centre and was beginning my ascent up a particularly treacherous hill that, I hoped,

---

78 Not enigmatic, just irritating.

would lead me up beyond the smattering of pretty, wooden houses, almost all of which were richly illuminated by festive lights, and into a deserted woodland of furs and pines.[79] It's extremely hard to explain the compulsion governing this bizarre series of moves. At times I don't feel quite right in the head, and I rebel against myself, others or just humanity in general. This was one of those moments. Rhys's absence had thrown me into a daze and, intoxicated by my newfound victim status (as well as by alcohol), I had decided that the only decent thing to do would be to isolate myself and spend the midnight countdown cut adrift in a wintery pool of loathing and self-doubt. I was no longer the adroit explorer breaking with years of unhappy New Years' experiences by doing something unique and unparalleled within his peer group. I was now the imbecile who had managed to cut himself off from his friends and family to stand alone in the Arctic Circle, a thousand miles from anyone with whom he could claim an acquaintance.

Yet as I neared the hill's summit, I snapped out of my 2003 self and realised the unbelievable folly of my plans. I am not that person; I don't need to treat myself as an outcast. I bolted back down the hill as quickly as I could manage without slipping and breaking my neck. My first hope was to get back to the centre of the town before the midnight fireworks display, however this had to be quickly downgraded. A quick look at my phone told me I had barely moments before the countdown began. I saw another group of people in the distance who seemed to be moving towards the harbour. As I drew closer I saw a great many cars parked up by the side of the river, with passengers disembarking and heading en masse for a small pier that stretched out in the water, affording a concurrent view of the island of Tromsø, as well as the Norwegian mainland. As I neared the pier, the bang of fireworks began pulsating across the sky. Amplified by the

---

79 Had I made it any further, I'd have realised that there is no deserted woodland in this part of Tromsø. In fact, I'd have hit a sizeable housing estate.

mountains which flank this deeply peculiar part of the world, the bangs seemed to be coming from all sides and angles. Visibility was low because of the ongoing blizzard, which had stepped up a notch during my descent back down towards the centre of the city, but I managed to catch a few fireworks and, crucially, I had managed to reinstate myself within a crowd of sorts before the New Year arrived. I didn't exchange so much as a word with anyone around me, but it was infinitely preferable to being alone with my thoughts at this, the mother of all arbitrary celebratory moments.

After the fireworks died down, I chose decisive action – I would wait it out for a further hour to be with Laura, virtually if not physically, as the UK welcomed in its own 2017. Consequently, and much to my own surprise, I ventured back into the Bastard Bar, ordered a beer and stood at the bar to await the return of the Fat Rats. Funnily enough, I was now stood next to Svein, the ageing Icelandic rocker from two nights ago. I said nothing – he was with his girlfriend and I was just happy that he was there enjoying the band alongside me.

I've said precious little about the Fat Rats thus far. They must be Northern Norway's finest rockabilly band, a high-energy, highly-skilled four-piece of fifties throwbacks led by a charismatic middle-aged Norwegian with a sensational Sun Studios American accent and impeccable dance moves straight out of Back to the Future. I greatly enjoyed both of their forty-five-minute sets, from their extended version of "Folsom Prison Blues" to their rather brilliant rockabilly take on Iggy Pop's "Real Wild Child". In another dimension, they could've been the soundtrack to one of the most rip-roaring and demented New Year's Eves I've ever had; in this one, however, they were the soundtrack to my salvation.

Weeks 31–34:
The Terror

The other day I admitted to Eleri that most days I feel quite scared. Does everyone feel like this? No doubt many of my compatriots are currently fretting about the big picture – the danger potentially posed by the US President-elect, the possibility of a Brexit botch job, the fact that all the great musicians are dying. But I'm equally worried about my inability to look after myself, my tendency to run myself into the ground by doing too much or living life too large, my increasing social anxiety and sense of isolation; perhaps above all else, my inability to fully visualise what my life might hold beyond the end of this gigging expedition.

It's strange given my recent complaints of exhaustion, but I'm viewing the expedition as increasingly vital to my mental health. Music grounds and balances us. It's a means of focusing intently on something other than inner turmoil, sending us off into delicious reverie and giving our hyperactive brains a bit of much needed downtime, especially if depression is continuing to claw at us for the bulk of each week. Even at the worst of moments, when anxiety takes control, or the sadness feels overwhelming, there is peace to be found within our favourite records or when the lights go off and a band we love prepares to take the stage. There was one occasion back in 2009 when, during the build up to Oasis at Wembley,[80] someone I know well and greatly respect launched into a comprehensive critique of my personality, emphasising my proclivity towards defensiveness, forgoing

---

80 Remember the reprobate throwing cups of piss into the crowd?

responsibility and assuming victim status at the slightest sign of conflict. There were many aspects of the resultant character assassination that I didn't fully agree with, and inevitably I was more than a little upset, but it didn't change anything. Once Liam Gallagher took to the stage, my eyes lit up and I, like ninety thousand others, bellowed my heart out for two hours. The gig undid the damage of the disagreement, at least for that moment. I could cite other incidents where music has helped me out of an unhappy spot at a show, but I'm worried about sounding too much of a victim.

As silly as it may sound, one of my growing concerns is that I won't make it to the end of the expedition – that something unexpected will hit me, forcing me to bail out and abandon my plans. It's become so important that I'm struggling to countenance the idea that it could still go wrong. This is of course a preposterous over-exaggeration given that I'm not climbing Everest, trekking to Antarctica or trying to make it through a Guns 'n Roses concert without tearing off my own ears (before gifting them to my lady-friends). There's no real reason why I should approach everyday anticipating imminent crisis, nor should there be any great concern that infirmity will strike me down. But the fear is there; it creeps, and it grows, and sometimes it's hard to keep at bay.

I've written a list of twelve mini-resolutions to try and achieve over the course of 2017. I say mini, but one of them is "go to India", which arguably requires a bit more of an investment; another is "go to the dentist", which may sound simple, but after a prolonged period of orthodontic hell during my youth, followed by an absence of more than a decade without a check-up, it may require some courage and fortitude. Overall, it's a good list and should serve as a signpost and motivating force as the year progresses.

Deep down, however, the only New Year's resolution that continually veers into view is one of survival. Survive the year, whatever else happens. And if I achieve said resolution, what then? Such questions are best left untended when the immediate future is shrouded with mental hazards and uncertainties, yet they enter my head with increasing regularity all the same. Laura told me recently that the key to mindfulness is stepping back and observing your thoughts, not getting wrapped up in them; treating them as clouds to be acknowledged from a distance as they float by. Good advice, except that I'm from Manchester and have thus grown up under permanent cloud cover. Our clouds don't float by; they're forever overhead.

Haiku Salut and Trust Fund, The Lexington, London, Thursday 5th January

- **Gig #40**
- **Musical birthdays:** Sam Phillips of Sun Records (1923), Brian Warner aka Marilyn Manson (1969)
- **Musical history:** Jimi Hendrix is temporarily jailed in Stockholm after going crazy and destroying his hotel room (1968)
- **Non-musical history:** Records from the day show 95,820 licensed pubs in England (1840)[81]

I've enjoyed many flavours of insomnia throughout my life, but this week has brought a new deliciously dark variant into my sleepless world; namely, an inability to get any rest because my pitch-black room lets in too much light.

This is the after-effect of a week spent in the Arctic Circle with barely a glimpse of sunlight. My resultant restlessness meant that, after two hard days back at work, combined with the chemical jolt of recommencing my medication after my accidental week's holiday from it, I arrived at The Lexington for my first show of 2017 feeling as morose in spirit as I was bereft of energy. Our misanthropic Tromsø receptionist had informed me on departure that, back in the comparative warmth and vivacity of London in January, I would feel an unabashed sense of refreshment.

She lied.

---

81 Today there are only half that number across the whole of the UK.

Yet as I arrived at a packed venue full of music lovers merrily sticking two fingers up at Dry January, I remembered what I've said on several occasions already: the show must go on *at all costs*.

Tromsø wasn't a life-changing experience in the way that my winter excursion to Australia had been eight years earlier, but it was damn spectacular, despite Rhys's continued glandular woes, which caused me to spend much of my trip alone reading, writing and trying to avoid breaking my neck as I navigated the perpetual snow and innumerable icy perils. Arriving back to Blighty with a minor sniffle as my only notable affliction, I felt proud of the resilience my body had unexpectedly shown to the sub-zero temperatures and excessive wind chill. I already cope well in the hot sun[82] and, it appears, I cope well in the extreme cold of the anti-sun. Admittedly, I have just started noticing new pain in the small of my back, but I'm attributing this to the planes, trains and automobiles I've been forced to endure over the Christmas break.

Having never broken a bone in my body (except possibly my nose)[83] I used to feel awkward and uncomfortable when engaging with peers in conversational comparisons about agonising pain. For years I had craved some form of physical vexation that would thus allow me to better relate to my maladroit friends, with their hilarious anecdotes of walking through glass doors, falling out of treehouses or being stung to death by swarms of bees.[84] Sadly, I was to avoid physical pain until well into my twenties when, in a few short years, I cracked a rib, almost went blind in one eye, and then suffered the indignity of being stung by a wasp in my mouth after leaving a beer can unattended while erecting a tent in South Wales. And then

---

82 Unlike early 90s Genesis.

83 We will never know the truth of this incident as it occurred aged fourteen whilst blind drunk when I fell face forward off a tall patio and passed out.

84 It's possible that I may be confusing my own childhood with the plot from My Girl.

there were the successive back problems, on each occasion laying me out flat (in my flat) for five days at a time. *Doing one's back in* ranks high on my list of ultimate social humiliations (Now That's What I Call Humiliation!). The first time it happened was at work surrounded by a hundred and fifty people. The second time was on a tennis court and resulted in my being carted out of the Caledonian Road Sports Centre in a wheelchair, cursing not only the embarrassing nature of the spectacle but, more pertinently, the fact that my injury had forced me to forfeit the tennis match. Yes, I had been losing anyway, yes, I was painfully unfit at the time, but I had until that calamitous moment maintained a degree of hope. My brother is notoriously awful at converting points during pressure situations. If I'd done the Grobbelaar spaghetti legs at match point, I'm sure I could've induced a double fault. As it was, it took a year for me to regain my physical confidence and get back out onto the tennis court. When I won the long-awaited rematch by two sets to love, I celebrated by drinking several pints too many in Kennington Square and accidentally left my tennis racquet behind in a nearby boozer, The Doghouse. Not wishing to pass up the opportunity to capitalise on this return to form, I hastily ordered a new racquet the following morning, only to find that I'd neglected to order any strings for it. In the time it took me to get the racquet sent away to be strung I was forced to leave my job, my mental health fell apart and I'd replaced all sporting urges with a PlayStation 4, a bottle of whisky and a copy of FIFA 16.

Eleri, who shares my love of tennis, and potentially also my love of whisky, was late for the gig. This is nothing unusual and I have become accustomed to it over the years, however it did mean that we missed the opening song by tonight's support act Trust Fund, a peculiar mix of Weezer, Yuck and Pavement, fronted by a singer with a crazily high voice who kept moving away from the mic and rending himself inaudible. One of the things that has taken me by surprise during my gigging expedition is the consistently high standard of musicianship I've experienced.

This evening gave me comfort, demonstrating quite conclusively that some musicians are indeed still human.[85]

Trust Fund had some decent tunes but seemed intent on playing them as badly as possible. It wasn't as shambolic as Pete Doherty, and certainly couldn't be described as offensive, but the performance felt under-rehearsed as opposed to playfully ramshackle – potentially too much time spent Christmas partying and not enough time in the practice room. That said, I empathised with them. I've gone on stage feeling under-rehearsed before, and it's excruciating, particularly once the first mistake unlocks the disaster door and your enjoyment quickly seeps out of sight.

Remarkably however, they were not the most chaotic act of the evening. This honour went to Haiku Salut, purveyors of beautiful ambient instrumental pop music performed appallingly. The three-piece was led by a fresh-faced young woman who looked a bit like a pixie, flanked by two of the most nervous-looking individuals I've ever seen on stage. The accordion player appeared as though she might be about to burst into tears and the piano/trumpet/drum player gave off an aura of such profound unease and discomfort that watching her was a deeply uncomfortable experience. One shouldn't judge a book by its cover, but they played so terribly that I'm convinced that they were genuinely on the edge of a panic attack. Cues missed, songs going out of time, drum patterns messed up, at one point the pixie slipped up and accidentally switched off the band's backing track. I'm currently waiting for the iTunes Store to load so that I can investigate their album, which I'm guessing will be full of ideas, intrigue and endeavour. Live, however, Haiku Salut were atrocious, which made for a disappointingly underwhelming first show of 2017.

Looking back through my earlier expedition notes, I've decided to blame Eleri for being a bad luck charm – most of the shows we've been to together in the past six months have been substandard (though technically the fault is clearly mine). I've just

---

85 Or are they dancer?

invited her to another one on Tuesday, again at The Lexington, so if it too proves to be a dud, then I'm going to start carrying a four-leaf clover or start wearing a dream catcher around my neck.

Baywaves, The Lexington, London, Tuesday 10th January

- Gig #41
- **Musical birthdays:** Rod Stewart (1945), Donald Fagen of Steely Dan (1948), Pat Benatar (1953)
- **Musical history:** Elvis records Hearthbreak Hotel as part of his first session for RCA Records in Nashville (1956)
- **Non-musical history:** Julius Caesar starts a civil war and coins a phrase as he crosses the Rubicon (49 BC)

This was the week that Mr. Kitten managed to upset Manchester United manager Jose Mourinho. At least that's what I'm telling myself. He certainly made one hell of a racket as I escorted him back down from Manchester where he'd been spending the Christmas holidays. With Mr. Mourinho just a few rows away, I'm confident that Mr. Kitten's incessant yowling did just enough to prevent the spiky football manager from switching off and relaxing. As we approached Milton Keynes a group of United fans began haranguing him (Jose, not Mr. Kitten), taking photos, getting shirts signed and eventually, once the train came to a standstill, filming him as he exited the platform and made his way across Euston. Which was weird, frankly.

Later in the evening I watched the BBC's Bowie documentary "The Last Few Years" and my thoughts returned to Mourinho as I heard Bowie's band pontificating on his relationship with fame and the rationale behind disappearing so completely from the public eye in the final decade of his life. Bowie had been in the limelight almost his entire adult life. Just imagine if there had been smartphones in the seventies – they could've sent far more stars disappearing over the edge and into the abyss.

The documentary marked what would have been the occasion of Bowie's seventieth birthday. Three days later I was still reflecting again on his passing as I made my way back to The Lexington to observe part of their "Five Day Forecast" new music showcase. My head way up in the Blackstars, I managed to get myself lost and turned up late; remarkable given that I'd been on the same route to the same venue just five nights earlier.

The one track I'd heard from Baywaves prior to booking the tickets, was full of promise. Sadly, the performance was full of meh. A relatively pleasant sound and energetic show couldn't make up for the lack of invention in the songs, each of which meandered on aimlessly, before inexplicably speeding up or slowing down at its close. This trick was applied to every song, so that it became progressively less fun, rather like the band itself. A year ago, I was dancing in the Effra to Bowie, casting off the gloom of his death by basking in the majesty of his back catalogue. I intend to mark the second anniversary of his death by observing something more interesting than Baywaves.

Type Two Error and Alphaduka, The Old Blue Last, London, Friday 13th January

- **Gig #42**
- **Musical birthdays:** Graham McPherson aka Suggs (1961), Wayne Coyne of The Flaming Lips (1961)
- **Musical history:** Frankie Goes to Hollywood's landmark single "Relax" is banned by the BBC, a move that in no way prevents its swift rise to the UK No. 1 spot (1984)
- **Non-musical history:** Keir Hardie forms the British Independent Labour Party (1893)

There's a Weezer song on the unfortunately named Raditude album called "I Can't Stop Partying". As I walked the two miles from the Phoenix Arts Club in Central London out east to the Old Blue Last, I felt a certain resonance with the track. I had no need for another gig, but I felt incapable of passing up an opportunity once it was offered to me.

Type Two Error came to my attention via Rhys, who has merrily informed me on more than one occasion that the lead singer used to be in cult indie-dance troupe Cooper Temple Clause, whom I once had the good fortune to see at the Astoria (London, not Waldorf) with my friend Natalie. Back then, she was dating their drummer and at the end of the show, which I vaguely remember being highly enjoyable, she disappeared upstairs to secure me a pass to the aftershow party, sending me into minor delirium – my first ever aftershow! Finally, I'd be cutting it with the who's who of the UK indie scene. My moment had arrived. Fifteen minutes later she made a fleeting appearance back in the foyer to tell me she'd failed in her mission, and thus my night petered out to a disappointing conclusion, tempered only by the purchase of an over-priced hot dog in Trafalgar Square on my way home in a fruitless attempt to try and abate my disappointment.

Cooper Temple Clause were, like Three Colours Red or Throwing Muses, one of those bands that you recall being quite good but whose songs you have regrettably forgotten over the passing of time. When Type Two Error took the stage, I was struck by my inability to recognise either the singer's appearance or voice. That said, it was fifteen years ago that I last saw him, and doubtless he didn't recognise me either. He seemed rather larger in carriage than when last I'd witnessed him on stage, but this has happened to the clear majority of us. Back when I used to frequent our local pub up north for the annual Christmas get-together of *people who formerly knew one another but didn't enjoy each other's company sufficiently to stay in touch*,[86] there would always be one person who had bulked up in the twelve months since our last meeting. Similarly, there would always be one person who had aged twenty years and hence was barely recognisable. Sadly,

---

86 These days I stay in with my mother and watch Christmas TV, despite the worrying sense that I might be turning into Bridget Jones.

I can no longer make this humour observation to my peers with any credibility, having battled weight gain myself throughout the previous year, whilst having been mistaken for a forty-year-old on three occasions in the past month alone, including by my own grandmother.

Type Two Error were middling, with occasional lapses into excellence. They retained the attention of the sizeable crowd throughout, though it was unclear whether any of the people surrounding me knew the singer's history or former glories. It must be strange playing in such circumstances, having once entertained thousands of festival goers on the Other Stage at Glastonbury, appeared on Top of the Pops and toured extensively across mainland Europe. So much time has elapsed since then. Is that five minutes of fame now nothing more than a distant speck of a memory on the horizon, or can he still reach it, touch it, feel it and relive it?

It made me think back to Tebby in Nassau, the other side of the world and, in this instance, the other side of the coin. On the one hand, we have an artist dreaming of making it out of her hometown to showcase her work to a wider audience, and on the other, an artist who had the platform, the moment of opportunity and a sense that the world was his for the taking, but is now regarded by audiences as no different to a band that's newly formed.

It's encouraging to see the drive to make new music continue undiminished, although I must admit that I preferred the support act Alphaduka. For 30 short minutes they entertained me with a lovely, accomplished blend of New Order, The Stone Roses and Kent, my favourite Swedish band whom, as I mentioned some time back, split up recently after a twenty-year career. The last track off the last Kent record is called "The Last Song." I don't expect that Alphaduka will have ever heard of Kent, predominantly because outside Scandinavia, no one under the age of forty appears to have heard of them.

This is very much Alphaduka's, and indeed, the world's loss.

I wonder how many artists are out there, in Europe, South America, Africa, South Korea, possibly North Korea (though this seems less likely) that could feature prominently in the list of greatest acts that you've ever heard, if only you'd been given the opportunity to hear them in the first place.

But that was Kent – a genius group of Swedes who never managed to get the global audience they deserved. One must question the sanity of a universe in which Kent couldn't make it in the UK, despite recording two English language albums, yet Gangnam Style was a global phenomenon.

Machiine and The Eskimo Chain, The Shacklewell Arms, London, Friday 20th January

- **Gig #43**
- **Musical birthdays:** Leadbelly (1889), Paul Stanley of KISS (1952), Nicky Wire of Manic Street Preachers (1969), Gary Barlow (1971), Will Young (1979)
- **Musical history:** The infamous Ozzy Osbourne bat-eating incident occurs after an audience member throws the animal onto the stage during a show in Des Moines. Ozzy attempts to bite its head off, wrongly assuming it to be fake, and is swiftly rushed to hospital for a rabies shot (1982)
- **Non-musical history:** The first opium war between Britain and China ends with the Brits making a successful grab for Hong Kong (1841)
- **Also:** For reasons that remain unclear to me, J. Edgar Hoover hands actress Shirley Temple a tear gas fountain pen (1949)

Today was the day I bought tickets to Evanescence. How this didn't happen earlier I do not know; though it may be their first UK show in five years, my inexplicable Stockholm Syndrome-esque obsession dates to 2004 and I can think of no reasonable excuse why I neglected to attend any of their performances during the intervening thirteen years. Emma has been roped into attending the gig with me as, perhaps unsurprisingly, I don't know any other Evanescence fans.

She doesn't sound enthusiastic at this juncture, but who knows, maybe I'll be able to convert her on the day. Should I really be trying to convert her though? Should an almost thirty-four-year-old really be listening to Evanescence at all? These are questions to which I have no answers; on a logical level I know that I should not like this band. The horribly misjudged nu metal rap section on the chorus of Bring Me to Life is a case in point. I concede it is dreadful, and yet I like it all the same.

Evanescence, in the grand scheme of things, do not matter a great deal, but the sentiment I've just expressed is a little concerning given that today was also the day of president-elect Donald Trump's inauguration. There appear to be a significant number of people who clearly recognised his failings, yet still gave him their vote.

I wiled away my afternoon following the BBC's live feed as it brought me up to the minute reports into the latest protests, Trump supporters being bottled, Washington Post reporters being thrown to the ground, and other such mania. This was already a muted backdrop for my forty-third live experience of the expedition, so I opted against watching the inauguration. I sent Emma a message, asking her to update me with any pertinent details that came from President Trump's speech. She didn't respond, so when I later went home I watched a few episodes of House of Cards, which felt altogether more fitting.

I decided to walk to The Shacklewell Arms, one of several New Year's resolutions aimed at hopefully shedding a few pounds. I've augment this exercise by attempting to eat as little as possible.

I shall not be telling my doctor.

Having shaken off my presidential malaise, I approached the venue with a sense of excitement and intrigue. Machiine was a band unknown to me until a week ago, but I had an inkling that I knew one of the band members, Lois, from way, way back when. I remember when I was fourteen or fifteen, going to see local musical heroes Cola Moon in Hawkshaw, the neighbouring village to my own. Somewhat inexplicably, they were performing in a giant marquee in the playing fields next to the primary school. Like most fourteen-year-olds, my social group was essentially confined to my school friends. Lois was one of the first people I ever remember meeting from beyond this narrow field of vision. I was intrigued by her hippy clothes, all seventies browns and oranges, and by her apparent ease conversing with strangers, which made me assume that she must be older than I was. A few years later, lo and behold, she showed up in my sixth form college.

I have nothing but positive memories of Lois. I remember her being a thoroughly down to earth and decent human being and I was quietly impressed when, over a decade later, I found out that she was in a band called Pins tearing up the Manchester music scene. I saw her briefly at an art exhibition in 2013 and she was unrecognisable, transformed into indie rock goddess, bleach blonde/pink hair and shiny clothes. I thought that was fantastic.

I met up with Joe on arrival at the venue and after a brief chat, Lois spotted me and came over. She remembered who I was and seemed pleased that I'd turned up to see them, though alas, the rest of the conversation was as predictably awkward as one might expect from two people that last had a proper dialogue when Tony Blair was still in his first term in office. We watched support band The Eskimo Chain, a very promising space-rock band, and were having a remarkably enjoyable time right up until the point Machiine took the stage. I wanted to like them so much. But alas, two hopelessly inept singers who looked like they belonged in Trainspotting let the side down with their incessant wailing, shambolic stage decorum and banter and general lack of musicality. Lois and her fellow Pins colleague, the guitarist, were great. The bassist was entertaining. The third Pins member played the tambourine, averagely. I lied afterwards and told Lois I'd thoroughly enjoyed it. She informed me that Pins would be in town in April so hopefully I could make that show and see her in more conventional pastures. Still, in many sense Machiine's confused and discombobulating performance was a fitting accompaniment to inauguration day.

The Flaming Lips, Brixton Academy, London, Saturday 21ˢᵗ January

- Gig #44
- **Musical birthdays:** Placido Domingo (1941), Edwin Starr (1942), Billy Ocean (1950), Jam Master Jay of Run-DMC (1965), Robert Del Naja aka 3D from Massive Attack (1965), Emma Bunton (1976)
- **Musical history:** Mika tops the UK charts with Grace Kelly, which goes onto become one of the five biggest singles of the year (2007)[87]
- **Non-musical history:** Having been convicted for high treason, Louise XVI of France is executed in Paris (1793)

It's the dreaded month of family birthdays, falling straight after the hideously expensive Christmas period (even more hideous if you spent part of it in Norway). Wednesday was my brother, next week is my step-mum, and at one thirty p.m. today we bought my sister Sasha her first legal cocktail. She ordered a cosmopolitan, which the barmaid got horribly wrong. I'm no cocktail connoisseur, but I know that when a cosmopolitan is clear, rather than pink, and tastes of pure sugar, something has gone awry in the preparation.

Sasha's coming of age was a strange moment for us given that most people's siblings tend to be relatively close in age and are thus unable to bestow the benefits of hindsight upon one another. My advice to Lew earlier in the week was that twenty-eight is a great age, but that he'll probably start to feel quite old by the end of it. With Sasha on the other hand, I've witnessed almost

---

87 This is significant for no other reason than my longstanding, ill-suffering band Silent Alliance were originally called Mica, until the shamefully terrible pop phenomenon Mika emerged on the scene. We were forced to change our name after people started showing up at our gigs expecting to see him. All I can say is, where is he now? Mind you, where are we now? History, it seems, favours the successful.

her entire life from the vantage point of alleged adulthood. I'd like to say that I've been able to pass on great pearls of wisdom and profound life-lessons over the past few years, but the reality is that buying her a cocktail may be the most constructive input I've had in some time. Alanis Morissette once sang that, *"You live, you learn,"* but I've seldom found this to be the case and, judging from her post Jagged Little Pill musical output, neither has she.

To prove this point, I filled my ears on my journey to our cocktail rendezvous with the glorious early noughties pop tones of Michelle Branch, an artist I'm far too old to be enjoying. Emma alerted me earlier in the week to Branch's pending comeback record and the two of us have since spent several days basking in nostalgia. Emma seems to have wholly retreated into her past, at least from a musical perspective. Perhaps this is because it reminds her of a happier and less tumultuous time. If so, I'm predicting the Michelle Branch record to sell by the bucketload.

Peculiarly, the reason I know about Michelle Branch is because, as teenagers, she was Rick's internet penpal and the two of them exchanged countless messages about their singer-songwriter aspirations. Unfortunately for him, while she was laying the groundwork for domestic stardom, Rick was busy whiling away the evenings recording comedy songs with me under the name The What?, a band who never quite caught the public's imagination and who only ever performed live once, a show that will go down as one of the most contemptible drunken embarrassments ever witnessed in the Summerseat area. A few years later I was amazed to discover that my uncle Tim was also in a comedy band of similarly low acclaim called Psychopath. It's comforting to know that this level of idiocy runs far and wide in the family, yet it's distressing nevertheless that Michelle Branch rejected Rick's offer to be her backing band. How different life could have been, had we been based in a different continent and not been utterly shit.

Our day was sufficiently joyous and celebratory, and by the time Lew and I made it to Brixton to meet up with our respective other halves, the positive spirits enjoyed with Sash ensured that we arrived at The Flaming Lips show in positive spirits.

Thank goodness for The Flaming Lips.

Just twenty-four hours after some deeply unprecedented events in world history, this show was a pure joy explosion, from the pyrotechnics of the first song through to the resplendent encore of "Do You Realise?". I'm the proud owner of a drinks coaster with *"Do you realise that everyone you know someday will die?"* emblazoned upon it, a gift from Emma who spotted the artefact on a trip to Ireland a few years back and duly purchased it for me. Admittedly, it's served to alienate me in quite a few office environments, with new colleagues leaping to the unfair conclusion that I'm either morose or bereft of my senses, so it's now decorating my desk at home instead. Of course, that's not the whole of the line from the song. It distorts the overarching sentiment of the track – that of making the most of the here and now. If you read the line in isolation, it's open to misinterpretation, a bit like the opening of Sinatra's My Way. Apparently, that was President Trump's choice of track for the inaugural dance at the inaugural presidential ball.

We need The Flaming Lips in our lives because they're the antidote to The Terror; ironic, given that was the name of their last record, and it is indeed terrifying. Wayne Coyle went on a long ramble midway through the show about the significance of their inflatable rainbow and how, though it was just a big dumb rainbow, the sort you might see outside a car wash, in this context it symbolised hope within the audience, and thus the band always worried on nights when it refused to inflate properly.

Tonight, there were no inflation woes, and over the course of the ninety-minute performance we were also treated to a giant unicorn, aliens, sunshine, bags of glitter, party poppers, confetti and scores of balloons. This is my third time seeing The Flaming Lips, and my favourite to date. If my description sounds demented, that's because they are completely nuts, and so much of what they attempt live isn't tied to a single theme or concept; it's not linked to the latest record and if there is a stage designer, my guess is they're about six years old. The experience is akin to being at a child's birthday party; the band gives you license to enjoy colours and sounds and imagery in an unadulterated state. We grow up so quickly – Sasha is the living, breathing proof of that – and it's awfully easy to forget how to have fun, how to be silly and how to keep things simple and unassuming. Laura's birthday is in May, and I think I'm going to suggest hiring a giant unicorn.

The Naked and Famous, Koncerthuset Studie 2, Copenhagen, Saturday 28th January

- **Gig #45**
- **Musical birthdays:** Ronnie Scott (1927), Sarah McLachlan (1968)
- **Musical history:** Backstage in Buffalo, Tommy Lee of Motley Crue knocks a fan unconscious after the unfortunate individual breaks the news that Lee's girlfriend has posed for the current issue of Penthouse magazine without his knowledge (1984)
- **Non-musical history:** Intent on turning an innocent fishing town into an international shipping hub, Sir Stamford Raffles first lands in Singapore (1819)
- **Also:** Russian explorers Fabian Gottlieb von Bellingshausen and Mikhail Lazarev discover Antarctica, the world's most pointless continent (1820)

Travelling abroad is considerably more difficult when you have lost your voice and no one can hear a thing you say. It's also damned near impossible to maintain conversation in a noisy Copenhagen bar.

I can't remember exactly when I agreed to go to Denmark for a single night to watch a band I'd already seen before, but I remember thinking that it didn't sound like such a bad idea. At five a.m. on the morning of the show, waking up to the realisation that I couldn't speak, I began to question the logic of the decision.

Fortunately, my doubt was short-lived and I embarked on what was to become twenty-four hours of decadence and mischief in the Danish capital. My partners in crime were Rick and his friend Joe, along with Eleri and her housemate Agatha, both of whom I'd invited in secret to spring one of my famous unsolicited surprises on Rick. One day someone is going to react badly to my deviousness and I'll give up my scheming, but today was not that day.

We arranged to meet at mid-afternoon. I lured Rick to the rendezvous point with an elaborately spun story about needing to revisit a bar I'd been in three years earlier. The trap was set.

As it turns out, the bar in which we staged the surprise was deeply peculiar, the walls adorned with black and white photography of Victorian men grabbing women's buttocks and bizarre drawings of demons excreting human beings. Several beers later however, any demons had been vanquished and the merriment continued back at the hotel, with the discovery that the ladies had purchased large quantities of vodka in a bid to reduce the overall cost of the night out, a tactic that backfired spectacularly, saving us zero money further down the line but ensuring that we were already blind drunk by the time we eventually arrived at the gig.

I've briefly touched on my love affair with overseas concerts previously. The more I go to, the more enamoured I become with the experience; the chance to see new venues, observe how crowds in different cultures react and respond to performances and catch a different side of bands than what you might get at their latest return visit to London or Manchester. I've been hugely fortunate in being able to attend Red Hot Chili Peppers in Milan, Bob Dylan in San Francisco, Neil Young in New Orleans, Muse and Mew in Munich, not to mention the wonderful and strange live experiences I've enjoyed during the expedition thus far.

Even stacked up against those wonderful memories however, tonight was special. It began with a taxi ride taking us out to the middle of nowhere and dropping us off outside what looked more like a contemporary arts institute cum modern office block. Once we were in we were greeted by a small but perfectly formed wooden studio space, a small bar selling dangerously strong pale ale, and a smallish crowd of attractive Danish people.[88] We were each of us hell-bent on living it up to The Naked and Famous's electro-pop tones, having pushed our way to the front and secured a near perfect vantage point. Plenty of fine music has emerged from New Zealand, however not much of it could reasonably be described as cool. The Naked and Famous are the closest thing New Zealand has to a cool band (apart from possibly Ladyhawke, who I'm going to see in a couple of weeks), and they seem to have become five percent cooler since I last saw them in Manchester in 2014. They're also tighter and more confident and, with a solid third album behind them, they have more to work with live.

Admittedly, rather like AC/DC they only have one chord sequence, but on the plus side, it's quite a good chord sequence and besides, on a night like this it didn't matter a jot. We were dancing and singing from the get-go, though in my case no actual sound was being produced due to the illness. Like Milli Vanilli before me, I was effectively miming. Further specifics about the performance itself are beyond my reach as the vodka had truly kicked in by this stage, suffice to say, it was one of the live highlights of the expedition and I'm sure at some stage I'll look for some footage on YouTube to see if the band was any good or not.

The night then descended into chaos, our group temporarily split in two after Joe and Agatha got in a separate taxi and went to the wrong bar. A pack of cards was produced, but I was unclear on the rules, or which game we were playing. I lost heavily (or so I'm told). I also made a moron of myself by repeatedly asking Agatha the same questions, and then compounded these errors by falling off my chair and covering Eleri and myself in beer. I am not sure how much longer we stayed out, but I recall being reliant on my peers to return me to the hotel in one piece.

---

88 On both visits I've made to Denmark I have been consistently struck by the good looks of the native population. Maybe they get special cosmetic treatment from the Government in return for their high taxes.

Getting up five hours later to go and get the plane home was not an enjoyable experience and my mood quickly sank through the airplane floor. I couldn't help but dwell on my continued predilection for over-indulgence. Was it a direct consequence of the expedition, or was it more intrinsically linked to my ropey mental health? Will my health – physically and mentally – hold out until June and the conclusion of this year of live experiences? I'd told myself I'd be more sensible in 2017, but one month in, very little has changed and, deep down, I feel increasingly unhinged. It's upsetting to think that this expedition might be doing me more harm than good. But it cannot be stopped.

Weeks 35–41:
Little Fictions

There was a girl, growing up, for whom I'd walk through rain, snow, Earth, Wind and Fire. Her name was Zoe, she had a blonde bob of hair, an excitable smile and ridiculously wide, innocent blue eyes. For a brief moment in time I'd have walked to the ends of the planet to make her happy. In retrospect, it's not clear why achieving such a feat could possibly have given her cause for satisfaction, but at that juncture in my youth, such was the strength of my conviction that I would gladly have abandoned any notion of the world being round in the hope of gaining her approval. She lived several villages over from mine and, pre-London walking pace, that meant a good hour and a half on-foot between my house and hers, down the old railway lines, back out into the dubious streets of Tottington, over the hill towards Walshaw and eventually my arrival at the sanctuary of her cosy suburban estate bedroom. Not that anything untoward was going on. We were friends, that was as far as it went. One night I braved the torrential downpour and near destroyed my discman in the deluge, the water seeping into my electronics and bringing The Cure's vastly underrated 1996 gothic masterpiece Wild Mood Swings – an album that does exactly what it says on the tin – to an abrupt halt. After a few hours curled up, wrapped in a towel, passionately chattering away about the horrors of teenage life, I ventured back out into the maelstrom, ready to play the album back once more as I braced myself for the desolate midnight journey home. These were my Wild Mood Walks, an impatient and hopeless young romantic, confounded by fate (Zoe had a boy in her life, a longstanding childhood friend of mine no less) and hence I was doomed to wander the streets contemplating the bitter loneliness of teenage singledom. At the time, I remember being confronted by the worrying sense that Wild Mood Walks might become a perpetual reality. How true the sentiment ultimately proved to be, not with Zoe, who sadly disappeared from my life, as did so many near-forgotten almost-flames, but with the countless other failed romances that would follow in the future, confining me to a never-ending sequence of epic late-night wanderings.

Morrissey probably did the same thing at my age, but whereas he found fame in music and militant vegetarianism, I found only the desire to keep moving, to keep listening, to keep pontificating and to keep hoping that, if I could only continue propelling myself forward, there would be greener and more pleasurable climes beyond the horizon. This sentiment rings as true today as it did back then; times may have changed, relationships may have come and gone, teenagedom may have morphed into adulthood, premature middle-age met with a resistance by naive rebirth metamorphosed into Peter Pan stasis, but regardless of my technical age, state and make-up, I keep walking, whenever I can, a musical accompaniment my steadfast companion along the way. I long for a simpler time, though at least now I crave only the freedom of being twenty-one, rather than endlessly trying to hark back and repeat the experience. Nevertheless, I find liberation in exploring my past desires, hopes, dreams and possibilities. I feel sated by a connection to the past and to the person I once was, as I try to build and shape my future direction. Having been thrown off course by the events of recent years, what choice do I have but to try and join up the dots between the then and the now, to better understand what made me who I am and the lessons therein?

And so I return to those long-distance walking albums, from The Cure to Marilyn Manson, The Beatles to The Smiths, New Order to New Radicals (I loved New Radicals), and I listen to them now with the same eagerness and earnest desire to learn from them, to have them guide me onwards wherever I might go. "You Only Get What You Give", New Radicals' moment of true pop majesty, became a track to which amazing things would invariably happen. The song that would spring an indie club dancefloor into life, that would randomly play amidst a profound conversation about love and death, the song with which I'd share an unexpected (but not undesired) kiss with a lifelong friend, after which I'd digitally stalk said friend until any hint of potential romance would be hastily extinguished following a blaze of *"What was I thinking getting with that guy?"*

I regret the digital stalking and misjudged text messages, of which there were rather more than I'd care to remember, but the memories intertwined with New Radicals are mine for keeps.

"You've got the music in you – don't let go." Now there's an adage for any nineties-indie kid to ascribe to.

Conor Oberst, Albert Hall, Manchester, Thursday 2nd February

- **Gig #46**
- **Musical birthdays:** Graham Nash (1942), Eva Cassidy (1963), Shakira Isabel Mebarak Ripoll (1977)
- **Musical history:** Buddy Holly, Ritchie Valens and The Big Bopper appear at the Surf Ballroom in Clear Lake, Iowa, twenty-four hours before a plane crash will kill all three of them (1959)
- **Non-musical history:** Austria pioneers an invention that will sadly fail to capture the imagination of the wider world, debuting the use of a rocket to deliver mail (1931)
- **Also:** Keith Emerson damages his hands after his stunt piano explodes prematurely during a San Francisco live show (1973)

"Manchester, so much to answer for."

This was my first Manchester show of the expedition, despite it being my home city and, in my not-so-humble opinion, the home of music (at least from the 1980s onwards). I'd like to be living in Manchester right now, having spent a successful nine-month stint there in 2013/14 that I regretfully curtailed after deciding to pursue a girl across the country.[89]

My sentiments were not always thus. When I was merely a pre-teen I was mugged in the centre of Manchester by some obnoxious Kappa-clad youths who delighted in taunting me and my neon pink wallet, as they made off with the four pounds I'd painstakingly saved up to purchase a CD single and still have enough for my tram ride home. Following this criminal act, I barely set foot in the city centre for the next fifteen years. This was pre-IRA bomb of course, so the centre of Manchester was not a particularly pretty sight. Today I have overcome my traumas, restored my four pounds of savings, and consequently have no qualms whatsoever about walking through the newly remodelled Piccadilly Gardens, the location of my brush with the criminal underworld, with its quirky, randomly patterned fountains, MOR chain restaurants and an inexplicable giant wall of concrete adjoining the gardens on one side. Yes, it blocks out the view of trams, but I can't help wondering why they didn't come up with something a little more inventive – a row of trees, a mural, mosaic or miniature aquarium, for example. Perhaps they splurged the budget on the fountain and had to make some cutbacks to the original vision. At any rate, it's a minor blemish on an otherwise transformed city that boasts a fabulous range of eateries, boozeries and giggeries, all within a two-mile radius, and the majority of which I managed to make my way around during my brief stint living there.

Rick and I were lucky, residing in the geographic centre of the city about thirty seconds walk from the town hall. If you exited our building via the rear door, you would also find yourself at the entrance to my favourite pub, The Vine. Happy memories indeed, and fitting that this decaying and distinctly old-fashioned public house was to be our meeting place prior to tonight's

---

89 To clarify, this was at her invitation. No one was stalked.

show. Walking the same route across the city as in those happy, heady days afforded me another opportunity to pass the flat and reflect on what might have been had my innate and overwhelming desire for female companionship not compelled me into some rash life decisions.

It's strange to think that I only saw Rick a couple of days ago in Scandinavia. This was a rather more routine meet-up, the first Rick, Brendan and Tom outing since Liverpool at the close of last year. But although I looked forward to seeing my oldest friends, I felt apprehensive about the gig itself. I haven't listened to Conor Oberst, aka Bright Eyes, much in the past decade. My ideal time to see him would have been thirteen or fourteen years ago, but I missed the boat. In fact, I missed the opportunity to see him play across the road from my house at the The Boogaloo, as I was on a plane to New York at the time. Philip and Alex met him and asked if he wanted to come back to our place and listen to some music. I have it on good authority that he was unnerved by the exchange and hastily declined the invitation.

Sadly, no one remotely famous, within music or indeed any other profession, has ever set foot in my home. Last year I had to interview Charlotte Church for a piece of work that I was doing on the Cardiff Festival of Voice, but despite her charm and easy-going nature, I opted against abusing my position and asking her over to hear some tunes. I still have her contact details, as good a reason as any to try and cut down on my alcohol intake. I have a track record of deliberately sabotaging my sober self while drunk, taking actions that I know will haunt me from the moment I wake up the following afternoon. The embarrassment runs far too deep for me to share the worst of these incidents. Suffice it to say that I once texted a girl asking if she wanted to go on a date, and after receiving no response, texted her a further thirty-five times with the same message. I then left a forty-five-minute gap, before replying with a profuse apology and citing a recurrent technical fault with my mobile. Remarkably, the plan worked. More remarkable still, she stuck around for a drink after our cinema trip, despite my ill-informed first-date choice of post-apocalyptic miseryfest The Road. Other mis-judged first dates I've chosen include observing a Frank Sinatra impersonator/dubious bingo session in a working men's club, and watching my uncle's comedy band Psychopath, whom I've mentioned before, and who remain to this day the only band I know to have turned up and performed at a wedding reception, despite no one asking them to play.

My catch up with Brendan and Rick was lovely, aside from the latter's revelation that during my night out in Copenhagen I had fallen off my chair on multiple occasions, smashing several glasses in the process and catching the attention and mirth of every patron and member of staff in the bar. Rather like myself in Denmark, Coner Oberst was hit and miss. I find acoustic-only performances tough going, especially when the performer in question has gone through their career submerged in a cloud of Dylan-apery. Turning up armed only with acoustic guitar and harmonica did not do Oberst any favours in this regard. When he's on form, he's fabulous, and selected solo tracks, combined with a couple of surprise Bright Eyes tunes, were electrifying in this intimate environment. Oberst himself was bright, witty and compelling to watch. He looks and acts the part of louche rock icon and, when he lands upon a brilliant tune, is unequalled in what he does. Yet too much of the set felt slow, stagnant and pedestrian, bereft of the inventive band arrangements from his records, and thus it proved to be the showcase of a songwriter that occasionally strikes gold, but is equally capable of striking mediocrity. I really wanted this show to be better than it proved, but like Killing Joke back in November, such matters are beyond my control.

Big Thief, The Lexington, London, Saturday 11th February

- **Gig #47**
- **Musical birthdays:** Eugene Craddock aka Gene Vincent (1935), Sheryl Crow (1962), Brandy (1979), Kelly Rowland (1981)

- **Musical history:** The Beatles record ten new songs for their first album "Please, Please Me" in a single day (1963)
- **Non-musical history:** After twenty-seven years of imprisonment, Nelson Mandela is released from prison by the South African Government (1990)

The biggest gap in the expedition for some time proved much needed. I spent the duration flu-ridden and excessively grumblesome. I didn't want to go to any more gigs; in fact, I didn't want to do anything if it involved breaking with the solitude of my bedroom. I wanted to retreat from the world. I felt like I'd expended an entire year's worth of energy in one shot during January and was now running on fumes, wings dipping and swaying as I made my way head-on into the side of a snowy mountain. Several days earlier I had cancelled all my social plans so that I could alternate in equal measure between my desk and my bed, this gloriously mundane routine punctuated only by the occasional trip to the Tesco Metro, two minutes down the road to buy coleslaw or potato salad, or both if I was in an adventurous mood.

Big Thief, an understated guitar band that forever wobbles along the narrow fence between subtlety and mundanity, was not the shot in the arm my life needed right now. But I set off to The Lexington regardless as the snowflakes began to fall around me, temporarily transporting me back to my Tromsø travails. Of course, snow in London is pointless. We'd need a Day After Tomorrow-esque covering to provoke a sustained shift in the essential character and make-up of the city landscape. It's a shame that snow rarely sticks here, as I'm getting well and truly fed up of walking back and forth to The Lexington. I've done everything I can to try and keep my venue choices varied, but this one seems inescapable. Some people thrive upon routine and a sense of familiarity. As I've grown older I seem to have rebelled against it, taking more and more extreme measures to keep daily life from assuming basic predictability. I must be a nightmarish boyfriend. Quite apart from my inconsistent and erratic mental state, I constantly second guess my own decisions and behaviours, the upshot being that no one ever quite knows (including myself) what I'm going to do next. This week, I started replaying a computer game that I last played seventeen years ago. I don't know why. The game is good, the decision born of confusion. On the plus side, it afforded Alex and me the chance to reminisce about simpler times gaming together in our early teens and wandering around Stockport, South Manchester, trying to sell old game cartridges and discs at part exchange shops to fund the latest releases. As we got older, the gaming obsession switched to music and our outings into town began to incorporate visits to Music Zone or, if things got desperate, Woolworths. I have a bizarrely vivid memory of the day we bought Mercury Rev's "All is Dream," Bjork's "Vespertine," and, arguably the pick of the bunch, "The Facts of Life" by Black Box Recorder, a bold left field choice I'd made after hearing their single earlier in the week as I sat awaiting the chop (in the hairdressers). Those Stockport times with Alex also brought back into sharp perspective my increasingly radical fashion decisions as I experimented with eyeliner, nail polish, suits and ties and bizarre hair colourings. It was in this period that my friend Louise, a girl who I had a crush on for at least a decade, but singularly failed to induce (or even indupe) into reciprocation, snapped me for the fashion pages of a youth-centric North-West lifestyle magazine. She caught me as I was wandering around Bury on a random sunny afternoon, wearing a checked red shirt, a black blazer jacket, beige cords, oversized Vans (I have huge feet), a Rage Against the Machine beanie, turquoise nails and matching sparkly earrings. I still have the clipping, and as one might imagine, I am beyond the ridiculous. Had I been the fashion section editor, I'd have sacked Louise for incompetence.

Wandering around my home town in those unenlightened times was challenging enough, however it was nothing compared to Stockport, where entrenched conservative views about appearance and gender norms led me to receive such consistent, relentless abuse from passing pedestrians (as well as several drivers who slowed down specifically to pour scorn upon my apparel), that eventually I lost it completely and swore my head off at a young family, simply for eyeing me up in a slightly suspicious manner.

At times of lethargy, confusion, demotivation and indifference, it's comforting to be able to cling to such enduring friendships as the one I've enjoyed with Alex. Back in those gender-defying days, Alex and I were cousins first, and friends second.[90] It could have been quite easy to drift. Instead, two decades down the line and we're still going to gigs together and arguing about music.

My evening out with him did me some good, although I was left with mixed feelings about Big Thief. The beauty of gifting, being bought albums by artists that you've never heard of before, is that you can form your judgement without preconceptions. You have the music and the lyrics and the artwork and precious little else to go on, hence my earlier formed view about Big Thief, their merits, their wobbly fence etc. Within minutes of the performance it became clear that Big Thief is not so much a band, but a brilliant soloist, Adrianne Lenker, padded out by a pedestrian supporting cast. Lenker was undeniably fabulous, to the extent that her talents totally overshadowed those of her bandmates who, by comparison, appeared all but redundant – ironic indeed given my Conor Oberst experience and the desperate need for a supporting cast. Had infirmity or stage fright struck down the Big Thief players, it would have made no discernible difference to my enjoyment of Lenker's skills. I came away thinking that she would do well to sack this band and get a better one, one that's capable of taking her music to greater heights. Harsh words perhaps but, having been to more than forty gigs since last June, I have fewer qualms about holding bands to loftier and more exacting standards. Besides, if my own current musical project ever gets off the ground,[91] Big Thief are welcome to turn up and trash my performance. I don't want to tempt fate, but I'm guessing we'll need the numbers.

---

90 Ironic, given that we're second cousins.
91 Five years down the line and my new band still hasn't played a show.

Walking back from The Lexington around midnight, I put the radio on to hear a news story about Austrian police on the hunt for a Hitler lookalike, who had been spotted in the failed dictator's hometown of Braunau. Impersonating Hitler is illegal in Austria, yet somehow it doesn't surprise me that this sort of thing is happening right now. The lookalike was posing for pictures, rather than annexing neighbouring territories or persecuting Jewish people, but against this international backdrop of populist uprisings, it's still not very helpful.

Ladyhawke, KOKO, London, Wednesday 15th February

- **Gig #48**
- **Musical birthdays:** Ali Campbell of UB40 (1959), Brandon Boyd of Incubus (1976)
- **Musical history:** In a move that could arguably have worked out better for all concerned, Glen Matlock is fired by the Sex Pistols, to be replaced by Sid Vicious (1977)
- **Non-musical history:** Socrates is sentenced to death in Ancient Greece for corrupting the minds of the local youth (399 BC)

It was never cool to like Crowded House. Less so to wander into Vibes, our hometown record store, and pick out a VHS of the final Crowded House show to occupy yourself with on a lonesome Friday night. Friends' eyebrows were raised at V Festival 2001 when I insisted we break off from Atomic Kitten's inaugural festival performance, to observe the second half of Neil Finn's career-spanning main stage set. All of this took place years before Flight of the Conchords expertly poked fun at the global perception of New Zealand's cultural output. New Zealand music has sadly always been, quite simply, the least cool thing outside of the German folk scene and thus, the arrival of Ladyhawke was a blessed relief for anyone who felt that the inhabitants of middle earth had been harshly treated over the years. Here was a nerdy young woman with a Prince fixation whom it was not in the slightest bit embarrassing to admire.

Yet despite a killer first single – My Delirium – she never quite propelled herself into the mainstream for long enough to become a permanent fixture. When news of her third album Wild Things reached us midway through 2016 I, like many others, reacted by logging myself onto the mobile interweb to investigate what the hell her second album had been about, and why I'd never heard of it. As it turns out, all her albums are solid, she remains as listenable as ever, and I went into tonight's show with a sense of expectation and excitement, particularly given the New Zealand pop high experienced just weeks earlier in Copenhagen.

My night's rest had been disrupted by red wine and unsolicited Valentine's Day stress, following a blazing row with a curry house over a missing order. I realise in retrospect that I was out of line for screaming my head off at the beleaguered curry proprietor, but in my defence, a two and a half hour wait for a takeaway is unacceptable, and besides, the same thing had happened to me less than a week earlier. There is probably a lesson here about needing to do more home cooking and placing less reliance on Just Eat, an organisation with some of the worst music-related advertising in history.[92] The on-demand economy shouldn't be allowed to endure it if the key service providers are a waste of space. I've yet to have an Airbnb host reply to one of my reservation enquiries, and I am losing count of the amount of times Uber drivers have refused to take me because I've been carrying Mr. Kitten in a cat box. When messaging Just Eat to register my complaint (the phone number they provided went unanswered) I began a lengthy rant on the folly of promoting

---

92 From 'I've had the Thai of my life,' to, 'Gimme gimme gimme a naan after midnight,' Just Eat's tube advertisements are almost certainly going to provoke someone into a killing spree in the near future. It's also surprisingly hard to get a naan after midnight as a lot of their restaurants close or stop delivering. I suspect it's far easy to get a man after midnight, though I have no first-hand experience of this.

restaurants blatantly incapable of meeting basic delivery require-
ments. This went on for fifteen minutes before I realised that I
was talking to a chatbot. At which point I abandoned my rant
and ordered a replacement pizza, also from Just Eat – surely the
sign of a desperate, broken man.

Eleri, Philip and myself went into Ladyhawke with much
positivity. What we got was a rather muted audience reaction to
a strong, sometimes exceptional musical display from a woman
with absolutely no stage presence or self-confidence. Ladyhawke's
music was performed brilliantly live, admittedly propped up by a
backing track.[93] She was everything I'd hoped for as a musician,
and yet she seemed so awkward and unable to communicate effectively that it was hard to engage in the show. The gawkiness was
undeniably quirky, but it created a barrier between her and her
followers, and though "Love Song", the first track of her encore,
temporarily brought us to unity, it was the only genuine connection made in the set. We enjoyed what we saw, we just couldn't
reach out and grab it in the way that we wanted. At one point
Philip, seeming to feel this disconnection more acutely than the
rest of us, cast Eleri and I aside and made his way to the front of
the crowd like a man possessed. Philip has never adhered to our
British social conventions (he's Swedish), so I'm assuming that in
his neck of Scandinavia it is general practice to wander off unan-
nounced as and when the inkling strikes you. When we hooked
back up at the close of the show, the three troublesome amigos
decided to do what we seem to do best, retreating to my house
for hard liquor, music and unabashed decadence.

Such is the story of my unpredictable, yet completely predict-
able life right now. I spent the morning after the gig throwing
away five bin liners of my possessions, all the while wondering
whether I might in fact be on the verge of running away.

---

93 It's easy for me to spot backing tracks, having spent the past decade in a
band in which the backing track is arguably our most important member.

The Divine Comedy, London Palladium, London, Tuesday 21ˢᵗ February

- **Gig #49**
- **Musical birthdays:** Eunice Waymon aka Nina Simone (1933), David Geffen (1943), James Dean Bradfield (1969) and Charlotte Church (1986)
- **Musical history:** Elton John becomes the first Western musical star to embark on a tour of Russia, playing eight concerts across the country (1979)
- **Non-musical history:** Jeanne d'Arc is called to the stand for the first time as her heresy trial continues (1431)

"This is the point in the evening where you start wondering if you've accidentally come to the wrong show," exclaimed Neil Hannon in-between the choruses of new album Foreverland's opener Napoleon Complex. It's the worst track of the album and not the ideal song to play second in the set; however it is markedly improved if the singer is dressed in a Napoleon outfit, as was the case this evening. I suspect Laura, unfamiliar with the band's idiosyncratic irreverence, did indeed wonder if she was at the right gig. In contrast, I managed to hold on steadfastly through a threesome of underwhelming opening numbers before track four brought us the mid-nineties classic "The Frog Princess", and the floodgates opened.

I've referred on numerous occasions now to the fact that some weeks are most definitely better than others, health-wise. This was the worst week I've had since beginning my expedition. Mentally, I went wrong, for want of a better term. Ladyhawke was the start; a hot tub party on Saturday, during which I was stuttering and shaking so much I could barely communicate, was the humiliating conclusion.[94] It was impossible to remain iso-

---

94 In the context of this anecdote, the hot tub is incidental. Nevertheless, I'm not convinced Brixton backyards ought to play host to grown semi-naked men huddled uncomfortably together in what is essentially an over-sized paddling pool.

lated and continuing hiding away my troubles from the world around me.

Everyone knew something was wrong and it was time to come clean. A series of awkward one-on-ones followed, and since then, the last few days have felt like an uphill struggle back in the direction of stability. One isn't supposed to describe mental health issues using words like shame or humiliation, but when waist-deep into the malaise they tend to be the overriding feelings, and they really do limit your ability to express your troubles to the wider world. They also limit the ability to have a good old cry – after all, the only thing more humiliating than feeling ashamed of yourself, is openly crying because you feel ashamed of yourself. Unless you soil yourself at the same time, but thankfully that's not something I've had the misfortune to experience.

Going to see The Divine Comedy for the first time, a band I've always greatly admired for their ambition, if not always for their execution, I did not soil myself, but I could not hold back the tears anymore. Everything was too overwhelming, particularly as beautiful song then followed beautiful song, Hannon's voice soaring, the band tight and energetic, the sound quality in the Palladium as pristine as you'd expect from a venue more commonly associated with questionable musical variety performances. When the Divine Comedy are at their worst they tend to resemble pantomime or cod-opera, but thankfully such misguided endeavours were at a minimum in tonight's set. It was hard to stay teary for too long either, largely because Hannon was so funny. He had costume changes, the first I've seen on the expedition since Sophie Ellis Bextor. And yes, I'm aware that with each additional sentence, I make The Divine Comedy's performance sound more and more like a variety show.

There's a decent gap between now and the next gig, enough time for me to regroup and hopefully return to my senses. On the plus side, having purchased a few more sets of tickets in the past seven days, my schedule for the remaining weeks of the expedition is practically complete. All I must do is keep showing up on the night, and the rest will take care of itself. Whether I can take care of myself is, of course, another question entirely.

Elbow, Hammersmith Apollo, London, Sunday 5th March

- **Gig #50**
- **Musical birthdays:** Eddy Grant (1948), Mark E Smith (1957), Andy Gibb (1958), Craig and Charlie Reid of The Proclaimers (1962)
- **Musical history:** Iconic early 90s rap artist MC Hammer bounces back from bankruptcy by becoming a preacher at the Jubilee Christian Centre in San Jose (2000)
- **Non-musical history:** Winston Churchill delivers his famously depressing iron curtain speech in Fulton, Missouri (1946)

Back on the gigging trail but under the weather, I arrived in Hammersmith feeling quietly proud of myself for managing to avoid being sick on the tube. This has happened to me before, in the most horrendous circumstances, between Angel and Old Street during Monday morning rush hour, surrounded by commuters. To make matters worse, I vomited down the glass barrier that separates the seating and standing areas, frightening the life out of the unsuspecting passenger who sat on the other side of it. A kindly onlooker handed me a couple of baby wipes, but they proved insufficient to clean up the mess, particularly since, on arrival at Old Street, I was sick a second time. In a strange twist of fate, my partner in crime on the previous evening had been Emma, tonight's gigging buddy. That was thirteen years ago, during my second week of full-time employment. I wonder just how much growing up I've done since then. When I started work, I was on anti-depressants and busily trying to coax myself out of an existential crisis induced by guilt and self-loathing. The parallels are a little disturbing. I'm wiser now, certainly, but I don't seem to be enjoying myself any more for my wisdom. Alex will become a father in a couple of months, and part of me thinks that's the sort of thing I ought to do to invoke tangible, substantive change in my life circumstances. But it's not exactly the most reasoned argument, and besides, I gather it takes two to baby tango.

Emma was my first girlfriend, more years ago than I care to remember. Yesterday evening, I recalled to Lew the tale of how I accidentally ended up dumping her at quarter to midnight on New Year's Eve, having spent the previous three hours hiding from her at a house party to avoid doing the sorry deed. I have also broken up with her by email, by telephone and face-to-face, though alas sadly never by fax. It is a wonder she is still speaking to me. Often at times when we reminisce, it feels as if we are talking about the lives of other people rather than the lives we currently inhabit. This affords us more opportunity to laugh at our past shortcomings, from the time a police officer asked Emma if she wanted to have me arrested for harassment,[95] to the time Emma lost her rag at me for hanging up on her, despite the legitimacy of my excuse (the house I was in was on fire).

The last time that Emma and I were in Hammersmith together was to see Status Quo, which must rank as one of the most disappointing experiences of my gigging life. Had we realised in advance that the much-publicised reunion tour would involve the band only playing tracks from their first four heavily-blues influenced albums, we would have refrained from shelling out £50 each for a ticket. It was a lifelong ambition of mine to see the Quo play "Rockin' All Over the World" live. They didn't, and now Rick Parfitt is dead. When I heard of his passing, I was incandescent with rage, before hastily recognising the need to dial down my frustration and adhere to the more conventional, well-practiced emotive response of sadness and grief.

It was around the time of Status Quo that the Kate Bush tickets went on sale. I was in a meeting when the moment of truth

---

95 I maintain I was not harassing her, I was merely being overloud in a public space. It did not help my cause that, at the time of the police officer's enquiry, a friend of mine was busy repeatedly bashing his head against a nearby shop shutter.

arrived, so I arranged for two separate sets of friends to join the virtual queues and to ensure at least some form of admittance was secured. When I returned forty-five minutes later, I found a series of increasingly exasperated emails complaining of web outages and erroneous claims about ticket availability. There was also a note from Philip explaining that he'd made it through to checkout but had eventually bailed on the basis that he had felt that it was too expensive. Having dreamt about seeing Kate on stage at her piano for many years, this was an unmitigated catastrophe, and, in a fit of panic, I began traversing a multitude of first-and second-hand ticketing sites, opening up endless browser windows, clicking refresh every other second, desperately flicking over from one site to the next in the hope of uncovering a single remaining unsold ticket. Fast forward six months and Nick and I could be found nestled up against a cramped trestle table at St Paul's Church in Hammersmith as we attempted to enjoy our pre-gig hospitality dinner, which featured a small picnic hamper containing a broad selection of artisan nonsense, a half bottle of wine, and a copy of the Before the Dawn show programme. We felt distinctly out of place; shelling out £450 per ticket may have guaranteed us entry to the show, but it had inadvertently elevated us into a social stratum with which we were both unfamiliar and somewhat uncomfortable. It had also caused a row in my relationship, forced me to curtail several potential holiday plans, as well as leading to two common misconceptions amongst my peer group that either a) I was now rich or b) I had gone insane.

But here was the thing. When I was sitting at my desk undertaking my desperate ticket search, it felt inconceivable[96] that I would miss out. I literally couldn't visualise a world in which I wasn't present for the Kate Bush gig, and when it became clear to me that this was how I felt, the question simply shifted from *if* to *how*. Struck by this compulsion, I acted as impulsively as I was decisive, to the extent that when I called Nick to let him know I'd

96 "Inconceivable!"

just spent £900 and could he possibly transfer over some money, I didn't know for which of the shows I'd managed to secure us entrance. Fate was on my side for, as it transpired, I'd purchased tickets in the second row of the circle for the opening night.

It's hard to compare any one single gig with another, unless all you listen to is seventies pub punk, so I can't say for certain whether Kate Bush was the greatest performance I've ever been to, but it was the most magical experience I can remember, and the only time that I've ever felt total music-induced emptiness in the days that followed it. There is little point to this story, other than to demonstrate the importance of trusting one's instincts when these key moments materialise. Outside Nick and myself, only one other friend of mine went to the Kate Bush shows and, in yet another strange twist of fate, he offered me a ticket which I readily accepted, thus affording me a second audience with my favourite female artist.

The reason why Emma and I were at Elbow was also down to instinct. I was always indifferent to them in the 2000s, but their performance at the Olympic opening ceremony impressed me and gave me the sense that they'd probably be half-decent live. This induced me to buy the tickets, which in turn induced Emma to rediscover them, which provoked her into nudging me to explore some of their recent albums. By the time we arrived at the show we were not-quite-fans, but not-quite-indifferent either. By the time we left, we had been well and truly converted, an experience so transformative that it wouldn't have felt out of place within a religious text.[97] This was an astonishing gig from one of the most evocative bands I've ever seen. Having always considered Elbow to be understated to the point of banality, I was mesmerised both by the richness and invention of the music, as well as by the depth and incision of Guy Garvey's lyrics, each song telling its own compelling mini-narrative in poetic fashion,

---

97 Funnily enough, Elbow have a song called Jesus is a Rochdale Girl, though they didn't play it.

irrespective of his wilfully mundane introductions, which ranged from, *"This is a song about arguing,"* to, *"This is a song set on a double decker bus."* I am hopeless at flowery language and utterly incapable of accessing the sort of superlatives that might adequately describe the swelling of my heart throughout the duration of their set. It has been a rough few weeks, but for ninety minutes Elbow reminded me that music still has the power to inspire the imagination, to offer salvation and comfort, and to infuse new meaning into the most tired of lives.

So Below, The Shacklewell Arms, London, Tuesday 7th March
- **Gig #51**
- **Musical birthdays:** Townes van Zandt (1944)
- **Musical history:** The head of CBS Records, John Hammond, holds a showcase gig to celebrate signing Bruce Springsteen to his label, but the night ends on a sour note after Hammond suffers a heart attack (1973)
- **Non-musical history:** Henry VIII's divorce request is denied by the Pope, triggering the creation of a new Church and, indirectly, triggering the unhappy demise of Anne Boleyn (1530)
- **Also:** Alexander Graham Bell patents the telephone, triggering the demise of face-to-face interaction and basic human engagement and, indirectly, triggering the rise of the selfie (1876)

Digital streaming accounted for more than fifty percent of online entertainment sales in 2016, which in turn accounted for 80p in every pound spent on entertainment. Ironically, in the middle of listening to this report on a BBC news podcast, my Amazon order of Elbow CDs showed up.

Over the past few weeks I've been painstakingly turning my lossless-quality digital audio collection, which took six months to convert from CD, into my own personal cloud-based streaming library. Doubtless my internet service provider is a little miffed at the unanticipated half-terabyte of data I've uploaded since our last bill. Occasionally I ask the question, why do I still buy CDs? I don't remove them from the CD rack unless it's to lend them to someone, in which case the likelihood is I'll never see them again. It strikes me as a mild form of madness, yet week in week out I persist, the reason being that in my crazy mind the only justification for being allowed to stream is to first own. The industry representative on the radio claimed that Taylor Swift and co. were bang out of order for arguing that artists lose out on streaming. She made the audacious claim that they receive the same revenues as via ownership, but drip fed over a longer period. Presumably she is anticipating that Ms Swift will live to be two hundred years old.

I can't argue with anyone who has chosen to invest their hard-earned cash in a monthly music subscription. The services exist, they offer good value for money, and although they're poor quality formats, most people don't seem to care about sound quality anymore as they're typically listening through crap headphones on a mobile device. I can't argue with this, but I can and I will gripe at an industry that failed to adapt and is now struggling to recompense the artists that it relies on.

How much are tonight's band, So Below, earning from streaming? People in the industry talk about licensing and the enormous commercial potential they can afford artists through synergies with gaming platforms, television, digital media and the like. Well, I've never met an artist whose primary creative goal was to write the soundtrack to a home appliance advert or to see their song featured within a mobile app involving rival clans of bears and pigs battling it out for ultimate supremacy.

In other news today, a smart meter user reported that on their first day after installation that they were told by their energy supplier that they'd used forty-four thousand pounds worth of energy. I ran a campaign a few years ago, espousing the benefits of smart meters; none of my client contacts raised this as a potential possibility. Perhaps one of the unrecognised benefits of smart meter technology could be curbing the pressure on the NHS by shocking our ageing population into an early grave.

I'm dwelling upon current affairs as I have very little to say about this evening's show. The smart meter story was more interesting than So Below, my diatribe at the music industry more worthwhile than the decision to put on this gig. And let's be very clear – my diatribe at the music industry is utterly pointless.

If I were to write a stern letter to the promoters, the questionably-named Lanzarote, I would highlight the drawbacks of dragging hapless music fans all the way out to deepest, darkest Dalston for a twenty-minute performance from a substandard pop reincarnation of Evanescence.[98] I would flag the need to give audiences more bang for their buck by booking at least one support band, rather than advertising doors open at seven thirty p.m. but failing to mention that your solitary act would not be on for a further two-and-a-quarter hours. I would cite the urgent need for a So Below band makeover to resolve the visual challenge having two of the least charismatic and engaging musicians I've ever seen. I would say all of these things, but to afford further energy to this cause would only add to the pointlessness.

So Below are not an awful band, but tonight was a total waste of time.

Adia Victoria, The Lexington, London, Tuesday 14th March

- **Gig #52**
- **Musical birthdays:** Quincy Jones (1933), Jona Lewie (1947)
- **Musical history:** The Rolling Stones head for France to escape paying English taxes (1971)[99]

---

98 For clarity, see my previous positive sentiments towards Evanescence, my acknowledgement of their musical shortcomings, and my reference to Stockholm Syndrome.

99 I've never liked them.

- **Non-musical history:** Following eighty years of unbiased and impartial journalism. the doors are finally closed on Soviet newspaper Pravda (1992)
- **Also:** Daft Goth pop band Dead or Alive are ejected from TV show The Tube, after they're forced to admit that they're incapable of playing live (1985)

My holiday to Japan beckons[100] and I am all bemusement, having no idea what to expect, and having done precious little research beyond a brief flick through my ninety-five-year-old Grandma's scrapbook last weekend. Her visit was in 1985, leaving some of her tourist information leaflets slightly out of date. She was unable to give me any local live music recommendations either. Nevertheless, I am intrigued about what the next fortnight may hold, safe in the knowledge that I'm accompanying a girlfriend obsessed with the Japanese and thus firmly in charge of our itinerary. All I know is that my tattoos could be misconstrued as evidence that I'm a member of the Yakuza, while coffee is pronounced "cohee."

As I arrived back at The Lexington for my millionth rendezvous at this behemoth of an unsigned bands' North London paradise, I could've done with a cohee, having spent several hours talking shop with a former client, now friend, reminiscing over the bizarre professional world we both inhabit. I had to fake it a bit, mainly because right now I'm focusing on life's minutiae rather than my career. If I get my task list sorted and manage to do the washing up or tidy the front room, then it's a successful day's undertaking. I've considered starting to read some Thoreau, but I'm worried it might be unspeakably dull. Walden my arse, let's rock!

---

100 I know, I go away *a lot*. For all of my day-to-day battles, I know I'm still unbelievably lucky to be in a situation where I can go to these weird and wonderful places. I have no idea how I'd survive if I weren't able to travel right now.

Eleri and I had showed up to watch some gothic country music, a genre I suspected to be a music industry invention. Not only was I feeling shattered, but I'd also been battling through the evening to mask an emotional tenderness brought on by reading a forty-page account by my uncle about his late wife Judith, who died either by suicide or accidental death (the coroner recorded an open verdict) when I was two. She suffered from depressive psychosis and spent the final months of her life obsessed with the idea that she was in danger, that someone within her family and friendship group was about to commit an act of grave harm upon her. It was one of the most astonishing and profoundly moving pieces of writing I'd ever encountered, one that gave me a vivid and indelible impression of an extraordinary person I was fractionally too young to know. I'd avoided reading the account for well over a year, through fear of the psychological impact it might have on me, and for some time afterwards I was lost in contemplation over the inherent trauma that occupies our very existence.

I'm not sure I can name a single person in my life who hasn't had to endure some sort of significant trauma. Is this the norm? My family has experienced moments of incredible pain and suffering, yet how different are we from the family down the road, around the corner, in the adjacent town? What's more, our traumas and afflictions are quintessentially first-world and can't possibly be compared to those in the grip of poverty or stranded within a war zone. I wish I'd done more to engage with some of these *bigger* issues. I wish I'd done more to support mental health awareness campaigning. I wish I'd known Judith.

Was gothic country music a potential escape from these regretful musings? Eleri and I went with a collectively open mind and an appetite for discovery. We were rewarded for our efforts with a show of incredible energy and charisma from Adia Victoria, an unknown artist whose star must surely rise, based on the evidence before us. Adia rocked, straddling the worlds of lounge, sad-core[101] and latter-day Dylan-esque electric blues, to beautiful effect. It was a fitting soundtrack to a day of strange reflections and emotional fluctuations, and by the time her set concluded, any remaining dark clouds had lifted and, as is our wont, my go-to companion-in-hedonism and I were all set to live the night large once again.

---

101 Yes, this is a real genre.

Weeks 42–50:
Finelines

Kasabian frontman Tom Meighan recently claimed that of all the post-2000 rock bands, only The Libertines, Arctic Monkeys and his own outfit had survived the death of twenty-first century rock and roll.

This is depressing on so many levels. I've expressed my feelings at length towards Pete Doherty, and I had the disadvantage of watching Kasabian support Oasis on no less than three occasions (I still can't remember any of their songs). I'll cut Alex Turner some slack, as at least his band seems to have evolved and tried new things, though I can't fully claim to be a fan. But where Meighan taps into a genuine truth, as opposed to a self-serving headline-grabbing statement, is the notion that modern rock music lacks heroes. I touched on this at the start of my expedition and, almost one year later it appears that Harry Stiles and Ed Sheeran are the best that the music industry has to offer, in terms of bona fide rock personalities.

At the close of Oasis documentary "Supersonic", Noel Gallagher remarked that events like Knebworth 1996 couldn't happen today as heroes simply weren't cut from the same cloth anymore – reality TV and narrow-minded radio playlisting had seen to that. Consequently, today's genuine music heroes are all either dead, past it or ageing fast, and we have no Benjamin Button trigger to reverse their inevitable decline into irrelevance.

This may sound like a prematurely middle-aged music fan's rant, but it's borne out by the promoters. The concept of discoverability in the music industry has become a nonsense. At a recent gig, I spoke to an independent festival organiser who explained that the reason we end up with the same headliners year-in year-out is because festival bookers are struggling with the increasingly limited shelf-life of all but the most established artists. Content is consumed, digested and excreted at an alarming rate. Festival bookers these days no longer have any idea who will still be relevant between booking the artists and the actual festival rocking up. When I was a teen, the NME was still a legitimate guide to the future icons and influences I should be tracking; today it's a gossip column more interested in tracking the tweets of the acts with the biggest social media following, than trying to trend-set and define the next generation of heroes for young people encountering music for the first time. I love Liam Gallagher, but his every twitter post does not constitute meaningful news.

Where are the true musical heroes, the true spokespeople and advocates for the millennial generation? Music itself has not suffered a decline, but the industry is so fixated on the short-term now that we are not being afforded the chance to nominate our long-term stars and icons. When I listen to the Muncie Girls album, the first band of this lengthy expedition, I hear lyrics that expertly tap into social discord and discontent, that inspire positive rebellion and speak-up for the things that matter to everyday people, dare I say it, the just-about-managing caricatured by Theresa May's government. If I was seventeen, I'd have a Muncie Girls poster on my wall, but I'd probably have to rely on Moon Pig to create and deliver it.

When I was growing up we had icons aplenty; today we have a trend-based, disruption-based economy, in which any artist can fall away with the same devastating speed that they rose to prominence, their impression temporal and doomed to fade as quickly as they establish meaning for themselves. The artists plastered on my bedroom walls when I was growing up remain as relevant today as they did in the nineties because no one has been allowed to replace them. I'm sure artists like Ed Sheeran are genuinely popular with their audiences, but there's a reason why they aren't held up as leaders or gurus for the modern age, and that's because our music industry has spent too long – from

Coldplay onwards – championing artists with nothing to say. This occurrence is not confined to music alone. Is it any wonder that young people on both sides of the Atlantic have flocked to Bernie Sanders and Jeremy Corbyn? I have nothing against either individual, per se; but it's hard to ignore the fact that they're both well over sixty-five, and thus occupy the realm of McCartney, Young, Dylan, Jagger, Ferry, Tyler and suchlike. Occupying the ever-so-slightly-younger age bracket we have Noel Gallagher, PJ Harvey and Damon Albarn, all around the half century mark, as well as artists like Madonna (58), Nick Cave (59), Paul Weller (450) and Billy Bragg (BC). Good music is out there, always, but it's not enough in of itself. We need legitimate spokespeople within music, capable of standing for something more than just the sound of their latest album. With this type of influence, music becomes a force to be reckoned with; without it, music becomes a pale parody of itself, its icons left to wither away without engendering anything like the same sense of belief or bedazzlement, ideas or ability to provoke meaningful action. We need musical heroes, and we desperately need to recapture a climate that encourages music-led subversion.

Palm Springs, Grease Bar, Kyoto, Thursday 23rd March
- **Gig #53**
- **Musical birthdays:** Chaka Khan (1953), Mark McLoughlin aka Marti Pellow (1966), Damon Albarn (1968), Beverly Knight (1972)
- **Musical history:** Alan Barton of Black Lace, the band credited by Q Magazine readers for writing the worst song of all time (Agadoo), passes away (1995)
- **Non-musical history:** The first tramcars begin operating in London, designed by the suspiciously named Mr. Train of New York City (1861)

Alongside the west bank of the Kama river in the brisk March twilight, it's possible to observe several young couples sitting, side by side, gazing out upon the water. There's a distinct absence of drinks, picnic mats, stereos or other appendages. Blessed with only each other's company, the scene creates the impression of being mating season in Kyoto. The river itself is unremarkable, but the human presence brings magic and warmth and further endears me to this unassuming, unimposing and outward-looking city. At the start of my expedition I did not expect to find myself wandering back and forth over Kyoto bridges in mid-March in search of live entertainment. But now that I'm here, I wouldn't miss it for the world. Less charming than the Kyoto coupling ritual, is the white surgical mask phenomenon. A sizeable proportion of the Japanese population adorn their faces with these bizarre protective devices. I am both pro-health[102] and pro-being-health conscious, but there's something creepy about seeing so many masks around you, in city and in countryside, as you go about your everyday business. It's as though a perilous airborne contagion has swept the nation and wearing facial protection is now the only means of sustaining human existence. It also obscures so much of the face as to render its wearer practically featureless.

I am not, as anticipated, the tallest person in Japan, although I'm likely in the top five percent, and earlier today I hit my head painfully on a low wooden archway (quite literally bashing my temple on a temple). Before we left the UK, I was worried about going to a Japanese gig, afraid that I might spoil the show for everyone standing behind me. As the week ran on and it became clear that finding a show would be easier said than done, I stopped caring. Anything would do, and if a few Japanese had their vantage point spoiled because of my endeavours, this would simply have to live on my conscience.

I've made the expedition more challenging for myself, by ruling out karaoke as a live musical experience. This is because, based on the past few days, it appears that anywhere in Japan can turn into a karaoke bar at the drop of a hat. Whether

---

102 I appreciate that I do not practise what I preach.

you're in a bar, café or restaurant, all it takes is one enthusiastic patron to put in the request and from nowhere a microphone will appear, the demented Japanese TV programming will be switched over to an autocue and everyone will start applauding. The microphone will then be ceremonially passed around the venue so that everyone can have a go, irrespective of their intentions for the evening.

My original plan was to go and see obscure US artist Jerry Paper playing at an obscure eighty-year-old public baths, but seeing a Western artist felt like a bit of a cop-out and so, after much deliberation and several false starts,[103] we decided on a half cop-out; a Japanese covers band playing western oldies in a fif-ties-themed venue featuring enthusiastic young waiting staff, an all-you-can-drink menu and multiple TV screens showing the first thirty minutes of Grease on an endless loop.

I always feel guilty when audiences are sparse or indifferent; thus, I actively applaud background musicians, lounge bar pia-nists, occasionally buskers, irrespective of their ability. There is no reason whatsoever why I should feel embarrassed for a house band that plays in the same venue, hour after hour, every day of the week, and yet as Palm Springs were about to take to the stage I looked around anxiously at all of the empty tables, punctuated by the occasional group of middle-aged Japanese friends pre-occupied in conversation and sharing not one iota of pre-show excitement or anticipation. As it turned out, my worries were not merely unfounded, but were light years wide of the mark. Put plainly, when the band took to the stage these middle-aged Japanese business people went mental. Our jaws dropped as liter-ally everyone in the venue bar rose from their seats and flooded the dance floor. This was no bumbling drunken wedding recep-tion shit-shambles; the audience was as tightly choreographed

---

103 Kyoto has a labyrinthine quality that, while endlessly intriguing, makes it nigh on impossible to find many of the music venues advertised on the web, even when armed with the arch-enemy of the modern explorer, Google Maps.

as a Michael Jackson dance troupe and neatly in sync with the band's own moves. I had never seen anything like it, and Laura and I were still speechless when, after two songs, the house lights went on and the band turned in our direction and started waving to us and applauding. Our round of applause was, as far as we could tell, a tribute to the fact that we were from out of town – it seems few Londoners make it to the Grease bar, and we received the same recognition and applause in each of the band's two subsequent sets, the closest I've come to feeling like a celebrity during the expedition. After the first performance, each band member came over in turn to personally thank us for our attendance. The lead female singer posed for a picture with us and, several hours later, escorted us out of the venue and waved us off into the night – again, this is the only time in the expedition that a band has walked me out following the show. All this combined to produce the most surreal night of my minor musical journey. To use a Lynchian term, Japan is a place that's both wonderful and strange, to the extent that I haven't even mentioned what Palm Springs sounded like yet. In brief, they were slightly ridiculous, yet massively accomplished purveyors of fifties and sixties rock 'n' roll classics, taking in everything from Chuck Berry and The Beatles to The Shirelles and Elvis. Particular shout-outs go to the insanely gracious and welcoming saxophonist, an outrageously talented guitarist who repeatedly played his instrument behind his own head (a delightful trick which has sadly died out in the Western music world) and a bassist who looked about twenty years older than everyone else and seemed perpetually bored throughout. Having struggled at first to find music in Kyoto, we ended up uncovering something deliciously weird and intriguing.

T-Bird, Ivory Coast Live House, Kanazawa, Tuesday 28th March

- **Gig #54**
- **Musical birthdays:** Stefani Joanne Angelina Germanotta aka Lady Gaga (1986)
- **Musical history:** A momentous day in my personal music history, as tickets for Kate Bush's first live shows in thirty-five years are released and ticketing websites across the world immediately crash (2014)
- **Non-musical history:** One of the great museums of the world, the Louvre opens to the public, in readiness for several centuries of being largely ignored, as visitors flock to a single room for a glimpse of the popular painting of a woman with an odd expression (1794)
- **Also:** Justin Bieber courts controversy once again after his monkey is quarantined on arrival at Munich Airport (2013)

Despite being technically an adult, I still fantasise occasionally about being invited to share the stage with my musical heroes. Usually it's Oasis, possibly because they're the only *hero band* I feel I'm competent enough to join. Unfortunately, the band broke up before they had the chance to make my dream come true, and with Liam and Noel currently refusing to speak to one another, I'm not holding out much hope for a reunion.

Yet remarkably, the waking world can from time to time turn fantasy into reality. Should my perpetual musical daydreams fail to come true before I retire from the live arena, I'll always have the memory of Kanazawa to fall back on.

The most unique moment of my life so far occurred at the Ivory Coast, a bar that bears no relation to the nation, but rather, is named so that, in the Japanese alphabet, it comes up on the first page of the phone book. Kanazawa had been a bit of a come down from Kyoto. One of the greatest cities I've ever visited had to be followed by something else and, in contrast, Kanazawa felt plain and ordinary, admittedly harsh words for a place with one of the top-rated Gardens in Japan, a huge imperial castle at the centre of town and an awesome backdrop of snow-dipped mountains rarely out of your eyeline.

Then we met Ryu Komuro, guitarist in seventies Japanese soft rock band T-Bird, and occasional session musician for The Allman Brothers, The Doobie Brothers and Cher. His interest in us grew when it became known that I played the guitar. Laura and I were the only two people in the bar at that point and Ryu delighted in regaling us with anecdotes of seventies rock 'n' roll life in Tokyo, before he quit the business and moved back to Kanazawa, citing professional exhaustion. Since then he's run Ivory Coast as one of the city's few live music venues, featuring a house band comprising the entire waiting staff. Regrettably, this means that you're unable to get a drink for the duration of each set.

Their first set of the evening was intimate to say the least, just a handful of us in the venue doing our best to pump out enthusiastic applause and good vibrations at the end of every song – predominantly western seventies and eighties standards. And then, my jaw dropped for the second time in a week, bad news indeed for anyone with a history of orthodontic woes. The moment came midway through the set, when Ryu exclaimed, *"Please welcome to the stage special guest Tom from London."* This was my dream – it couldn't really be happening. And yet it was. He was gazing in my direction, beckoning me onward. I had no choice. I had to obey, and so I made my way with trepidation over to the stage and picked up a gorgeous, battered old 1969 Stratocaster (Ryu told us he bought it while hanging out with Rory Gallagher). Before I knew it, Ryu had started the intro to "Wonderful Tonight", a song I hadn't played since attempting it during a guitar lesson in 1995. Muddling my way through the first half of the track, Ryu invited me to play a solo. After muddling my way through that too, we finished the song to rapturous applause from Laura and the other random Japanese men sat at the bar. As I prepared to exit stage right and swiftly return to my red wine, we were joined by the barmaid who led us in a rendition of "Englishman in New York". Finally, my work done, the set was over, I made my way back to Laura in a bit of a daze and was offered a scotch on the house in reward for my efforts.

The night lapsed back into normality for twenty minutes but then the second set commenced, and I was plunged back into the spotlight. The crowd was bigger, Ryu was on a roll and so, apparently, was I. This was my destiny calling, and so I once again assumed my place in the band.

This time I didn't recognise the songs they were expecting me to play. Thankfully, several years of improvising at a weekly jam night at Rawtenstall's premier music venue, The Rhythm Station, has equipped me with the tools necessary to fudge my way through such situations. The whisky had taken its toll and my solos were becoming increasingly experimental, but the audience didn't seem to mind – the sheer novelty of seeing a gawkish, oversized Westerner up on stage was enough of a draw. My final appearance of the night arrived post-midnight, feeling much the worse for wear and managing to totally botch "Let It Be", throwing our lovely singer off by playing the wrong chords and reducing her to a giggling mess. Still, I felt the satisfaction of knowing I had finally achieved one of my musical dreams. It wasn't Oasis, but it was a special, special moment. I went to Japan hoping for nothing more than a bit of a break and a chance to see some temples; but this is a magical country, and it's given me two of the most joyous and memorable nights of my life.

Volomusiks, Nao Kawamura and Irene Diaz, Mameromantic, Tokyo, Friday 1st April

- **Gig #55**
- **Musical birthdays:** Rudolph Isley (1939), Jimmy Cliff (1948), Susan Boyle (1961)
- **Musical history:** After a parental dispute over misplaced business documents, Marvin Gaye intervenes and is shot dead by his father (1984)
- **Non-musical history:** Hitler is sentenced to five years' labour, following his role in the Munich

putsch, a move that backfires after he spends his time under house arrest penning a racist classic (1924)

- **Also:** A near miss, as Halley's comet comes within 0.0884 AUs of Earth (374 AD)[104]

My height makes Tokyo in the rain a deeply hazardous place to navigate. I could've lost an eye to a low flying umbrella at many a point on my five-mile walk from Ikebukero to Daikanyamacho. Eventually the rain, which had begun to fall just moments after I set off, became untenable and – fearing the onset of trench foot – I was forced to escape into a small and dimly lit German themed café. I settled into an alcove to enjoy an overpriced wheat beer, flanked on one side by several photographs of former German footballer Michael Ballack, and on the other by a series of framed advertisements for overpriced wheat beers. Unsurprisingly, I was the café's only patron, German culture once again proving its inability to adapt to lands outside das Vaterland.

Japan has been very good to me, but it's nearly time to move on and have another crack at day-to-day living. I've wandered the Tokyo streets these past forty-eight hours a little wearied from so many days' relentless tourism. Our trip had proved such a success that, by the time we arrived in this iconic city we were already sated, unable to visualise how the holiday could be made any more memorable. The German café did little to further Tokyo's cause. All I had left to be excited about was the final show of my expedition's unanticipated Japanese leg, a "Look Up Japan" showcase for women in music. Beyond this, I knew little about the event, a shortcoming of an incomprehensible Google translation. I also feared Laura might be getting as tired of Japanese gigs as I was of origami shops. Yet for all their undeniable joys, the last two shows had to all intents and purposes been novelty acts, western-themed sets performed by house bands for partially

---

104 Approximately this is half the distance between the Earth and the Sun, so "near miss" probably depends on who you're asking.

interested patrons. This show promised legitimacy – something for the bona fide young music fans in Tokyo – if we could find the damn thing. One of the prevailing memories I'll take from Japan is the immense challenge of locating the places you've researched in advance. You look up a bar that sounds promising, only to find that when you arrive at the stated location on Google maps, the venue is either a) not there or b) on the fifth floor of an unsignposted, generic apartment block. It took us twenty minutes to find Mameromantic; like something out of a Douglas Adams novel, we located it behind an unmarked door at the far end of a random second floor basement.[105]

First up was Irene Diaz, a minuscule pianist and singer from LA whose presence at the gig was a bit of a mystery. Her woozy piano was relatively enjoyable, and an inspired electric ukulele player brought some colour to the songs, all of which dealt with issues of love, relationships, break-ups, missing the one you love, struggling to be with the one you love, recognising when the person you're with might not love you back, and so on. The most appropriate term, regrettably, is "generic", hence why I was so perplexed to see her opening the show in a random venue in South West Tokyo. I will admit to a pang of jealousy, having earlier that day scoured the shelves of Tower Records in Shibuya in the hope of finding the Silent Alliance debut album, which we released in Japan in late 2008. A friend of mine was at the same store a few years back and managed to locate a single remaining copy. She didn't buy it.

The whole business of our album release was a bit of a mystery to us – an approach via the then popular social networking site Myspace back in February of 2018 led to us spending six months putting together a ten-song record in my bedroom, using shoddy recording equipment, second-hand mics, busted amplifiers and often out of tune instruments. By early 2009, we'd sold close to one thousand records in Japan, been played on Japanese radio and

---

105 All that was missing was the sign saying, "Beware of the leopard."

extended our album licensing arrangement to the Philippines, though we were never sent any sales figures, so I can't say whether we achieved the same cult status there. At the time, the big question was whether we'd be willing to come over and try and play some shows to capitalise on the interest generated by our minor Japanese indie level. Sadly, we all had full time jobs and considered it too big a risk. Looking back, I regret the decision to play it safe. Gigging in Japan would not have made the slightest bit of difference to the overall trajectory of our wonky musical career, but it would've been a fucking cool thing to do all the same. Irene Diaz wasn't as good as we were in our heyday, but she had made it one step further than anything we'd achieved. Such recollections were promptly cast aside when Nao Kawamura took to the stage. Kawamura was, for want of a better word, crazy, as well as brilliant. The music was half Stevie Wonder, half experimental jazz, with Kawamura frantically singing and occasionally wailing over the top of it. It was prodigiously well-executed – people so young shouldn't be able to play such complex music, and I was in awe. Things got better still with the final act, Volomusiks, combining the vocal gymnastics of the previous act with slightly more conventional beats and clearer pop sensibilities. A virtuoso pianist and over-enthusiastic slap-bassist played second fiddle to a charismatic singer electing to sing in Japanese, a refreshing change that befitted her band's quirky arrangements. Much though Irene Diaz had to offer us, it was amusing seeing a Californian so totally upstaged by two eccentric Japanese singers, both of whom better commanded stage and audience, offering the gravitas and unabashed confidence you'd normally expect to lie with the well-established Western artist, despite the relative ignominy of the surroundings. Watching music in Japan has been such a pleasure, not to mention a genuinely relaxing experience (at least when I've been in the audience rather than serving as an unexpected member of the band). I'd happily have gone to a show every night if I'd been allowed, and goodness knows how many great artists are out there in the pubs and bars of Japan's cultural centres, just waiting to be discovered. How sad that in the UK we tend to associate Japanese music either with J-pop or with ridiculously large drums. Sometimes our field of vision can be so narrow, affording us only a fraction of a glimpse into the totality of the musical universe.

Under the Skin, Royal Festival Hall, London, Tuesday 4th April

- **Gig #56**
- **Musical birthdays:** Muddy Waters (1913), Johnny Borrell of Razorlight (1980)
- **Musical history:** After Elvis plays at San Diego Arena, police issue a warning that if the singer ever performs in a similar manner, he'll be arrested (1956)[106]
- **Non-musical history:** Gun enthusiast Charlton Heston wins his Academy Award for Ben Hur (1960)
- **Also:** Michael and Karolina Tomaro run into trouble with the Swedish tax authorities after attempting to name their baby "Metallica" (2007)

There was no time for post-Japan blues, thanks to an impulsive decision to purchase tickets to a live orchestral accompaniment to the Jonathan Glazer film, Under the Skin. I went along to the Royal Festival Hall thinking this would be my gig for the week; I left feeling fifty shades of Natalie Imbruglia, unable to decide if such an understated musical endeavour could be legitimately included as part of the expedition. The film is so absorbing that by the second hour I'd completely forgotten about the presence of the orchestra.

In her Q&A prior to the screening, Mica Levi came across as a person utterly flabbergasted by her sudden and meteoric rise from total unknown to acclaimed composer. It must be bizarre

---

106 I'm disappointed that British police didn't issue a similar threat after Pete Doherty's December performance.

suddenly finding yourself on stage at one of London's most iconic venues, taking questions about your artistic processes and how you go about mapping complex arrangements to imagery – this was after all her very first film score. Glazer had to carry her through the ordeal, translating her garbled explanations into a clearer understanding of what she'd been attempting to achieve. Fortunately, once the film began, her music spoke for itself. This wasn't really a legitimate gig, but it was a breathtakingly beautiful spectacle all the same.

Lena Laki, The Old Queen's Head, London, Wednesday 5th April

- **Gig #57**
- **Musical birthdays:** Agnetha Faltskog of ABBA (1950), Pharrell Williams (1973)
- **Musical history:** R.E.M. play their first ever gig at St Mary's Episcopal Church in Athens, Georgia (1980)
- **Non-musical history:** Oscar Wilde, accused of homosexual practices, loses his libel case against the Marquess of Queensberry (1895)
- **Also:** Kurt Cobain kills himself; on their Monster world tour, each night R.E.M. will dedicate the song "Let Me In" to Cobain (1994)

Since his last appearance in this expedition, Rhys has been both married and mugged. The two incidents are not related. Sporting a black eye and accompanied by the most well-dressed homeless person I've ever met, a delightful gent named Lemmy, Rhys's presence was much appreciated after Eleri was struck down by a cold at the last minute. Everything about tonight was last minute in fact. I had no idea who Lena Laki was – nothing new there. But it hadn't occurred to me until I arrived at The Old Queen's Head that the last time I'd been to the venue was for the launch party for the Silent Alliance debut album. This was one of the most significant nights of my musical life, having given such an excessive amount of my time to producing the record. We'd put on an album completion party at my flat a few months earlier, but it had been poorly attended and was memorable only for me losing my voice trying to impersonate Michael Jackson. The Old Queen's Head launch party was the real deal, the week that Japanese record shops began stocking our record and the week that a box with a hundred copies of the CD showed up at our front door.

Unfortunately, we couldn't read the lengthy blurb on the back cover as it was in Japanese, so to this day we still have no idea what they said about us.

As I made my way into the venue to meet Rhys, I remembered the buzz of taking the stage that night in 2008, buoyed by the blissful notion that we were at last a bona fide band with an album, playing to a packed-out crowd of punters. Lord knows how we managed to sell out our gig, I can't recall us being popular at the time, but there we were, selling CDs, signing autographs and generally feeling as though the world was our oyster. I even managed to get a date out of it, the first time this had happened in nine years of playing live.

Tracy and I went on a series of dates over the next few months, parted, met up again, parted again, and so on and so forth. After some time without contact, and just a few days after Christmas 2010, I got a text from a mutual friend telling me that she had died. An epilepsy sufferer of the most reluctant kind (i.e. unwilling to truly accept the condition), Tracy had passed away in the middle of the night following a fit. The first person to ever make me feel like a genuine rock star was gone. We were barely together, but she made an indelible impression. Such a spirited, wry and effusive person, with a huge passion for music, I miss her, and I hope she'd be proud of me for my gig-going efforts.

Memories aside, we had a show to watch, which amounted to thirty minutes of middling minor key folk music. There was little to distinguish the music from the thousands of other folk artists currently gracing stages around the UK, save for a cellist who played beautifully but gave the impression of being imprisoned against her will. There was technically nothing wrong with Lena Laki. She was perfectly pleasant, but we found her repertoire to be a little lacking in invention and generally forgettable, a shame given my memorable associations with the venue. I came away feeling as though I'd experienced two half-gigs this week, neither of which had particularly done the trick but, when combined, kind of justified their inclusion.

My Vitriol, Scala, London, Wednesday 12th April

- **Gig #58**
- **Musical birthdays:** Herbie Hancock (1940), John Kay of Steppenwolf (1944), David Cassidy (1950), Sarah Cracknell of Saint Etienne (1967), Bryan McFadden of Westlife (1980)
- **Musical history:** Rock 'n' roll is about to be unveiled to the world for the first time as Bill Haley records "Rock Around the Clock" at Pythian Temple studios in New York City (1954)
- **Non-musical history:** Yuri Gagarin becomes the first person to orbit Earth, and will later inspire Public Service Broadcasting's second album "The Race to Space" (1961)

My Vitriol were first brought to my attention on the back seat of the 477 bus from Bury to Summerseat, courtesy of my friend Luke and his Discman. Back in 2001 Luke and I used to routinely skip our heavily Catholic sixth form college assembly on Friday mornings to head into town and spend what remained of our lunch money on (mainly Prince) CDs. That week, Luke decided to branch out and, on playing me the first couple of tracks from My Vitriol's debut album Finelines, I was filled with acute jealousy at having been beaten to their discovery. Within ten days I'd bought the album for myself and introduced them to a further four people, claiming the act as my own. Alex made it out to see them that summer in Manchester. He bought a hoodie – that was what you did back then.

My Vitriol's plight gives a whole new meaning to the phrase "difficult second album". After eighteen months on the touring circuit, promoting their singles on the usual TV slots and hastily compiling a B-sides collection, the band disappeared. Since then, other than a brief reappearance later in the decade to promote an EP that I've never heard, they were decreed missing, presumed dead. An article published last year documented what went wrong, namely that the band had made it big before the line-up was complete, forcing them to hastily recruit additional musicians to capitalise on their demand. However, when they came to record their second album, things didn't go according to plan, and it became obvious that the band lacked the rapport to carry on together. Henceforth, line-up changes occurred, sessions were abandoned or scrapped, gigs were cancelled, the band were dropped by their label (understandable given these circumstances) and My Vitriol faded into oblivion. Repeated attempts by singer Som Wardner to revive the band fell by the wayside, and it's fair to say that the fan base was as surprised as anyone when in 2014 a campaign was initiated to raise the funds for the recording of a new album. This information passed me by at the time because, in classic My Vitriol style, the band failed to deliver the album. It took a further two years and much outcry from the fundraisers before the material finally surfaced, in the form of "The Secret Sessions." To make it clear, that's a fifteen-year gap between debut release and sophomore effort.

I can empathise with difficult second album syndrome. Silent Alliance had one member quit the band and another permanently leave the country as we tried to get ours recorded. It ended up taking five years, by which time the genre and sound we were aiming at had long since ceased to be cool. However, I can take some small comfort from the fact that we still finished the record in less than half the time it took My Vitriol to finish theirs.[107]

---

107 Remarkably, My Vitriol managed to take even longer between albums than both Stereo MCs and Guns 'n Roses, neither of whom should have bothered with their more recent efforts (nor indeed their earlier work).

The day of this most unlikely of gigs, my computer died, leaving me unable to work, in a miserable mood and struggling to reclaim the excitement I'd felt on booking the tickets a few months earlier. Fortunately, I had Emma for company, bolstering my spirits with her fond recollections of gigs we'd been to see at the Scala some eleven years earlier. By the time My Vitriol took to the stage, I was back in the zone, although of course I had no idea what to expect from such an enigmatic and puzzling group of musicians.

What we got was an occasionally sparkling performance that also served to reemphasise the huge sense of missed potential and opportunity surrounding the band. The struggle to keep the band alive is ongoing – they presented themselves as a three-piece, bereft of a bassist (a shame, as I'd heard that Ringo's granddaughter had been playing with them, which might have been interesting) and reliant on a backing track to fill in the missing instruments. Wardner was full of energy, overly-enthusiastic, and at times slightly insane – most notably a crazed and largely incomprehensible rant about Syria. It was clear that he was basking in his return to the live arena. Yet one couldn't help but sense the tremendous difficulty the band had faced in making it back as far as the Scala, hardly the loftiest of auditoriums for a band once heralded as the new Foo Fighters.

And then, after Emma and I had retreated to one of the balconies for a change of vantage point, we saw below us a small but uniquely demented group of diehard fans, bouncing away as they attempted to release fifteen years of pent up energy and longing. I love My Vitriol, but that was the moment I realised the show was put on for the pogoing loonies, not for me.

Chelsea Wolfe, Heaven, London, Tuesday 18th April

- **Gig #59**
- **Musical birthdays:** Mark "Bez" Berry of Happy Mondays (1964)
- **Musical history:** An LA hospital plays host to Michael Jackson as he undergoes surgery after his

hair catches on fire during a Pepsi commercial shoot (1984)

- **Non-musical history:** Colonial hero, explorer and anti-slavery campaigner David Livingstone's journey finally comes to an end as he is buried in Westminster Abbey (1874)[108]
- **Also:** The Natural History Museum opens for the first time in South Kensington; a young David Attenborough is at the front of the opening day queue (1881)[109]

Did Chelsea Wolfe save my life? Probably not, although she did more for my cause than any DJ ever has. At the close of 2015, her bleaker-than-bleak industrial-gothic record Abyss felt like the musical realisation of the cliff edge over which my life had descended. The track "After the Fall" became my signature song.

Wolfe was one of the first steps on my path back into music, though she provoked a mixed reaction when I attempted to share her with family and friends. Alex was nonplussed. Joe said Abyss was too dark even for him (and he'd introduced me to her in the first place). Lew said hearing the album made him feel like he was dying. I didn't bother playing it to my dad, for fear of sending him to an early grave.

And so, Chelsea Wolfe became my personal, private, undisputed Queen of Goth. Not that I ever expected to see her in the flesh; most of the US bands Joe introduces me to have precious few fans to speak of, and thus find it difficult to accommodate transatlantic touring plans. Far less expected was the notion that she'd feature within the expedition itself – some things are just too unlikely to wish for. But this expedition has taken on a life of its own, and with that comes inherent unpredictability. Hence, around the turn of the year Chelsea Wolfe

---

108 To clarify, he was dead..
109 Probably.

announced a single, seemingly random London date, and I knew that I had to be there.

My time back in the UK these past few weeks has been dispiriting, a combination of the inevitable back-to-work comedown and a general lack of direction. How can you find the motivation to proceed forwards when you don't know which way forwards is? I needed a lift. Granted, most people don't turn to Goth sounds to give them such a lift, but then most people are not me. The morning of the gig saw the announcement of the UK's latest General Election, news that was never going to get me on my feet, skipping, jumping or singing "Songs from the South". I found it hard to concentrate once news of Theresa May's unanticipated U-turn broke. It became a matter of counting down the hours until show time and a chance to distract myself from the political apprehension subsuming me.

Joe had been kind enough to accompany me, despite his reservations about Abyss. I was grateful for the company. When I left my job and my foundations felt the shakiest they'd ever been, he was pretty much the first person I told. Sometimes it's comforting to be around people who *know*, who understand, accept and don't feel the need to dive into your psyche and poke around for answers and clarity you don't necessarily have.

Heaven has not shaken off the smell of vomit in the many moons that have passed since I showed up for The Japanese House. It remains regrettably dingy. It's also unbelievably difficult to access the main auditorium if – God forbid – the artist you're seeing commands any sort of a fan base. Which, astonishingly, Wolfe did.

As with The Japanese House before her, Heaven was heaving, and for the first half of the set we had to settle for a troublesome, distant vantage point. Ultimately though, I cared little – the sound, the aura, the experience was what I had come for. Looking like Irma Vep meets the Corpse Bride, Wolfe glid across the stage, commanding a haunting presence that was only broken when she spoke, revealing a US teen rom-com accent totally at odds with the proceedings. This mattered not; in every other respect she was the perfect live representation of her music. It was dark, brooding, distorted, menacing and unbelievably loud. It's possible that this combination unsettled Joe, but I was too wrapped in my own eerie bliss to pay any attention. He emerged unscathed, I know that much, and seemed happy that I'd enjoyed myself. This wasn't the best show I've been to on my expedition – I still think Wolfe needs one more quality record[110] to add to her catalogue before she has the complete live set – but it felt like one of the most important, a show that connected the dots between the fall, the aftermath and my ongoing attempt at a recovery.

Pins, Moth Club, London, Wednesday 19th April
- **Gig #60**
- **Musical birthdays:** Marion Hugh "Suge" Knight Jr (1966)
- **Musical history:** Delightful Geordie Brian Johnson joins AC/DC, after the death of Bon Scott, as the band prepare to go stratospheric with Back in Black (1980)
- **Non-musical history:** The American revolution gets underway at Lexington Common (1775)
- **Also:** After forty-five years in power, Castro resigns from the Communist Party of Cuba's central committee (2011)

It's been a busy week, with barely a chance to draw gothic breath between Chelsea Wolfe and Pins, the day-job of my long-time acquaintance Lois, whom last I encountered at The Shacklewell Arms post Machiine gig.

Once again, I didn't tell Lois I was coming.

Given that Pins featured on BBC 6 Music earlier in the week and were playing sold-out shows up and down the UK, I figured she wouldn't especially care. One person I did tell was my friend Rebecca. Unfortunately, I gave her the wrong date and so she was

---

110 She has since released one further quality record, 2017's Hiss Spun.

unable to attend. Fortunately, another friend Yulia could deputise, despite having hopped straight off an early morning flight from Moscow into a busy day of soliciting (she is a solicitor).

Is "binary music" a legitimate musical term, or have I finally coined my own phrase? Either way, this is what Pins sound like. Choppy, repetitive, full of octaves, the more I try and describe it, the less it bears any relation to the aforementioned terminology. Pins were a one-trick pony, but it was a highly enjoyable trick. At the end of the show I parted company with Yulia, who was on the verge of collapse after a long weekend of excessive travelling, and I decided to stick around to congratulate Lois on a remarkably intense, animated and brilliantly received performance. As before, she seemed pleased to see me and suggested that I join the band for a drink. Flattered, I accepted her invitation and returned to the bar, only to discover that what the offer translated into was a thirty-second exchange of pleasantries before I was passed onto Pins' promoter, who seemed as unhappy about the introduction as I was and spent ten minutes informing me that my musical expedition meant precious little to anyone who worked in music for a living.

I stood at the bar for a few more minutes after his hasty exit before being ushered towards the door. It transpired that the club was closing, save for the Pins aftershow. Already feeling slightly embarrassed, I then subjected myself to the ultimate humiliation, wandering up the stairs to the private room where the party was being staged and nervously creeping inside. What did I expect? I was spotted but not approached by Lois, I stood on my own for ninety seconds or so, and then I made my retreat. I felt like a moron, although I suspect nobody else noticed either my arrival nor my exit, so incidental and inconsequential was I to the proceedings. I bear Lois no ill will. Years of being in less popular bands have taught me that post-gig meet and greets are endlessly distracting, frustrating and ultimately unsatisfactory for all parties involved. One can only imagine what it must be like being in a popular band and having to deal with hangers-on like me.

Jaws, Scala, London, Wednesday 26ᵗʰ April
- **Gig #61**
- **Musical birthdays:** Niomi McLean Daley aka Ms Dynamite (1981)
- **Musical history:** UK comedian Bernie Clifton is left fuming after a printing error sees the tracklisting for his new CD replaced with a list of tracks by death metal band Abhorrent Decimation (2016)
- **Non-musical history:** Brazil expels its Jewish population (1654)[111]
- **Also:** A gunman makes off with a $50,000 Porsche after mugging Rod Stewart (1982)

My love affair with Hannah began this evening.

Not an actual love affair. It's advisable not to write that sort of thing down in case it is later used as evidence against you in a court of law.

No, I speak purely of my platonic adoration of this new compadre. Since first meeting one another at the hideous Pete Doherty show, our friendship has blossomed and, if my year-long expedition achieves nothing else, I can take from it the satisfaction of forming a delightful new acquaintance along the way.

Hannah left home at age fourteen, an event I can barely comprehend, let alone contemplate.[112] It is a minor miracle, and a huge credit to her that she has made it this far with faculties, intellect and a sense of humour still intact. She also looks a bit like Kate Bush, though she claims she doesn't.

We began our evening talking about our respective recent encounters with the homeless (last week I gave a homeless person a fiver; they asked for more). We ended the evening sharing our life stories while being thrown out of The Fellow for grossly outstaying our welcome. This was the night I needed (how

---

111 The rotten ride for the Jews just keeps on going.
112 Retrospectively – I am not fourteen.

often have I said that of late?) following four days of trauma and emotional discontent – from Saturday morning's inexplicable, unprovoked, teary, blubbering mess through to Tuesday's lacklustre and frustrated band practice. These downward spirals have been happening once a month for well over a year and it's a pain in the arse, but sometimes life is an endurance test and my unpredictable, impulsive and often overly indulgent lifestyle doesn't exactly do me any favours. It was a rough start to the week, but I'm still here, alive and kicking.

After a few pints in the Lucas Arms spent chatting to a gentleman who was lucky enough to have been present at Oasis, Maine Road '96, sat in an executive box where KD Lang and Heather Small from M-People sang karaoke into the small hours of the morning, we ventured down the road to the Scala equipped with what Hannah described as a "road beer". This is not a good idea and I would not recommend it if, like me, you're trying to watch your alcohol intake and you know you have four hours of back-to-back meetings the following morning. We were also in a rush to catch support act Kagoul, an enjoyable mix of pleasant indie meets angular alt-prog guitar stylings. I have literally no idea what I mean by that, though it's not the first time that I've used the word angular and doubtless it will not be the last. It's a useful, faintly nonsensical descriptor.

As with every trip I've made to the Scala over the past year, the venue was bursting at the seams, though this time predominantly populated by a younger demographic with an apparent selfie fixation. I don't feel like mincing my words right now, so fuck the selfie, fuck the selfie stick, and fuck the state of pathetic narcissism it has induced upon the world.

Unfortunately, I didn't take any kindlier to headline act Jaws, a meandering guitar band incapable of writing a chorus, fronted by a guy wearing what can only be described as chef's trousers and flanked by two individuals who looked more like they belonged in Rage Against the Machine than a lacklustre indie combo. Sadly, this show was not raging against anything (not even the selfie stick), yet the level of crowd enthusiasm was dialled up to eleven from the moment they took to the stage. Crowd surfing, moshing, circles of death – never have these live phenomena seemed so out of place. Before the end of the set, Hannah and I had abandoned our vantage point and gone for a chat at the bar. My assessment: dull, *must try harder.* I'd love to pass this report card onto Jaws but it's not worth it. Maybe I'm just out of touch, a fading dinosaur incapable of understanding what's getting the millennial up and out to gigs. Whatever the case, I'd take Oasis at Maine Road any day of the week.

Honey Lung, Camden Assembly, London, Tuesday 2nd May
- **Gig #62**
- **Musical birthdays:** Engelbert Humperdinck (1936), David McAlmont (1967), Lily Allen (1985), Justin Hayward-Young of The Vaccines (1987)
- **Musical history:** Joy Division appears live for the final time at Birmingham University, just two weeks before Ian Curtis commits suicide (1980)
- **Non-musical history:** Anne Boleyn is imprisoned in the Tower of London; things don't get much better for her thereafter (1536)
- **Also:** Japanese rock star Hideto Matsumoto hangs himself in his Tokyo apartment, aged just thirty-three (1998)[113]

There are many important lessons that present themselves when walking excessive distances. My main learning from the past weekend is that the rough and ready northern town of Halifax is not, contrary to the views of Vice Magazine, one of the worst

---

113 I must confess I've never heard of him, but apparently his funeral was attended by more than seventy thousand people and required one hundred police officers, one hundred and seventy security guards, police boats and helicopters.

places to live in the UK. At least, it did not give the appearance of being, for want of a better word, a shithole. Indeed, for any fans of international boxing, Halifax on Saturday night was the place to be – the whole town was out in force to watch the shining light of British boxing, Anthony Joshua, knock down the mighty Wladimir Klitschko. Unfortunately, I am no fan of international boxing, but it would be unfair to level this complaint at the townsfolk of Halifax.

We were staying in Halifax in a desperate bid for overnight recuperation following a day's trekking over the Pennines and in advance of another lengthy sojourn required to complete our mission from Bury to Leeds. I love long-distance walking and, before I die, my aim is to have walked the entire length of England. I've already covered the glamorous stretch from Croydon to Coventry, and though I appreciate that this latest excursion is not necessarily the right direction, it does at least set me up for a pleasant hike through North Yorkshire in years to come, where I anticipate it being excessively windy.

The downside of long-distance walking is that it tends to render one unable to walk, hence making gig-going a troublesome and energy-sapping exercise. Once again, I had heard of neither band nor venue, but I was encouraged by Eleri to get over my physical ailments and buck up my ideas. Eleri, it seemed, was buoyed by the recent revelation that she is second only to Rhys in gigging expedition appearances. That did not, however, stop her from being late, and left me contemplating my exhaustion alone in The Enterprise, a nearby pub where I once had the good fortune to enjoy that rarest of moments – playing a genuinely well-received show.

The gig in question stood out not so much for our performance but for the fact that every band member spent the evening trying unsuccessfully to flirt with headline artist Rose Elinor Dougall, formerly of The Pipettes fame. I made it further than some – I was at least identified by her as being a member of the band. But her star well and truly eclipsed our space debris; I was unable to resist the urge to fall into fandom and, as is inevitably the case with such imbalanced interactions, within minutes a devastating silence had ensued. I know not what has become of Rose; like The Pipettes, she appears to have disappeared into obscurity. Gwenno, the lead creative force of the band, last surfaced a couple of years ago with a Welsh-language album that pertained to many of the most pressing and resonant contemporary socio-political themes. Unfortunately, knowing no Welsh whatsoever, I didn't connect with her message, and thus the poignancy of her musical statement was largely wasted upon me.

When Eleri eventually showed up, we made our way at leisure to Camden Assembly, an excellent little venue held back by a suspiciously sticky floor. As for Honey Lung, they were unexpectedly fantastic – so young I could have fathered them, had I been more popular in my teenage years, but so talented. Sounding like early Smashing Pumpkins crossed with Weezer and a bit of screamy grunge thrown in for good measure, their set oozed potential and encouragingly, their new songs were the best tracks on show. If music tastes don't deviate too much in the next twelve months, I expect to see them ascend from height to height; by the end, we were true fans, bopping away as those in front of us displayed all the quintessential headbanging one tends to associate with positive youthful zeal. We were the oldest members of the audience, save for the band's parents, but this music combined past and future, blissfully overlooking the present, for of course, so much of the present is a shambles.

Bob Dylan, Wembley Arena, London, Tuesday 9th May

- **Gig #63**
- **Musical birthdays:** Billy Joel (1949), Dave Gahan (1962), Paul Heaton (1962)
- **Musical history:** The Beatles sign their first contract with EMI Parlophone (1962)
- **Non-musical history:** Barack Obama pledges his support for same-sex marriage (2012)
- **Also:** A sad day in musical history as Jimmy Page appears on US TV's "Saturday Night Live" with

rapper Sean "Puffy" Combs, performing "Come with Me" from the "Godzilla" movie soundtrack (1998)

"You know something's happening, but you don't know what it is."

I've always been able to empathise with Mr. Jones in this regard.

Wembley Arena hasn't typically been a happy hunting ground for me. An Oasis gig punctuated by deeply unnecessary fan violence, a completely underwhelming Deftones show in which they played approximately none of the songs I liked, a Smashing Pumpkins farewell tour show in 2000 that was cut short after they came on late and overran the curfew. And then of course there was The Cure. Such anticipation and excitement, such an incredible start, such mid-set fervour as hit after hit was rolled out. And then such creakiness, disintegrating into outright exhaustion, as the band continued to play and play and play (and play and play). I am a huge fan of The Cure, but three and a half hours is just too much misery. Half of the audience were gone by the end, we missed the last tube and we ended up getting home in the early hours of the morning, utterly depressed and running short on sleeping time.

This is no exaggeration.

The Cure played more than fifty songs, despite Robert Smith looking like he'd spent the past twenty-four hours in an induced coma and wearing what looked suspiciously like pyjamas. The sound engineer, clearly flagging by the third hour, decided to exit the building during the second of three encores, leaving renditions of "Why Can't I Be You?" and The Lovecats all but unrecognisable. And there were still several songs to go.

On the plus side, delving back several years further into my Wembley Arena gig archive, we also saw Avril Lavigne twice on successive nights, genuinely life-changing experiences for Philip and me, and ones for which we've been roundly ridiculed ever since. The first Avril gig was a drunken eBay decision, back in the days when you could use a secondary ticketing website without being rinsed for everything you own. The second gig was a last-minute compensation plan enacted after Philip, over-enthused by the quality of both music and lager, tumbled down a flight of stairs, splitting his head open and forcing him to spend the final thirty minutes in the medical area before hastily departing to hospital to have his wound glued up. Our otherwise perfect evening had been ruined; our only option was to do a Gatsby and repeat the past the following night thanks to a further eBay purchase. It's reasonable to claim that we fared rather better than Gatsby, enjoying the same evening as twenty-four hours previously, but avoiding any further trippery or bleedage.

More remarkable still, from that moment, our recently formed musical project had a clear objective: to become famous and meet Avril. This motivation would spur us on for at least the first five years of Silent Alliance, arguably up until the point Avril met Chad Kroeger and we seriously began to question her credibility as an artist.

People may mock Avril for her perceived lack of authenticity and tendency to team up (and on occasion marry) awful musical collaborators, but what we witnessed during those two performances was an artist who could sing, play and effortlessly captivate a crowd for ninety minutes, not to mention exiting on a high, leaving said crowd wanting more, rather than The Cure's controversial approach of leaving them wanting less.

One week after witnessing the honeyed lungs of Honey Lung, Eleri was upbeat about the prospect of her inaugural Dylan concert. She was also curious about meeting my dad, our resident Dylanologist, and an individual I described to her as "extremely daft". In contrast, this was my ninth Dylan show, a run that started with arguably the most memorable concert back in 2003 at Brixton Academy, when my dad got stuck in traffic, leaving me hanging around in a pub for two hours, where I was accosted and later threatened by an irate drug dealer. Fast forward a few years and I saw Dylan in San Francisco on my lonesome, just hours after landing, suffering extreme jet lag to the point that I momentarily drifted off and fell over in the middle of the crowd. I had to spend the final five songs pacing frantically around the back of the venue trying to stave off this unwanted slumber.

In many ways, it seems my relationship with Dylan is as unpredictable as his live shows, which have ranged from the resplendent (Albert Hall, 2013) to the diabolical (Finsbury Park, 2011). Though his set list barely changes these days, you never quite know what to expect from the great man.

Despite our rather distant vantage point, this Wembley Arena show was one of the gems of the expedition. Dylan has in the past two years achieved the remarkable and unexpected feat of relearning how to sing, and it's hard to look back at his lengthy growling period without a sense of regret about the glory and majesty we might have witnessed, had his shows been interlaced at any stage with a discernible hint of melody. Having recently surprised the world by releasing three separate cover albums celebrating the great American songbook, one of which ranks as the most uninspiringly-titled triple album in history,[114] Dylan's set veered randomly from crooner to folk classic to twelve bar blues to legendary rock song. It's very hard to describe my emotions watching him play, because it no longer really matters whether he's playing well – I am forever overcome by my sense of delight about the very fact that he's still with us. When I first saw Bob, I did so at great cost (for an undergraduate student at any rate) because I was worried that he might die at some point soon. The same insecurity governed us through shows two, three, four and five. By show six, I began to wonder if he was in better health than I'd given him credit for. That was five years ago, and I look forward to him confounding, befuddling and bemusing me for many more years to come.

---

114 Triplicate.

The Japanese House, KOKO, London, Wednesday 17th May

- **Gig #64**
- **Musical birthdays:** Taj Mahal (1942), Enya Ni Bhraonain (1961), Trent Reznor (1965), Josh Homme (1973), Andrea Corr (1974)
- **Musical history:** The legendary "Judas" audience heckle to Bob Dylan occurs at Manchester's Free Trade Hall (1966)
- **Non-musical history:** Herbert Asquith's Government falls, the last time that the UK has had a Liberal Prime Minister (1915)
- **Also:** Life becomes infinitely more complex as British Summer Time is introduced (1916)

There is just something about this girl. Something that lingers in the mind long after she's left the stage. It's hard to put my finger on, other than to reiterate once again the strong sense that Amber Bain aka The Japanese House is destined for greatness. Why else would I have chosen to go see her for a second time in six months, barely hours after landing back in the UK, following a ridiculously intense four-day work trip to Delhi?

How I wish I'd been able to round off my gigging expedition with a concert in India. Alas, time did not permit it, and none of the people I spoke to (predominantly taxi drivers) had much advice on where one might be able to come across live musical entertainment. One of them claimed that Delhi is not much of a music town, although with eighteen million citizens I found this information rather suspect. That said, it mattered little. I'd unexpectedly been able to meet one of my New Year's resolutions after all (though I still haven't been to the dentists). Having braved the forty-three degree heat to see as many of the sights as I could – from Humayun's Tomb to the small group of monkeys that have commandeered their own street around the corner from the Prime Minister's residence – I also managed to avoid an upset stomach and achieved a commendable two hours' sleep on the plane home (commendable given the screaming child and bear-sized gentleman who flanked me on either side).

I spent my day trying not to pass out, all the while contemplating whether I should buy a ticket to Amber Bain's biggest show to date. I'd given my tickets away to Eleri and her sister, but just an hour before the starting time, I decided that I could not not be there. This emotion has always proved influential – it's led me to Kate Bush hospitality tickets, to Steely Dan in New York, to Neil Young in New Orleans, to being soaked in urine watching Oasis at Wembley Stadium, even to frankly absurd shows like Britney on the "Oops! I Did It Again" tour, Sophie Ellis Bextor at Nottingham Theatre Royal and Avril Lavigne on five separate occasions. This list could go on for some time; as soon as I mentally visualise myself at the show, the decision is made, and I am there.

Once again, The Japanese House did not disappoint, sparing my blushes after both Eleri and Catrin had expressed pre-gig confusion at my Amber-obsessed ravings and adulation. On record the songs are enjoyable; live they are transformed. Both of my esteemed Welsh friends left the venue full-blown Bain converts, singing focus track "Face Like Thunder" to themselves in reverie as they wandered over to Mornington Crescent, leaving me to dash hurriedly in the direction of my bed for fear that a crash might be imminent. If only I could make all my choices the way I approach these shows – I'd surely be the most interesting man in my life. There's also a decent chance that I'd be either broke or dead. Still, just for tonight, it was totally the right call. You see, there's just something about this girl.

Red Sun Revival, Islington Academy, London, Saturday 20th May
- **Gig #65**
- **Musical birthdays:** Joe Cocker (1944), Cherilyn Sarkasian aka Cher (1946), Busta Rhymes (1972)
- **Musical history:** Pete Townshend and Roger Daltrey take to a Windsor stage with members of

their opening act after John Entwistle and Keith Moon fail to show up in time. When the two of them arrive, a huge fight breaks out on stage, which concludes with Townshend hitting Moon on the head with his guitar (1966)

- **Non-musical history:** Portuguese explorer Vasco de Gama completes his mission to become the first European to reach India by sea (1498)
- **Also:** Heavy metal lunatics Lordi win the Eurovision Song Contest for Finland while dressed in horror costumes (2006)

Except for the Steely Dan gigs, both of which fell within days of one another, I've managed to go almost the entire year seeing a different band each week. Four days ago, I risked breaking this amazing run by returning to The Japanese House. I still had time to recover, yet all I ended up managing to do was check out another band I'd already seen once during my expedition.

It wasn't supposed to turn out like this.

I was supposed to be seeing Chameleons Vox, the continuation of cult 80s Manchester band The Chameleons, who were being supported by Red Sun Revival, our former babysitter's Goth band. Unfortunately, I misjudged the timing of the show; at the same time my proposed show accomplice for the evening, Hannah, misjudged the location of her phone and promptly went AWOL. I just about made it to Red Sun Revival on time, but by the conclusion of their set at five past seven p.m. (too early for any respectable gig goer), I suddenly found myself facing three hours alone in Islington Academy watching a band with which I had no prior connection. I appreciate that I'm supposed to be a bit of a muso and thus ought to be more aware of The Chameleons, but I'm not, and I was a little perturbed on visiting their website to see them claim to be, *"The most influential band ever to hail from Manchester"*, a statement that is plainly untrue. By seven fifteen p.m. I had left the venue and was wandering aimlessly around Highbury and Islington, trying to find something to do.

This rather unsatisfactory experience was tempered somewhat by my reflections on a second date with Red Sun Revival, a band that seems to be equally cursed and blessed with their gigging arrangements. An amazing support slot for them was made problematic by their drummer suffering a biking accident earlier in the week, leaving them reliant on a slightly cheesy drum machine for the duration of the set. Funnily enough, back towards the end of 2016 when I first saw them, they were missing their bassist, who had endured some sort of similar misfortune. They've also ditched the Meatloaf-lookalike rhythm guitarist, who contributed precious little to either sound or aesthetic, but whose absence left me with the sense that I was now watching an entirely different line-up. I still very much enjoyed their performance, but the timing and circumstances made this feel like possibly the most un-gig-like gig of the entire year.

Weeks 51–53:
No More Stories

Leo Tolstoy once said that, *"The only absolute knowledge attainable by man is that life is meaningless."*

I haven't read any Tolstoy and I had to check whose quote this was on Wikipedia. In part, this is because I am not an intellectual; it's also because I've spent most of my time going to gigs, rather than reading the classics. Nevertheless, the quote has always resonated with the optimist in me. If life is essentially meaningless and the only certainty is that we're all going to die, it's up to us to instil some meaning, to create purpose for ourselves and reasons to go on living.

Is music a good enough reason for living?

I don't know, but it's a decent start.

I was also inspired earlier today by a quote from Tom Asacker, a marketing expert who has transformed his world view over the past few years and now sounds more like a motivational speaker than a marketeer.

"Don't become so wedded to your story that you can't break out of it."

Sometimes I hear observations or insights that feel like they're aimed directly at me and me alone. When I heard Asacker speak I recognised instantly that two years ago I had become too wedded to my story. I was a London-based, services industry-oriented careerist, motivated by the idea of being successful but still remaining everyone's best friend, busily pursuing the goal of becoming an employee-centric managing director of some communications agency or other, not to mention haplessly searching around in my scant free time for a meaningful relationship to hurl myself at. I had perhaps a vague sense back then of how narrow my parameters for success had become, but no real comprehension of how I could reset my course or do anything differently. Then, in little over a single month, everything changed, everything fell apart, and I suddenly found myself facing an alien reality in which success was suddenly defined not by title or pay grade but by whether I could manage to extract myself from my bed-shaped coffin before the sun went back down. When I look back at everything that I did and everything that happened to me, I see plenty of evidence suggesting a subconscious effort to break out of my narrative, but one that always stopped short of truly definitive action, despite the growing realisation that my current narrative was becoming ever more impossible to sustain. As it turned out, life would eventually seize the initiative and make the decision for me.

I've deliberately avoided placing too much emphasis on the facts and circumstances of my breakdown. A large part of this reasoning is because, at the start of the expedition, it was too painful and traumatic to contemplate. In fact, this is the first time I've ever referred to it as a breakdown, though in retrospect, it's quite hard to see it as anything else. Yet as time has elapsed, and gigs have accrued, I've started to realise that there's another reason for my desire to address the aftermath rather than the fall itself, and it's that I'd rather be defined by my response to my problems than the problems themselves. My mental health regularly troubles me and shouldn't be obscured, overlooked or glossed over. However, while I may not be a motivational speaker (and this is certainly not a self-help book – it's full of dubious opinions, terrible advice and Lord knows how many ill-judged decisions), my expedition, for better or worse, is my response to these troubles.

There was a second quote of Asacker's that drew me in: *"The narrative is not who we are, it's just the past"*.

This expedition has been my attempt to free myself from the shackles of my own narrative, to connect the dots between my past and my present in new ways to reveal a different way forward, a story less beholden to conventional social, professional and societal measures of success. My aim was to go to a gig every week, to see what it felt like and to see what I might find along the way. I had no idea that I'd end up seeing shows in Norway or Denmark or Japan or the Bahamas. I wish that I'd been able to see some live music in India, not because it would've made the expedition more meaningful, but because I really like that Indian bongo sound,[115] and because I have periodic dreams in which I find myself playing lead dancer in the Bollywood-themed Basement Jaxx video for Romeo.[116] I don't consider myself to have achieved anything miraculous by attending sixty or more shows in the past twelve months. After all, the rather obnoxious promoter I met at the Pins gig expressed in no uncertain terms just how unremarkable he felt my endeavours were by any quantitative measure. What I have done, however, is to try and realise a goal that holds true personal significance; to redefine, in some small way, the manner and method in which I approach my life, in the hope of opening myself to new opportunities; to redefine what it means to be me, in the hope of arriving at a new frontier, alive to possibility and unencumbered by the baggage of my past. I have not yet succeeded; I am a work in progress. But maybe that's how it should be. Where I go next is unclear. I could write another book. I could emigrate to Singapore. I could buy a boat. Maybe I *should* buy a boat.

The only thing I can say for definite is that wherever I go and whatever I do, music will continue to define and shape me. Whatever my life may hold, it must be a Pop Life. That's the legacy Prince has left to me.

---

115 I believe it may be called a Tabla.
116 Sadly, that song aside, they are a rubbish, rubbish band.

**Mew, Shepherd's Bush Empire, London,
Tuesday 23rd May**

- **Gig #66**
- **Musical birthdays:** Maxwell (1972), Jewel Kilcher (1974) Blaine Harrison of the Mystery Jets (1985)
- **Musical history:** Led Zeppelin are presented with the Polar Music Prize by the King of Sweden in Stockholm (2006)
- **Non-musical history:** Fabled outlaws Bonnie and Clyde are finally killed by police in a Louisiana ambush (1934)

Today was no day for gigging. I missed the news of the Manchester bombing late last night after deciding to settle down to a film, rather than carrying on browsing the web. I awoke to a concerned message from one of my clients asking whether my family was safe. Five minutes later I'd been able to confirm that my family was indeed safe, but the true horror and pain of the incident was beginning to dawn on me. Somehow these things feel more personal when it's your home town. At the time of writing I don't know anyone who was injured or killed at the Manchester Evening Arena, but it's almost certain that some of my peers and acquaintances will. What I do know is that there were many different cultural events going on across Manchester last night, and yet the attacker chose to target a pop concert attended by kids and their parents, young teenagers and their best mates, people who aren't yet old enough to make their own life decisions, to choose where or how they want to live. If that's the definition of a "Crusader" then it's a fucking stupid definition.

Manchester was in my heart all day, the memories of my own unique experiences at the Arena resonating with renewed strength and poignancy. Oasis in 1995, my first ever gig, Radiohead in 1997, James in 1998, Garbage in 1999, R.E.M. in 1999, right the way through to Prince in 2014, the last time I'd ever see him perform. I'm due to go back there this summer to see Radiohead touring A Moon Shaped Pool. No one who goes to the Arena hereafter will ever be able to separate it from this tragedy. I don't know anything about Ariana Grande, but I still have my memories of what it's like to encounter live music for the first time, of going to see your heroes for the very first time. So many years down the line, these memories remain crystal clear, and my expedition has reacquainted me with such sensations, reawakening the beautiful naivety of teenage discovery. As one parent was quoted as saying this morning, *"This was my daughter's first ever show – she's hardly likely to want to go to another is she?"* Even if they do continue to embrace live music in the years to come (and my goodness I hope they do), the mark that the bombing will leave on these kids' lives will be indelible.

My home city will endure; we're a resilient bunch, but irrespective, today was no day for gigging, and yet gigging is exactly what I found myself doing, partly out of obligation to my friends, partly because I was unable to think of anything else to do to take my mind off the horrific event.

As it turned out, we made the right call. Mew was a cathartic experience that served to remind me of many great nights out spent watching them with family and friends over the years. Not only are they one of the most incredible live bands – five Danish guys capable of creating soundscapes of enormous complexity and majesty – but they're a band who have always had a uniquely personal resonance for me. Philip introduced me to the band in 2003.[117] Since then, I've spent more than half of the intervening years with him as my housemate and one of my closest friends. When I saw them in 2010 they were the headline act at Truck Festival, the one festival my band was ever invited to play at. We opened the day's music; Mew closed it. In 2015, through sheer serendipity, my friend and former drummer Giles and I, saw them at a tiny club in Southern Munich, playing to an audience of approximately a hundred and fifty; one of

---

117 A night that will live long in the memory after I unwittingly tried to down a glass of wine that had been doubling as an ashtray.

the most breathtakingly beautiful and intimate shows I've ever seen. Mew are a band who always seem to rock up at significant life moments. Tonight, was no exception and they didn't disappoint – they never do.

A few shows back I reflected upon Philip's lamentable Avril-induced head injury. This Mew gig was also notable for a second regrettable incident, although fortunately not one that caused the daft fellow to miss any of the music. Instead, he brought the evening's catharsis to an abrupt end by getting an earplug stuck in his ear. Finding the venue's medical team entirely unable to assist him in its removal, we were whisked away from Yulia and Laura in an Uber to go in search of tweezers, no doubt infuriating our driver in the process due to the indeterminably raised voices required to sustain conversation with someone who has, all of a sudden, become partially deaf.

The Afghan Whigs, KOKO, London, Tuesday 30th May

- **Gig #67**
- **Musical birthdays:** Nicky "Topper" Headon of The Clash (1955), Marie Fredriksson of Roxette (1958), Tom Morello (1964), Stephen Malkmus (1966), Tim Burgess (1968)
- **Musical history:** Singer Finley Quaye narrowly avoids a jail sentence after his mobile phone rings while he's in the dock (2003)[118]
- **Non-musical history:** Aged just nineteen, Jeanne d'Arc is burned at the stake in Rouen, France (1431)
- **Also:** John Francis tries and fails to assassinate Queen Victoria (1841)

---

118 He was waiting to be sentenced having been found guilty of assault and not, as one might have suspected, of crimes against music.

This weekend I achieved a minor personal goal by reaching John O'Groats and seeing, for the first time, the northern coast of the British Isles. It was an astonishing trip, stunning scenery, deer running across roads, seals idling their way across deserted bays, glorious mountains enveloped by comforting white clouds and everything else one might expect from this most evocative of domestic landscapes.

Yet as Laura, my mother and I navigated our way across the terrain in our white suburban hire car, we were collectively unable to extract ourselves from the poignant scene we'd witnessed at our most northerly bed and breakfast. Thirteen weeks earlier the daughter of our elderly Scottish proprietor had lost her husband, aged just thirty-five, hit by a car in undisclosed, tragic circumstances. Gordon was weary from working back-to-back seven-day weeks in the B&B, no longer able to rely on the support of his youngest daughter who now faced widowhood and the sizeable challenge of bringing up her four children, aged nine, seven, six and five, on her own. We never managed to establish whether his own wife was dead or an absentee – it wasn't our place to ask – but the palpable loss he was suffering was evident, not to mention the clear demise of his appetite to go on doing a job he'd been busy with for decades previously. Long in the tooth, scruffy, beleaguered and lacking in sleep, Gordon's plight was no one's fault, and yet we felt a sense of guilt simply for accepting his hospitality, given that here was a man so plainly in need of a rest.

The whole of this Scotland trip felt overtly personal, a series of intimate encounters with people and places so totally unlike many of those foreign hotelling ventures in which greetings and reception are par for the course, one-to-one connections are few and far between and service, rather than interaction, is the order of the day. I left Scotland feeling as though I'd partaken in a mini-series of local documentaries – micro-narratives about individual lives, trials, tribulations and hazards, people trying, struggling and succeeding, to some degree, in their own personal universes. The significance of such endeavours resonated with me as I approached my final week of gigging, a chance to reconnect with one of my all-time favourite bands, The Afghan Whigs, whose longstanding guitarist Dave Rosser is currently battling pancreatic cancer. I don't know Rosser personally, although Emma has met him several times and reliably informs me that he's a true gent and a blissful human being, but I know that singer Greg Dulli, one of my idols, will have been hit hard by the news of his diagnosis.

Dulli is a musician who once ditched an entire solo album upon hearing news of filmmaker and friend Ted Demme's death back in 2002, returning to the studio to record an altogether more intimate and engaging new record that served as a reflection upon mortality and a glowing tribute to the passing of a lost loved one. He's a musician who spoke with unbelievable elegance at the loss of another friend, genius songwriter Elliott Smith, just twelve months later, doing more than any other commentator I heard at the time to emphasise the innate humanity and compassion present throughout Smith's curtailed oeuvre. Greg Dulli, perhaps over and above any other musician I admire, understands the language of music and the vitality and energy of true friendship. He speaks of his wildly varied musical influences as one might a close confidant and comrade. When he pontificates about Prince, I feel like he truly knows the man and his motivations, not just the artist and his output.

Waiting for Emma and Lew in the pub pre-Koko, I wondered whether Dave Rosser was well enough to tour with the band or whether his absence on the stage might be reflected in the stage banter or choice of tunes. I wondered whether Greg could find the words to articulate his emotions or his sense of the inevitable loss to come, particularly given that one of the tracks of the Whigs' new album, written in response to Dave's illness, has the telling title, "I Got Lost."

As it turned out, Greg gave the most apt response I could have imagined, drafting in a long-time associate of the band and an expert songwriter in his own right, Ed Harcourt,[119] both

---

119 See the Sophie Ellis Bextor Bush hall show for further musings on Ed.

to support the band on the tour as well as to play the role of extra guitarist during the Whigs show itself. Both artists acknowledged Dave's absence, drawing upon their personal memories of working with a brilliant guitarist and a true friend to create a tribute that genuinely celebrated the wonderful contribution he has made to their lives.

The Afghan Whigs are an incredible band with an incredible body of work, a band almost destroyed by drugs and booze, but resurrected after a lengthy absence, with two recent albums that have given them enough confidence to reclaim their mantle as one of indie rock's most authentic and most engaging, underrated treasures. Tonight's show was built on a setlist comprised predominantly of new material. The old songs, when they occasionally surfaced, felt workmanlike in comparison to the vibrancy of their recent output. Though into their late forties, here was a band staking a meaningful claim upon the contemporary and doing so in a way that made me feel both glad to be alive, and excited about the possibility of what might come next.

We go through our lives bearing witness to innumerable difficulties, tragedies, sheer travesties, but we have nights like this to fall back on when times are hardest, and Greg Dulli seems to understand this better than anyone. Here is a band dedicated to the business of feeling, experiencing, being alive.[120]

Depeche Mode, Olympic Stadium, Munich, Friday 9th June

- **Gig #68**
- **Musical birthdays:** Cole Porter (1891), Les Paul (1915), Jackie Wilson (1934), Ed Simons of The Chemical Brothers (1970), Matt Bellamy (1978), Tom Kirkham of largely unsuccessful pop band Silent Alliance (1983)

---

120 Dave Rosser sadly passed away, aged just 50, on June 27th, 2017.

- **Musical history:** MC Hammer achieves the longest uninterrupted run at the top of the Billboard charts since they were created (1991)
- **Non-musical history:** Bhumibol Adulyadej becomes King of Thailand and will go on to become the longest serving monarch in history (1946)
- **Also:** A fight breaks out between Liam Gallagher and Mick Hucknall at London's Metropolitan Hotel; it is unclear who emerges victorious (1998)

It's astonishing how much can happen in a single week. This is made more incredulous when the week in question already marks the conclusion of a year-long gigging expedition. It's the fifty-third week of my musical travels, so I've overrun by seven days, but after being forced to miss a session back in autumn, I felt it only right to atone with one last, unique hurrah.

Yet now that the moment has arrived, it's hard to describe this hurrah as anything other than muted, tempered as it has been by the unprecedented events of the past month. I began week fifty-three in Manchester, paying my respects to those who lost their lives in the terror attack by visiting the incredible memorial in St. Ann's square, just around the corner from my former flat. It was comforting to meet up with Brendan and learn that he shared my pain in response to what felt like a uniquely personal attack, not just on our homes and our community, but on our upbringing. We were the same age as the bombing victims when we first went out on the town for our inaugural live experiences; we will keep a candle burning in our hearts for them, because we know what it means to grow up a gig-goer, not to mention our pride in Manchester and its unique resonance with music.

Later in the day, as we played pianos and guitars together in honour of Rick's birthday, news reached us of the latest attack at London Bridge.

I worked in London Bridge for a decade; it's one of my favourite places in the country and I've frequented every bar and restaurant in the area, including all of those caught up in the attack. The news left me desolate and beyond the reach of those around me. It felt painful beyond words; I couldn't begin to articulate my anguish for the lives of those unalterably damaged by being in the wrong place at the wrong time. The twisted irony of my decision to make a pilgrimage to Manchester that weekend was equally hard to bear.

Fast forward twenty-four hours and I was lying on my bed in floods of tears as the One Manchester concert aired on the BBC, with artists I despise like Robbie Williams and the Black-Eyed Peas still proving themselves to be surprisingly capable of inducing wave after wave of waterworks. Two weeks ago, I had no idea who Ariana Grande was. Today, I can relate to the father of one of the injured girls who admitted that he was now a bit in love with Grande, following her poignant visit to the hospital where the victims were being treated.

I hope Ariana Grande is given the freedom of the city. When she next arrives in Manchester, she will walk on water,[121] for she is one of us now: the most honorary of honorary Mancs. If she sets foot in the city centre she'll be mobbed by an unbridled, unstoppable, Richter-scale force of pure, positive energy. What she did in galvanising our city's young after a seismic shock of pure hatred, to get them back on our streets, smiling and celebrating again, was one of the most inspirational things I've had the good fortune to witness. When she next plays, I'll be queuing for tickets. I even bought her re-released charity single "One Last Time" and I like it, though admittedly I've lost all objectivity when it comes to these Grande matters.

Credit must also go to Chris Martin, not only for Coldplay's life-affirming performance, which ran contrary to my previous anti-Coldplay sentiments in its sheer joy and sense of collective defiance, but for getting our favourite Manc son Liam Gallagher to come out and light up our world at this time of suffering. Liam

---

121 Not literally, as this would involve traversing the Manchester Ship Canal, and I don't want Ariana Grande to be taken ill.

never does straight empathy in the way Chris Martin does; it's not his style and, as an Oasis die-hard, I'd be disappointed if he ever changed his ways. But his presence was a reminder of our city's blistering musical heritage, not to mention something for the dads of all the pre-teen girls to get up and dance for. In the "Supersonic" documentary last year Liam corrected one of the great misconceptions about himself, explaining that his statuesque, seemingly indifferent presence at the front of the stage was not, as had been levelled at him, an act of supreme arrogance, but rather, was his way of attempting to comprehend the mass spirit of togetherness before him. In the One Manchester concert, he sang straight and pure, and for anyone that has ever felt that they know him, they *knew*. He is ours, and we are his, and this was further proof (if proof be needed) that when times are hard, music can serve as salvation for us all.

All of which leads neatly on to the back end of week fifty-three, which saw me wandering in a discombobulated fashion around the streets of central Munich with my absent friend Giles, formerly of South West England and now a resident of neighbouring town Augsburg, trying to contemplate the madness of a General Election outcome that absolutely no one seemed to be expecting. Laura and I had flown over to Germany for my gig finale shortly before polling had concluded; indeed, I'd cast my vote in sombre early morning circumstances, with no hope of anything other than more doom, gloom and dark political clouds overhead. So much has happened since the start of my journey, but in the political realm at least, the major events of these past twelve months have delivered only an increased sensation of dread and foreboding. Seeing the exit poll as we headed for passport control, led to two immediate conclusions; firstly, that *something was happening*, and secondly, that I would have to stay up all night and watch events unfold, an act I'd sworn never to repeat after the double disappointment of the 2015 election and Brexit in successive years. This decision proved to be as momentous as it was exhausting, hence the state of disrepair I found myself in as we attempted to take on an Impressionist art gallery around the corner from Hitler's old house. It was hard to give much thought to the idea of another gig, let alone the idea that I was rapidly homing in on my final outing of this lengthy expedition. Too much was happening too quickly, and it was proving impossible to take it all in. To add to the complications, it was also my birthday, which meant twenty plus concurrent phone conversations about Corbyn and Coalitions of Chaos, in addition to the usual unwanted mortality check.

Only by early evening, taking an accidental stroll through a park north of the city centre after we'd set off on the wrong way to the venue, did I begin to relax and move from weighty and intense musings to quieter and more satisfying contemplation. Giles and I were on our way to see Depeche Mode at the Olympic Stadium, a band whose most recent work "Spirit" poured a scornful and despondent light on the state of UK affairs. The band sounded the angriest they'd been in decades, spitting out lyrics such as, *"Where's the revolution? Come on people you're letting me down!"* along with the rather more doom-laden, *"We're all fucked!"*

"Spirit" came out before the General Election was called, its release overshadowed by the need for the band to spend time and energy publicly rebutting totally unfounded accusations of neo-Nazi extreme-right sympathies. Depeche Mode are not the cheerleading music outfit of the extreme right; they're a smart, textured, dark and atmospheric band, hard to place musically, extremely lucky to be alive, and still capable of illuminating a sixty-thousand-capacity stadium, despite being well into their fifties. Dave Gahan remains the most ludicrously camp but brilliantly compelling frontman; Martin Gore still has the voice of an angel and still looks like he's harbouring a family of field mice in his hair. Fletch's role and purpose in the band is still gloriously unclear, but he wears his sunglasses and stands quietly at the back of the stage with the same undiminished pride.

As the band broke into "World in My Eyes", I thought about my cousin Alex. Back in October when I heard the news that Alex and Louisa were expecting a child, I spent an inordinate amount of time fretting over the prospect of introducing a new-born baby to such a disastrous mess of a planet. As it turned out, Baby Ada was born barely twelve hours after the London terror attack, a sleepy little angel to provide us with some respite from the tumultuous realities of the outside world. I was honorary Uncle Tom and my first visit, shortly after casting my vote, was one the proudest moments of my life.

Now, watching the band tear through the classics, I was filled with an incredible sense of optimism. I *had* to be optimistic – for Ada, for Alex, for every one of my gig-going sisters and brothers.

Depeche Mode had just released an album pleading for a revolution and, finally, it felt as though life might be changing.

Epilogue

I am a machine that cannot be switched off.

I whizz and whirr and continue to plug away without the slightest hint of cessation.

Times may change, years may come and go, politicians may rise and decline, trends and movements may emerge and disappear, and yet here I am, the perennial musical explorer, calendar mercilessly blocked out with one show after another.

Things weren't supposed to work out this way, but this is my life and I need to own it, even when it's exhausting, pointless, debilitating or plain ridiculous.

As Emma and I head to Hammersmith Apollo to see Evanescence, ready to come good on a decade-long ambition and revisit the scene of my inexplicable obsession all those years ago,[122] I know that – at least in the eyes of my peers – I've planted a flag firmly in the realm of court jester. Last night I had another dream about singer Amy Lee. What is happening to me, and should I be worried?

I know that I shouldn't be doing this; I should be staying home and resting after a relentless year spent flirting with exhaustion. But I can't help myself. Gigs have become my life once more. A life on the road is my calling, my means of resisting the lure of dull, settled martyrdom. I'm Peter Pan, weary of forever knocking on the closed windows of ageing peers and former comrades. This is where I belong. I may be older, more tired

---

122 See Prologue.

and painfully aware of the perils that lie in wait should I continue along this path indefinitely, yet as I wait for the band to take to the stage, I know that I must keep going. I don't want this to end. Not just yet.

I can't wait for Evanescence. I can't wait for the next show to begin. I can't get enough of the vibe, the beautiful sound of every venue as an audience pines for its heroes, the cheer of the crowd when the lights go down and everyone enters their own internal countdown to ecstasy. It doesn't matter how many times you observe this spectacle; whatever your age, musical preference or sense of world accomplishment, you can still be transfixed in reverie as you await the start of the show. Just look at my dad – he's been going to gigs since the mid-sixties and yet, when we await Dylan or The Dan, or James, I can sense the same youthful fervour that he must've encountered five decades previous. It's the same fervour the Ariana Grande fans delighted in, that night at the Arena, before the attack. I hope that they can find it again, as they, and indeed all of us, move forward in these troubling times. My fervour tonight is for the silliest of bands, but it is real, and it resonates, and I won't allow anyone to take it away from me. We are all alive and we all need meaning, and Lord, I've found it in this expedition. Beautiful meaning, beautiful purpose: a reason to be.

In the first ever around-the-world yacht race in 1968, Frenchman Bernard Moitessier shocked his home nation, not to mention his family when, ten months in and nearing the finish line, he abandoned his leading position and set off in the direction of Tahiti, intent on circumnavigating the globe a second time. He announced his decision by firing a message to the London Times, via slingshot, onto a passing ship in the middle of the Southern Atlantic. The explanation he gave for his surprise decision is something that I've been quietly contemplating of late.

"Because I am happy at sea and perhaps to save my soul."
I should buy a boat.

EIN HERZE FÜR AUTOREN A HEART FOR AUTHORS À L'ÉCOUTE DES AUTEURS MIA ΚΑΡΔΙΑ ΓΙΑ ΣΥ
 HJÄRTA FÖR FÖRFATTARE UN CORAZÓN POR LOS AUTORES YAZARLARIMIZA GÖNÜL VERELIM
CUORE PER AUTORI ET HJERTE FOR FORFATTERE EEN HART VOOR SCHRIJVERS TEMOS OS A
ZÖINKERT SERCE DLA AUTORÓW EIN HERZ FÜR AUTOREN A HEART FOR AUTHORS À L'É
FUNÇÃO BCEЙ ДУШОЙ К АВТОРАМ ETT HJÄRTA FÖR FÖRFATTARE Á LA ESCUCHA DE LOS AU
AUTEURS MIA ΚΑΡΔΙΑ ΓΙΑ ΣΥΓΓΡΑΦΕΙΣ UN CUORE PER AUTORI ET HJERTE FOR FORFATTERE E
YAZARLARIMIZA RLI SERCE ZÖINKÉRT SERCE DLA AUTORÓW EIN HERZ
SCHRIJVERS FUNÇÃO BCEЙ ДУШОЙ К АВТОРАМ ETT HJÄRTA

The author

Tom is a 30-something music obsessive and part-time explorer who hails from the North West of England. In the real world, Tom is a self-employed marketing and communications consultant, but is happiest watching bands perform, following Liverpool FC and thinking about his hair. A multi-instrumentalist and songwriter, Tom has released two albums with his band Silent Alliance, who are passably big in Japan. Tom lives in North London with his feline companion of 12 years, Mr Kitten. Pop Life is his first book.

The publisher

*He who stops
getting better
stops being good.*

This is the motto of novum publishing, and our focus
is on finding new manuscripts, publishing them and
offering long-term support to the authors.
Our publishing house was founded in 1997, and since
then it has become THE expert for new authors and
has won numerous awards.

**Our editorial team will peruse each manuscript
within a few weeks free of charge and without
obligation.**

You will find more information about
novum publishing and our books on the internet:

www.novum-publishing.co.uk

Printed in Great
Britain
by Amazon